Gift and Duty

Other Titles in the SEANET Series

Vol. 1
Sharing Jesus in the Buddhist World

Vol. 2
Sharing Jesus Holistically in the Buddhist World

Vol. 3
Sharing Jesus Effectively in the Buddhist World

Vol. 4
Communicating Christ in the Buddhist World

Vol. 5
Communicating Christ Through Story and Song: Orality in Buddhist Contexts

Vol. 6
Communicating Christ in Asian Cities: Urban Issues in Buddhist Contexts

Vol. 7
Family and Faith in Asia: The Missional Impact of Social Networks

Vol. 8
Suffering: Christian Reflections on Buddhist Dukkha

Vol. 9
Complexities of Money and Missions in Asia

Vol. 10
Developing Indigenous Leaders: Lessons in Mission from Buddhist Asia

Vol. 11
Becoming the People of God: Creating Christ-Centered Communities in Buddhist Asia

Vol. 12
Seeking the Unseen: Spiritual Realities in the Buddhist World

Vol. 13
Restored to Freedom from Fear, Guilt and Shame: Lessons from the Buddhist World

Gift and Duty

Where Grace and Merit Meet

Edited by
Paul H. De Neui

RESOURCE *Publications* • Eugene, Oregon

GIFT AND DUTY
Where Grace and Merit Meet

Copyright © 2017 Paul H. De Neui. All rights reserved. Except for brief quotations in critical publications or reviews, no part of this book may be reproduced in any manner without prior written permission from the publisher. Write: Permissions, Wipf and Stock Publishers, 199 W. 8th Ave., Suite 3, Eugene, OR 97401.

Resource Publications
An Imprint of Wipf and Stock Publishers
199 W. 8th Ave., Suite 3
Eugene, OR 97401

www.wipfandstock.com

PAPERBACK ISBN: 978-1-5326-3869-5
HARDCOVER ISBN: 978-1-5326-3870-1
EBOOK ISBN: 978-1-5326-3871-8

Manufactured in the U.S.A.

Contents

Contributors | *vii*
Introduction | *xi*

Part I Religious Foundations

Chapter 1
  Can Christians Use Karma Theory? | 3
  —*Russell H. Bowers, Jr.*

Chapter 2
  An Adaptational Dialogue in Reading Luke 16:19-31 for Thai Buddhists Followers of Jesus. | 29
  —*C-S Abraham Cheong*

Chapter 3
  The 'Karma' of the Old Testament as a Bridge to Communicate Grace to Karmic Communities. | 48
  —*Cristian Dumitrescu*

Chapter 4
  Contextualization of Merit-Making and Grace for Christward Movements in the Karmic World. | 67
  —*David S. Lim*

Chapter 5
  From Karma to Grace: By Merit or Mercy? | 93
  —*Alex G. Smith*

Part II Cultural Perspectives

Chapter 6
The Nature of Merit-Making of Pure-Land Buddhism and Zen (Shang) Buddhism within Chinese Naturalism | *123*
—*Tae-Yun Timothy Hwang*

Chapter 7
An Indian Christian Dialogue with the Karmic Community. | *135*
—*Bouvert Regulas*

Chapter 8
How Cultural Reciprocity Practices Reinforce Merit-Making Affecting the Experience of God's Grace. | *155*
—*Sheryl Takagi Silzer*

Chapter 9
Christian Charity Viewed Through Karmic Eyes in Sri Lanka. | *175*
— *G.P.V. Somaratna*

Chapter 10
Prapheni Heet Sibsong: The Tradition of Merit-Making with Ethical Commitment to the 'Other.' | *194*
—*Dipti Visuddhangkoon*

Contributors

RUSSELL BOWERS earned his PhD in systematic theology from Dallas Theological Seminary. His published dissertation compares the thought of Keiji Nishitani with that of historic Christianity. He has pastored churches in the USA, led a Cambodia project targeting senior Christian leadership development, and taught college and seminary in Singapore and the USA. Russ's recently-published *Finding Home* demonstrates how the gospel fills the needs and aspirations of the world religions. He and his wife Glenna live in Texas. They have three married children and seven grandchildren.

C-S ABRAHAM CHEONG is an associate professor of the New Testament at Baeksuk University, South Korea. He has worked in this position since 2003. Dr. Cheong studied Theology at Westminster Theological Seminary in Philadelphia, USA, earning his M.Div. He was ordained in KAPC in California, and achieved his Ph.D. at the University of Sheffield, UK. He served a local church in Seoul as pastor for three years, along with his wife, Sarah, and two children, Jason and Christina. He has written papers in English and Korean, and published three novels. Over the last twenty years, he has taught local pastors and theological students in Thailand, China, and Japan. His main focus is on contextual Biblical interpretation, particularly for non-Christians in Buddhism and Donghak - a traditional Korean religion.

PAUL DE NEUI is an ordained minister with the Evangelical Covenant Church. He and his wife served as missionaries with church planting and community development organizations in northeast Thailand from 1987-2005. He completed his PhD in Intercultural Studies at Fuller Theological Seminary. Paul has been involved in SEANET for over ten years. Presently he is the professor of Missiology and Intercultural Studies and the director of the Center for World Christian Studies at North Park Theological Seminary in Chicago, Illinois."

CRISTIAN DUMITRESCU is particularly interested to help people rediscover the beauty of the gospel through their local worldview and value system. This passion was born during his ministry with nomadic Gypsies in Romania. Cristian earned his BA in Theology at the Romanian Adventist Theological Institute (where he later taught), and a license in Theology at the Babes-Bolyai University in the same country. After serving as a pastor in post-Communist Romania, he pursued an MA in Religious Studies at Newbold College in the UK. His PhD is from Andrews University in the US, where he taught for ten years. Dumitrescu raised awareness about the plight of immigrants in Europe long before this issue had become news. He has taught in Indonesia, Myanmar, Mongolia, China, and Indochina and held evangelistic presentations on three continents. Cristian currently teaches 'World Mission' and 'Intercultural Studies and Research' at the Adventist International Institute of Advanced Studies in the Philippines. Cristian is married to Alina, and they have been blessed by God with two daughters: Ingrid and Celine.

TAEYUN (TIMOTHY) HWANG has been a missionary to the Philippines since 1981. He is now a missionary-at-large of Global Mission Society, where he served six years training missionary candidates. He earned an MA and a PhD in Asian Studies and Philippine Studies from the University of the Philippines. He has held various teaching positions and now serves as the chairman of the Asian School of Development & Cross-cultural Studies.

DAVID S. LIM is from the Philippines. He has served as academic dean at the Asian Theological Seminary in the Philippines and Oxford Centre for Mission Studies in the UK. His PhD in New Testament Theology was earned from Fuller Theological Seminary. He now serves as the president of the Asian School of Development and Cross-cultural Studies, president of China Ministries International- Philippines, board chair of Lausanne Philippines, and coordinator of the Asian House Church Movement. He has authored several books and articles on non-Western missiology, theological contextualization, and transformational development.

Contributors

BOUVERT REGULAS started preaching as a teenager. He has received a B.Th. from Bethel Bible College, Punalur, an M.A. from Mysore University, an M.Div. from C.O.T.R. Theological Seminary, Visakhapatnam, P.G. Diploma in Journalism and Mass Communication from IGNOU, Delhi, M.Th. and PhD in Religion and Philosophy and in Missions from Acts Academy of Higher Education, Bangalore. Being the author of eight books, he has written more than a hundred articles in Christian magazines and publications. He works as the Principal of Mission Theological College, President of Mission of God and the Chairman of the Writers Association. Bouvert and Maheswari Regulas are blessed with four children - Boncy, Blessy, Bitsy and Blessert Regulas. At present he resides in Chennai, India.

SHERYL TAKAGI SILZER is a multicultural consultant with SIL International. She is a third generation Japanese American whose ancestors were Buddhist. Her paternal grandfather became a Christian through his immigration experience in the early 1910s and passed on his faith to his family. Sheryl leads Cultural Self-Discovery workshops for multicultural teams working in cross-cultural ministries. She also teaches as an adjunct professor at Talbot School of Theology in Asian American ministry. Her specialty is the influence of Asian religious thought on Asian cultural practices. Sheryl received a PhD in Intercultural Studies at Fuller School of World Mission. She and her husband Pete served for several years with SIL in the Asia-Pacific area as Bible translators. They have two married sons and five grandchildren.

ALEX G. SMITH was born and raised in Australia till age 21. In Canada he graduated from Prairie Bible College and later, in Kenya, Africa, the International Institute of Christian Communication. In the USA he earned the DMiss and MA degrees at Fuller Theological Seminary and an MDiv from George Fox Evangelical Seminary. Veteran missionary to Thailand, he founded the Thailand Church Growth Committee, and co-founded SEANET (South, East, Southeast, and North Asia Network). He served as Adjunct Faculty at Multnomah University USA for eighteen years. He is also visiting professor to several Asian Seminaries. Presently he serves as International Trainer and Advocate in the Buddhist World for OMF International, under which he has served in various roles for more than five decades. He has published numerous books and articles on ministry in the Buddhist world. His Thailand church planting experiences deepened the conviction that multiplying movements of local indigenous fellowships and training local lay pastors are priority strategies for mission. He is committed to effective communication of God's grace, truth and biblical theology in Asian Buddhist contexts. He resides with his American wife, Faith in the USA. They have three adult sons and four grandchildren.

G.P.V. SOMARATNA is from Sri Lanka. He has an MA in Missiology and an MA in Theology, as well as a PhD in South Asian history from the University of London. He served as head of the Department of History and Political Science, professor of modern history at the University of Colombo, Sri Lanka, and is now serving as senior research professor at Colombo Theological Seminary. He also served as adjunct professor at Trinity Theological College, Post-Doctoral fellow at the Hebrew University of Jerusalem, and Global Research Institute of Fuller Theological Seminary. He has published numerous articles and books on the history of Sri Lanka and the impact of Christianity upon Sri Lankan Buddhism. He is widely regarded as one of Sri Lanka's leading scholars on Ceylonese history.

DR. DIPTI VISUDDHANGKOON is an associate professor and full-time faculty member at the Department of Foreign Language, Mahachulalongkornrajavidyalaya University, Khonkaen Campus in Thailand. She has a PhD, and has completed several research studies about Buddhism. Dr. Visuddhangkoon has presented papers at several international conferences, helped Buddhist monks learn English, and published several books about English for monks.

Introduction

IN JANUARY 2017 a group of practitioners, scholars and reflective thinkers gathered in Chiang Mai, Thailand to discuss the intersecting points between Buddhist Merit and Christian Grace. The results were surprising. Karma, as it turns out, is a curious thing. Those living under what is sometimes referred to as the "Law of Karma" are labelled in the literature as "Karmic Communities." As far as this author has been able to observe, no one has put up a sign in their village, "Welcome to the Karmic Community." In fact there is no tangible evidence of any people group, to whom others have given this label, who have claimed it as their own. If it is a law, karmic law is unwritten and holds its sway through non-discursive perpetuation inherited through worldview transfer from generation to generation. It is perhaps one of the most defining etic generalizations given to many forms of high-context Buddhist cultures.

Karmic communities are tangibly evidenced by the outward expression of merit-making. In many places today, merit-making remains an essential component to the social and religious balance of society. It is the motivation that drives an on-going obligation to perform millions of deeds in response to the past, in participation with the present, and providing hope for the future. And here is a curious intersecting point where the understandings of followers of the Buddha and followers of the Christ may meet.

Is the Christian concept of grace anathema to the social structure of merit-making found in Buddhist karmic communities? Most Christ followers would be quick to respond that the performance of good deeds is the response to divine grace and in fact compels a lifestyle of generosity and compassion. Are there not several warning references to coming judgement reserved for those who claim to follow Jesus and do not tangibly show their care towards others? Are all Buddhist forms of merit-making purely

Introduction

for religious purposes to assuage cosmic consequences or are there other reasons? Are there not Christian churches who operate under a legalistic view of God's divine wrath and are in essence living as karmic communities of the Christian type?

The result of discussions about these and other questions is the volume you now hold in your hand. SEANET proudly presents what is number 14 in its series of missiological reference texts, "Gift and Duty: Where Grace and Merit Meet." Each of the ten authors presented here represent a particular perspective, both Christian and Buddhist, that can inform the other. SEANET is extremely grateful to each author who contributed her or his time in researching, presenting and re-writing the chapters included. It has been my privilege to interact and learn with each of you. Thank you for your inspiring and insightful efforts.

Special thanks go to all of our SEANET steering committee for organizing the initial conference, especially David Sheahan for his detailed work as registrar. I am deeply indebted to my assistant Benjamin Wickstrom for his follow up with each author and for Tina Hileman who was a gift of God's grace to help in the detailed editing of each chapter. I want to especially thank those at Wipf and Stock for their continual extension of grace as we created this volume together. The work of Dwight Martin printing the volume in Asia for regional distribution must also be acknowledged.

May this volume lead to a deeper understanding of the significance of diverse religious and cultural perspectives. And may this cognitive understanding be embodied in mutual movements of social transformation beginning in the heart of every reader.

To the glory of God and the good of all humanity.

PAUL H. DE NEUI, EDITOR

Part I

Religious Foundations

'Therefore everyone who hears
these words of mine
and puts them into practice
is like a wise man
who built his house on the rock.'

MATTHEW 7:24

1

Can Christians Use Karma Theory?

RUSSELL H. BOWERS, JR.

OBSERVING TWO OCCASIONS WHERE the Bible employs outside imagery to articulate its own ideas, this chapter concludes that non-Jewish and non-Christian thought can provide legitimate tools for evangelism. For many adherents of other religions, Christianity appears arcane and abstruse. What may help them understand are analogies to ideas they already accept. Using non-biblical thought to illustrate the Bible's message does not imply the former to be either authoritative or entirely true. It is therefore not syncretism. The chapter then outlines one learned Buddhist exposition of karma. It proceeds to identify parallels and differences between karma and grace, and to suggest why the latter provides a hope for humanity that is more satisfying both logically and existentially.

Citing Outside Sources

Were the Buddha to stand before us today and declare, "Friends, two plus two equals four," what would you say? I hope you would agree he is right. Acknowledging that he is would not make you a Buddhist, because two plus two does in fact make four. "Four" is the answer not because Buddha says so; it just is. Were we to argue that the answer is four because Buddha says so, that would be considering him an authority figure. We would then be Buddhists. But this is not the case in simply acknowledging when Buddha gets something right. As lovers of truth, we should be glad when anyone gets anything right. It does no good to allege that his accurate math is a demonic ploy to lure Christians into lowering their defenses and accepting his whole system. He simply happens to be right in his addition; we can gladly agree that he is, and remain neither syncretists nor compromisers.

The Bible is not embarrassed to acknowledge when non-Christians in the New Testament or non-Jews in the Old are right. Sometimes these unexpected truth-speakers speak or act better than do their more orthodox contemporaries. Josiah, for example, was one of Judah's most godly kings. One day his southern neighbor, Egypt's Pharaoh Neco, set out for war against the Babylonians, to the north and east. Judah lay between, and Josiah marched to confront Neco. Pharaoh queried, "What quarrel is there, king of Judah, between you and me? It is not you I am attacking at this time, but the house with which I am at war. God has told me to hurry; so stop opposing God, who is with me, or he will destroy you." The Old Testament pharaohs are not generally presented as paragons of truth and piety. So whom should we believe is right in this case—a godly Judean king, or a pagan Egyptian pharaoh? Granted, Neco said that God told him to hurry, but why should we imagine he was talking about the one and true God? Was it not more likely to have been a deity from his own pantheon? The answer emerges from what follows: "Josiah, however, would not listen to what Neco had said at God's command but went to fight him on the plain of Megiddo. Archers shot King Josiah, so they put him in his other chariot and brought him to Jerusalem, where he died" (2 Chr 35:20–24). Neco of Egypt was right; godly Josiah of Judah wrong. Josiah "would not listen to what Neco had said at God's command." So he died, and Judah declined into apostasy and captivity. God had indeed spoken to Pharaoh Neco, not to King Josiah. What matters is truth, not the one who happens to speak it. The sons of this age at times do prove more shrewd than the sons of light (Luke 16:8).

Sometimes the Bible employs imagery—including philosophical and religious imagery—from outside Jewish and Christian circles to articulate its own ideas. Genesis 1 is the Bible's most straightforward account of earth's origin. God speaks, logically and sequentially, and formless vacuity acquires shape and inhabitants. Although the earth was "formless and empty" (*tōhû wāḇōhû*) before God's speech, Genesis 1 envisions no sentient opposition to his work of creation. No one or no thing (other than inanimate watery chaos) stood in God's way and needed to be defeated.

Not so with neighboring mythology. The Sumerians and their neighbors invoke Tiamat. She is the roiling, primordial sea, often personified as a dragon. After giving birth to various Mesopotamian gods, Tiamat is killed by Marduk. Marduk then uses Tiamat's corpse as raw material to create the earth—half to form a dome to separate waters above from waters below, and half to form *terra firma* itself. Certain themes in this myth parallel Genesis, such as the primordial chaotic waters, and a dome created to separate upper waters from lower.

Though Genesis envisions no such sentient serpent whom Yahweh must first conquer in order to create, other biblical passages do. A dozen times in Job, the Psalms, and Isaiah, biblical writers refer to Leviathan or Rahab. Leviathan—"the twisted one," perhaps derived from the Arabic root *lwy* "to twist"—is found in Job 3:8; 41:1; Ps 74:14, 104:26; Isa 27:1 *bis*; Rahab—"the proud one," from *rāhav* "behave proudly"—occurs in Job 9:13, 26:12; Ps 87:4; 89:10; Isa 30:7, 51:9. These are "different names for the same monster."[1] "Rahab" is "an alternative for 'Tiamat,' the Babylonian name of the dragon of darkness and chaos."[2] "Though this is not mentioned in Genesis, fragments of a creation story known from Ugarit, where God subdues the sea, are found throughout the Bible and in rabbinic literature."[3] The above biblical passages mirror three themes common to various non-Jewish creation myths: a repressive monster who restrains creation, a heroic god who defeats the monster and releases the forces necessary for life, and the god's ultimate control of these forces.[4]

Does, then, the Bible teach that this monster, Tiamat, actually existed, and that God had to defeat and dismember her to provide raw material for what he created? Or is this rather "a shared conceptual world which serves as a medium of communication,"[5] "a helpful metaphor to describe Yahweh's creative activity"?[6] Surely it must be the latter. Mythopoeic allusions in Job, for example, "are merely borrowed imagery from the ancient Near Eastern cultural milieu,"[7] not borrowed theology. "It is inconceivable that these strict monotheists intended to support their view from pagan

---

1. Wakeman, *God's Battle with the Monster*, 79.
2. Bacher and Lauterbach, *Jewish Encyclopedia*, "Rahab."
3. Berlin and Brettler, *Jewish Study Bible*, 1291.
4. Waltke, "The Creation Account," 33.
5. Wakeman, *God's Battle with the Monster*, vii.
6. Waltke, "The Creation Account," 34.
7. Parsons, "Literary Features," 219.

mythology, which they undoubtedly detested and abominated, unless they were sure that their hearers would understand that their allusions were used in a purely figurative sense."[8] Stories such as these were used simply because "Canaanite mythic imagery was the most impressive means in that ancient cultural milieu whereby to display" the point that the author was trying to make.[9] This is simply "[a]n old myth concerning the triumph of good over evil" that "was taken over from ancient Canaan and transformed by the Hebrews."[10]

So though in this case Israel's theology did not derive from the myths of her neighbors, the imagery in which that theology was expressed did. This is the point for the present chapter. Biblical writers were conversant with their audience's ideas, and comfortable in communicating their own convictions by means of them.

This example may seem oblique or unique, so let us consider a more straightforward one. The apostle is alone in Athens. As he awaits the arrival of his associates, Paul observes and then examines the Athenians' idols and altars. The verb is *anatheōreō*, "look at again and again." On this occasion at least, Paul studied to understand his hearers' ideology before articulating his own to them. He was thus able to introduce his gospel in terms of their altar "To an Unknown God," and in the words of their poets, "'For in him we live and move and have our being.' As some of your own poets have said, 'We are his offspring'" (Acts 17:28). Here Paul possibly alludes to Epimenides or Euripides in the first line, and more clearly to Aratus in the second. Aratus himself may have been quoting a hymn to Zeus from Cleanthes; hence Paul's reference to "poets" in the plural. Though the core of his message to the Athenian philosophers was identical to that of his sermon to Antiochean Jews four chapters earlier, the two addresses are distinctly framed with imagery and quotations appropriate to each audience.

So, if the Old Testament cites Babylonian myths, and Paul pagan philosophers, then we in Asia may quote the Buddha. Doing so does not suggest we consider him our authority. Nor does it elevate his words to the status of scripture, or imply that we consider his whole system correct. But because our hearers know and believe Buddha, citing him introduces our new ideas in their familiar, comfortable terms. It shows that we are honest enough to acknowledge when Buddha got something right, humble and

---

8. Waltke, "The Creation Account," 35.

9. Day, "God and Leviathan," 436.

10. Gordon, "Leviathan," 1.

secure enough in our own faith to celebrate when he did, and interested enough in them to try to put our message in terms they easily understand. Buddha's words can serve as our starting point, just as a pagan altar and Greek poets provided Paul's starting point for the Athenians. In this way, our message will be couched in words and ways that immediately resonate.

Karma: Traleg Kyabgon

As the apostle examined the Athenians' *sebasmata* before speaking, so we would do well to contemplate karma before employing it in our evangelism. Two paths may lead toward understanding: study of Buddhist writings, and interaction with living communities. These paths may end up in different destinations, but both can aid our ability to accurately address our Asian audiences. This chapter will focus on the first path—classic Buddhist belief as articulated in selected writings. Starting with this common foundation, Christian emissaries can blend in the unique flavor of their specific communities to produce locally appropriate elixirs for evangelism and discipleship.

The Tripitaka ex *Abhidharmakośabhāṣyam* extensively discusses karma. A standard edition of the abhidharma alone devotes one chapter of 215 pages to the subject,[11] in addition to passing references. The sutra *pitaka* likewise contemplates karma. An exhaustive examination of these exceeds the needs of this chapter. Instead, its understanding of karma will derive from Traleg Kyabgon's 2015 *Karma: What It Is, What It Isn't, Why It Matters*. This work brings traditional Buddhist philosophy into conversation with Western philosophy and psychology. What follows in this section is a précis of that book.

The Buddha preoccupied himself with suffering—its prevalence, cause, and cure. He neither suggested that all life is painful, nor offered to take others' suffering upon himself. Instead he outlined how people elicit so much of their own angst, and offered a way beyond it altogether. As the source of suffering is our own doing, not a divine hand, so its pacification must likewise come from us.

Buddha did not teach linear causal relationships—i.e., that a single cause always yields a single result—but referred to causes and conditions in the plural. He thus painted a complex picture of how things work. It takes a web of causes and conditions to produce results, not a single, simple antecedent.

---

11. See *Abhidharmakośabhāṣyam*, 550–765.

Part I: Religious Foundations

Karma is action. Past actions are responsible for our current condition in the world, and present thoughts and actions determine our future. Critics of such individual responsibility object that it produces an unsympathetic attitude toward others in difficult situations. But Buddhism does not fault individuals for all their circumstances. For example, though many of our illnesses may arise from karma, not all do. Thinking that the poor will stay poor until their karmic debt expires cannot be reconciled with the idea of interconnectedness. There is no need to wait for karmic imprints to evaporate before working to change things. Buddhist karmic theory is neither fatalism nor predetermination. We have real choices to make in our affairs. If this were not so Buddhist teaching would be less inspirational and effective than it is. True, we are who we are because of our karmic inheritance, but this does not mean we have to remain as we are. Karmic theory is supposed to encourage us to think, "I can become the person I want to be, and not dwell on what I already am." It should urge us forward, not bog us down in guilt and its associated malaise. So the real Buddhist perspective of karma entails attaining freedom from a variety of karmic hindrances, burning the seeds of entrenched habits and rendering them impotent.

Mindfulness practice enables us to see what sort of karmic patterns we are creating. No divine being maintains a worldly order to which we must conform. Hence we need not struggle with external judgment, nor fear becoming a deviant, since no fixed standard exists by which to define deviancy.

Buddha's understanding of karma is often confused or combined with other interpretations. Before the Buddha's time, karma referred to the performance of sacrifices by Vedic priests as a way to restore harmony in the universe. What one individual did could affect his family, his community, and even the dead. A moral connotation developed only later. The idea of rebirth also emerged later and strengthened over time, extending reaping into succeeding lifetimes. Having a soul bestows spiritual immortality. The Hindu *Bhagavad Gītā* posits a soul or *jīva* that remains the same through many incarnations, as an individual remains identical though repeatedly changing clothes. The jīva exits the mind-body at death and faces all its deeds. Buddhism, by contrast, denies any soul, and stresses that we process our mixed karma gradually and incrementally.

Until the Buddha's time people considered a person to be composed of mind-body (itself comprised of the five elements of earth, fire, wind, water, and space) plus a soul (jīva or ātman). Buddha accepted the fivefold composition of the body, but added four additional complexes of feeling, perception, disposition, and consciousness. Together they comprise five skandhas or bundles of phenomena. We are these five skandhas and nothing more. An imagined, unchanging jīva would not help us perform any kind of mental function, such as seeing, smelling, or tasting. The skandhas themselves are always changing. Thus when one creates karma, it is not an individual with a fixed nature who does so. A person becomes either noble or ignoble through his or her own deeds, not through birth. Everyone has the opportunity to excel.

Buddha often employed the analogy of seedlings. A seed requires the right environment if it is to sprout—sufficient moisture, sunlight, warmth, etc. Even when these are present we can make no certain prediction about when or if a particular seed will germinate. Thus, according to the *Samyutta Nikaya*, even individuals who commit terrible things will not necessarily go to hell. What we think about at the time of death is determinative, since thinking proper thoughts near death can mitigate much negative karma. Even then we might not avoid the outcomes of past karmic deeds. Their seeds may remain dormant, only to germinate once the effect of the good karma created at the moment of death wears off.

To summarize to this point: We are personally responsible for our actions in life. The consequences of these actions are not fixed. Character is crucial: in trying to develop character, an individual becomes a different person. The point is not to discover "who I am," but to see things differently and become different. Character should be constructed upon selflessness. Character is important because we do not have a stable, fixed self-identity.

We can become different from who we were. By contrast, the idea of a fixed self disallows deep, essential change. Actor and costume are the same: we are what we do. Performers are not agents disassociated from their actions, but are transformed by them. We perform actions because preexisting causes and conditions incline us toward doing them. But we are still responsible for what we do, unimpelled by divine governance. We become what we are as a result of what we are doing.

Because the agent is in a constant state of flux, we take rebirth. Even while alive we are not the same person from moment to moment. The reborn "individual" is not identical to the one who lived the previous life, but only carries forward dispositional properties, etc., from the past. Hindu reincarnation teaches that exactly the same person comes back in a new life. Buddhist rebirth, by contrast, implies that the new person is the same but different. What takes place is continuity rather than the persistence and transfer of a fixed entity. The idea of continuity pervades the Buddhist canon, encouraging us to reinvent ourselves. This understanding constitutes a middle way between eternalism and nihilism.

Karma functions in a collective as well as an individual sense. Mutual karmic experience can influence even our natural environment. This collective idea underlies the "power of prayer," which is recognized in Buddhism as helpful.

Buddha believed in what may be called soft determinism. That is, past deeds do influence our current lives, but we have the capacity to change course. Free will and determinism go together: preexisting conditions predetermine our action, but free will enables us to contravene that predetermination. What persists of our own personality is the character we build over the course of our lives. Character constitutes the sum total of what we are as human beings.

The full fruit of one's karma ripens in a next life. Intention matters more than the action itself, though Hindus and Jains would disagree. Doing something in ignorance is not as consequential as doing it intentionally. Other mitigating circumstances might also modify the fruit of otherwise deleterious deeds.

The Buddhist emphasis on character underlies its devotion to virtue, the pillars of which are morality and ethics (*śīla*), meditation (*bhāvanā*), and generosity (*dāna*). We need all three. Patience is primary in śīla and surpasses love and compassion in value. Patience means that we do not flounder when things go wrong, but, with intelligence and in a wiser direction, try again. We do not rid ourselves of bad karma in one fell stroke, but rather gradually wear things down. We need to persist and not be too impatient. The very attempt to eliminate past patterns creates new positive karmic propensities.

The correct approach to karma is not to conceive of it too mechanically, but rather to consider the fabric of our karmic experience. Karma is not determinism or fatalism, but encourages improvement and movement forward. Its complexity and infinite subtlety enshroud karma in an aura of mystery.

Karma theory continued to develop after the passing of the Buddha. Hindus pressured Buddhists to explain how there can be continuity without a "self." Yogacarins proposed the idea of an *ālaya-vijñāna* or "storehouse consciousness" as an answer. This is a repository, at an unconscious level, of our karmic traces. The ālaya-vijñāna is a more permanent state than our conscious states, but is not itself permanent and can be transformed. There are five sense consciousnesses. The input from these is processed by the sixth—mental consciousness or the thinking mind. Its conclusions are then appropriated by the seventh—the egoic mind. The egoic mind mistakenly thinks that it is a self, a "me." The egoic mind leaves imprints on the eighth—the ālaya-vijñāna or storehouse consciousness. Here the perfume of the impressions (*vāsanā*) is retained. In this way karmic imprints, of which we are not conscious, remain alive yet dormant. The ālaya-vijñāna can transport these to another life.

Tibetan Buddhism teaches that if we cannot achieve clear light mind at the point of death, karmic forces propel us to take rebirth. Even then, if we stay aware, we will be able to choose our parents. Death provides an opportunity for awakening and working through karma. A conscious and helpful journey is more likely with a capable guide. Understanding that what we see at death with the mind's eye lacks substantial reality is to see emptiness.

According to Madhyamaka, founded by Nāgārjuna in the second century CE, karma is created through mental fixation and our tendency to reify, ascribing to things more attributes than they have. We even imagine the existence of what does not exist, such as God and the soul. But because all things dependently arise, nothing has inherent existence; everything is empty. Karma also, being an interdependently arising phenomenon, lacks inherent existence and can be overcome.

Buddhism distinguishes between intellect and insight (*prajñā*). Even while seeking prajñā through contemplation, we do so through our karmic inheritance. On the ultimate level, prajñā destroys karma. But on the relative level, prajñā depends on preexisting karmic causes and conditions, so that some people may be predisposed toward greater insight than others. Cause and effect are mutually dependent, as are agent and actions. Both karma and agent are real on the conventional but not the ultimate level. We are not tied to karmic reality in such a way that we are condemned to saṃsāra. Prajñā can help us break through our karmic bondage as we learn to balance between what is relatively and what is ultimately real. Through cultivating ourselves and accumulating merit, we attain the form body of the Buddha. Through cultivating insight and accumulating wisdom, we attain the formless aspect of the Buddha's being. Our ultimate goal is freedom from both iron shackles (bad karma) and gold (good karma). We try to overcome negative karma by cultivating positive, working toward eventually overcoming even positive karma.

Life has no meaning—predetermined by God, for example—that we need to discover. It has only whatever meaning we assign it, and nothing beyond. To make life worthwhile, we need to become more enlightened as to its purpose. Coming to terms with death is part of that. Life without death is impossible; death and life give rise to each other. Our aim is not to conquer death, but to accept it as a consequence of our impermanence. In Protestant theology, death is unnatural, tied to sin. Jesus' conquering death in his resurrection becomes our hope. In Buddhism, we die not because of sin, but because we are a product of causes and conditions. A Buddhist does not think of living forever.

On the one hand, we may have a predetermined time to die, as our karma determines. But on the other, death depends on many causes, and can sometimes be delayed. So a Buddhist does not shun necessary medical care. Whether we pursue Tibetan Buddhism's detailed contemplation of death in order to help us focus on the present, or Zen's almost ignoring of it, the ultimate end is the same—greater acceptance of death in the here and now.

Buddhist rebirth needs to be distinguished from Hindu reincarnation, Greek immortality, and Christian resurrection. What is transferred from one life to another is not an unchanging psychic principle, but rather different psychic elements all hanging together. What we find is continuity but not identity; simultaneously the same individual and yet a totally different individual. It is the karmic impressions that are transferred. The various concepts of "soul" are mental constructions, not based on anything empirical we can find. That is why the word "soul" has different definitions.

To be aware of things is to be conscious. To be enlightened is to be far more conscious in our waking state than normal. There is no need to posit an extra entity. We are quite real, though we lack an inner essence. Though the five skandhas are enough, the idea of a "self" that integrates our various phenomena is useful.

In Buddhism, the mind is not a container with thoughts in it. Without conscious processes there is no consciousness as a separate thing. The skandhas have existence but not reality. It is they, apart from the first or body that are reborn and together comprise the self. If we are thus a bundle of processes, change makes enlightenment possible. This is achieved through the cultivation of mindfulness and awareness. We lose nothing by abandoning the idea of an underlying, unchanging psychic principle.

Karmic theory provides a possible foundation for ethics. In theism, moral action consists of conformity to the wishes of the Almighty. But such thinking does not actually result in moral behavior, since obeying rules is not a moral act. To act morally we must make choices. Secular ideas fare little better: no one has yet been able to build a firm ethical foundation in the ideal of human rights and justice. Karma provides a better foundation. Buddhism teaches the wholesome or beneficial thing to do, not what is right and wrong. Real moral or ethical values must emerge from within.

There is no one who acts with full consciousness. Most of us do stupid things out of ignorance. As such we are not as fully responsible for our actions as we would be if we acted in full knowledge of what we were doing. Intentionality makes a difference in the nature of our deeds: accidentally hitting a deer while driving differs from going hunting and shooting one.

We should be moral because of the kind of beings we are. Acting morally is in our own self-interest. By doing so we are being true to ourselves; when we behave unethically, we are being untrue. It is not our sinful nature that prompts our less-helpful actions, but our inner corruption. We imagine a certain action will benefit us, when actually it will not. We can learn to observe this fact and change course. We should see ourselves as works in progress with very elastic human nature. Taking a more functional or structural view will help us do this. We need to see the effects of our actions on our environment and on others, and how karma is being generated in the process.

All things are laden with meaning; a hammer is a hammer because it drives nails. Karma is created by restoring meaning to what we experience. Everything we see means something to us. Our emotions are aroused, and karma is created. That meaning we give to things has to do with the interconnectedness of phenomena. A profound understanding of this leads us out of karmic bondage.

We objectify things through not seeing interconnections. To see things dualistically is to see them unclearly. Karma is created through perceiving others in an objective manner, subjectively. Individuals create karma, but almost always in an interpersonal setting.

Psychology and morality are inseparable. What we think about is what we become. Karma is created because we act on our thoughts in one way or another. Morality based on natural law is foreign to how Buddhists ground ethics and dangerous because it encourages moralistic, dogmatic, and puritanical thought and behavior. In addition, such ethics feed moral neuroses and obsessive behaviors. In Buddhism, even heinous acts may be rendered less reprehensible through mitigating circumstances. It is the effect of our actions upon ourselves and others that determines whether they are good or bad. It is not the action, but the effect; not what "feels good," but what genuinely promotes well-being; not right or wrong, but what is beneficial or harmful.

Equanimity is important. Becoming calm and observant reduces the impetus of our unthinking behavior. Pacifying unbridled thinking is fundamental to mental cultivation. It both reduces negative habits and cultivates positive karma.

Expressing love helps us become more spontaneous and less scripted. Negative thinking is narrow, structured, constricting. Positive thinking is expansive and brings us out of ourselves. Cultivating good karma helps us extract ourselves from the effects of bad karma: we need to use karma to free ourselves from karma.

To access our true nature requires insight. Gaining insight requires conscious cultivation of the mind and its faculties. Thus positive karma is necessary for insight, since the mind cannot produce insight out of nothing. We must cultivate the body as well. An agitated body contributes to a poorly functioning mind. When we perform wholesome actions we become more relaxed and attuned physically, more expressive verbally, more creative mentally, and more diverse in the range of our emotions. Insight results in greater capacity to communicate on multiple levels, and the ability to employ skillful means in helping others. Developing good habits results in overcoming first bad habits, and then habits altogether.

Our ultimate goal is to transcend good and evil, to think beyond these terms. Buddhism does not need to explain the problem of evil, as does Christianity. Buddhas return out of compassion to work with others and decrease their suffering. They are not, however, able to remove another's karma, alter what another does, directly alleviate the suffering of the world (since each is responsible for his or her own life), or magically remove another person's karma. A buddha can only assist others do so.

Through reflection on ourselves we open up more and see how important it is to harmonize with the environment, the world, and others. Thus, Buddhism emphasizes the development of both wisdom and compassion.

Karma is not a complete metaphysical abstraction, as is Christian resurrection, but also enjoys empirical support. This allows for and encourages the role of science. The phenomena of near death experiences (NDEs) and recollection of previous lives may buttress the position that an aspect of a person, or consciousness, continues after death to reattach to a new body. Visions of Jesus or Buddha during a NDE may be only products of the mind, as are visions described in the *Tibetan Book of the Dead*. Such phenomena are compatible with the idea that things come into being, persist, and disintegrate, with new form coming into being out of the remnants. A continuity of conscious identity, or a conscious continuum, can travel to a next life assuming a different form. The old person is gone, except for faint traces; certain propensities are transferred.

We may have inherited a propensity, but such propensities do not predetermine our future. We must be responsible to work things out. Karmic theory is not meant to encourage conjecture about previous incarnation(s).

Consciousness is like a light that changes and transforms itself—brighter, dimmer; expansive, restrictive—depending upon the vehicle in which it finds lodging. It is like a stream, not a thing, "shining" differently in different media. Thus, the same conscious entity can at one time be a human and at another a pig. After we die, our consciousness looks for and decides on something to which to cling. We take rebirth in a variety of ways, mainly due to our psychological impetus corresponding to the six realms of anger, greed, ignorance, desire, jealousy, pride. These six correspond to hell being, hungry ghost, animal, human, demigod, god.

The world we perceive and inhabit is largely constructed through a shared karmic vision. All humans, for example, see things in a similar way, one that is quite dissimilar to how cats see things. Rebirth occurs precisely due to these tendencies within us. Whatever our predominant poison is, we see the possibilities of it for the future. Greedy people, for example, are living the life of a hungry ghost, never satisfied. Ultimately we need not be reborn driven by karmic propensities: highly realized beings "come back" through the powerful forces of compassion and wisdom, not karma.

One should first work at reducing negative karma one step at a time. Abandoning overly ambitious self-improvement projects, in which we try to do the whole thing at once, in itself produces positive karma. When in time we do turn to positive efforts, the new habits we attract are not strictly speaking habits. Practicing good results in spontaneity, not mindless repetition. A non ego-centric mentality is key.

Part I: Religious Foundations

Human nature has tremendous potential that is seldom explored, stifled by bad habits. The more we repeat such habits, the more we suppress our near primal urge for awakening. Wealth is available to us, both material and internal, consisting of a life led with real satisfaction. Hence, Buddhist icons are laden with jewels. This is meant to convey a sense of enrichment. The more enriched we feel, the less attached to things we become. The approach we take will carry into our next life. If we feel enriched, we attract richness at a multitude of levels.

Generally, we have little willpower, which is why karma is created. We act out of ignorance, not knowing the implications of our acts. Proper cultivation of karma gives a more unified perspective on our lives. Fixation on the self results in undesirable, self-destructive behaviors.

If we understand what we need to be and do, what more is needed? If we feel satisfied and fulfilled, then we do not need anything more. Such satisfaction and fulfillment is the aim of life. We should unburden ourselves from what is extraneous, acquire only that worth having, and enjoy our surroundings in peace and harmony. In our normal mode of creating negative karma, we are accumulating junk, not treasure. Ethical cultivation resembles embarking on a big cleanup job. We have to start now and work incrementally. No one becomes a guitarist overnight.

Liberation requires both leading a good life and meditation. Wisdom, unlike intellect, does not arise from mental activity alone. A wise person knows about all kinds of things, including how to live well. This emerges from cultivating ourselves. Buddhism does not teach eliminating all desires, but progressively liberating ourselves from fixation. Feeling enriched automatically produces a willingness to let go of grasping, upon which karma depends. We still need to eat and drink; a buddha knows what is necessary. Through compassion and skillful means, buddhas can talk and live in any situation.

Openness to karma may free us from the impasse between religious fundamentalists and secular humanists. We do not believe in waiting for others to do things for us if we can do them ourselves.

Karma is integral to Buddhism. It is a complex concept with clear fundamentals. Karma is not purely metaphysical, but has an empirical grounding and a pragmatic aspect. It is one of the many things we cannot directly see or verify.

Karma: Other Views

Some of Kyabgon's exposition may strike people who live among Buddhists as inaccurate or incomplete. Buddhists they know imagine karma more negatively, as something that dooms to disease or disaster, with little hope of escape. Popular karma does at times generate disdain toward "lower" classes of people and unfortunates undergoing calamities. Kyabgon barely mentions merit, and neglects entirely the idea of transfer of merit, a matter of great importance to many Buddhists.

Many view karma in a mechanical, linear fashion, in contrast with Kyabgon's complex web and his talk of seeds that may or may not germinate. For them, a one-to-one correspondence does link deeds in a present life to consequences in the next. Such ideas are popularized in *The Cause and Effect Sutra*. In a series of cartoon pairs the booklet asks and answers such questions as: "Why you are a Government Officer in this-life? Because you have built Buddha's images in your previous life." "Why in this-life you have cars and various transportation facilities? Because you have repaired broken bridges and paved roads for the benefit of others in your previous life." "Why in this-life you are an orphan? Because you were a bird-shooter in your previous life."[12]

Such disparities illustrate the impossibility of defining "the Buddhist position" on karma. Different schools of Buddhism teach conflicting ideas on many issues. Similar fluidity characterizes other faiths. What is "the Christian position" on church government, or principles of Bible translation, or current use of the charismata, or divine sovereignty vs. human responsibility? All Buddhists share a basic core of beliefs, just as all Christians should share a core of their own. But outside these non-negotiables flourish numerous nuances.

Anyone attempting to communicate the gospel to a specific Buddhist community should understand that community's slant on the dharma. It may differ from the views of other Buddhists. Nevertheless, any evangelist must start where his audience actually is, not where he thinks they should be. That includes learning what the local ideas are about karma.

It is helpful to erect all such parochial superstructures on a foundation of classic Buddhist thought. We open a door to significant opportunity when we know our audiences well. Daniel and companions were promoted to government positions from which they were permitted to introduce

---

12. *The Buddha Speaks of*, 8–9, 14–15, 36–37.

PART I: RELIGIOUS FOUNDATIONS

Yahweh, God of Israel, to the most powerful king of their time. Had they declined to study "the literature and language of the Chaldeans" and failed to become "ten times better than all the magicians and enchanters in [Nebuchadnezzar's] whole kingdom," they would have enjoyed no such opportunity. We similarly might find that knowing Buddhism better than our audiences opens otherwise closed but significant doors for witness. Hence, our reflection in this chapter upon Kyabgon. Not all he writes may immediately reflect our specific milieus but he does attempt to outline the classic Buddhist concepts of karma.

Karma and the Bible: Parallels

As Paul could quote Aratus and Cleanthes without implying acceptance of all they said, or as Jesus could observe that one of the legal experts was "not far from the kingdom of God" (Mark 12:34), so we may cite Buddhism on karma when it parallels biblical truth.

A first parallel is that we reap what we sow. This phenomenon is unapologetically biblical. In addition to such straightforward passages, the truth of reaping what one sows plays out in such stories as Jacob the deceiver (Gen 27:35–36, 31:20, 26–27) being deceived—most obviously by his father-in-law (29:25) and his sons (34:13, 37:31–35). So while interacting with Buddhists we certainly can affirm some aspects of getting back what we give out.

A second is the power of repentance to transform one's future. The Bible often urges repentance, though in some circles repentance is insufficiently discussed. We can change our lives for good or for ill (Ezek 18; 33). Ahab repented and avoided personal punishment (1 Kgs 21:27–29). Nineveh was spared. Jesus' initial message, as well as John's before him, was "Repent, because the kingdom of God is at hand." When asked, John suggested specific examples of what that meant (Luke 3:8–14).

Third, though we may be inclined through genetics, upbringing, or habit to think and act in certain ways, we are neither fated nor compelled to do so. We have choice. The Bible presents humans as responsible for the choices they make and the paths they follow. "Choose this day whom you will serve," not "You have been chosen this day for whom you will serve." "Choose life," not "Some of you have been chosen for life." "Whoever wants to may come," not "Whoever has been predestined will inevitably come." So to the extent that Kyabgon urges that we intelligently and willfully reject past inclinations and patterns in favor of what is true and wise and good, Christians gladly agree. When he urges abandonment of an ignorant and errant past in favor of an enlightened future, we say amen.

Fourth, we can agree that both karma and Christian resurrection are faith positions. Karma is "one of the many things we cannot directly see or verify" (Kyabgon 2015:149). Kyabgon wants to adduce empirical evidence to buttress karma's claim to validity, then deny any to Christian resurrection. But although the resurrection of Jesus is not a repeatable, measurable phenomenon, neither is any other historical event. The eyewitness accounts of many people on different occasions, none of whom expected Jesus' physical resurrection, and one of whom violently opposed the idea, must at least be granted a hearing. These accounts provide evidence that goes beyond the mere metaphysical speculation that Kyabgon allows. They do not prove the event, just as neither do eyewitness accounts prove the murder of Julius Caesar.

Karma and the Bible: Misunderstandings

Kyabgon repeatedly rejects the idea of a human soul, since he believes that the soul is by definition unchanging. But this misunderstands the soul's nature. In Hodge's theology, "[T]he human soul is a spirit. The essential attributes of a spirit are reason, conscience, and will."[13] Reason, conscience, and will are activities or functions, not entities or substances. These functions apparently emerge gradually as a fetus develops and is born, and continue to evolve throughout each individual's lifetime. They together form what might be called capacities or activities of the human soul. But much less is said in scripture regarding the vehicle or substance or substratum, if any, in which these capacities or activities inhere and operate. The very fact that no such capacities existed or functioned before the individual who exercises them came into being argues against any notion of the soul's being an unchanged, eternal substance. People's reason, conscience, and will fluctuate constantly, and the Bible describes in detail no substratum for them other than the body. Kyabgon seems to have conflated the Bible with the *Bhagavad Gītā*. The *Gītā*, as he rightly notes, does in fact teach such an eternal, unchanging soul: "You were never born; you will never die. You have never changed; you can never change. Unborn, eternal, immutable, immemorial, you do not die when the body dies.... As a man abandons worn-out clothes

---

13. Hodge, *Systematic Theology*, 96.

and acquires new ones, so when the body is worn out a new one is acquired by the Self [or soul], who lives within ."[14] However we understand what the Bible means by "soul," it is not what the *Bhagavad Gītā* means.

A second misunderstanding seems to be an innuendo that God's directives are arbitrary and not entirely for our best interests. If this accurately reflects Kyabgon it represents a sad but not atypical etic assessment of the Bible. Kyabgon does acknowledge that there are some who have gained inspiration from theism to lead more moral lives, and he applauds that outcome. A theistic ethic, he says, compels one to conform "to the wishes of the Almighty ... and it is up to us to find and work out our role within God's natural law."[15] Of course for him "simply obeying the rules ... does not constitute a moral act,"[16] which consists of making a choice. Kyabgon's reiterates his fear that any discussion of ethics might be hijacked by religious fanatics. Karma, he confidently asserts, provides a better foundation for ethics.

Such a view ignores the Bible's repeated assurances of God's love for those he has created, and his desire for their well-being. God does not, for example, demand sacrifice out of self-interest—because he is hungry or needs anything (Ps 50:12). His proscriptions against murder, rape, rampant materialism, etc., are imposed not to restrict but to free people to become their truest selves. We need not, as Kyabgon suggests, replace the concepts of "right and wrong" with "beneficial and non-beneficial." This kind of outlook echoes Eden: "Did God really say ... ?" with its implication that God is withholding something good when he forbids eating the fruit of one tree.

Karma and the Bible: Problems

This leads us to introduce selected problems with karma, at least as an all-encompassing theory that excludes God and grace.

If God created humanity, he should know what is best for it. A loving, righteous God would urge and forbid only what conduces to his creatures' ultimate well-being. If so, then theism as well as Kyabgon's version of karma promotes human *shalōm*. It arguably does so better. Neither individuals nor societies, even those rare thoughtful ones, consistently know and promote what is best. They inevitably tweak and sometimes reverse their theories

---

14. *Gītā*, 63.
15. Kyabgon, "Karma," 105.
16. Ibid., 106.

about what "best" might be. In the 1930s, "best" for millions of Germans was to label Jews subhuman, and exterminate them. "Best" in this case led to disaster: terror for the murdered and dehumanization of their murderers. Today's Western medical community provides another example. For decades doctors warned that butter is bad and margarine good. Now it is the opposite. Eggs were dangerous but now are nutritious. Our enemy was fat, not sugar; now sugar is more suspect. Artificial sweeteners designed for weight loss encourage obesity. Not long ago the medical community touted the health benefits of cigarette smoking. Do we really always know what is best?

If we can get things so wrong in nutrition, despite all we invest in research, might we also get things wrong in the more subtle realms of morals and philosophy? Toddlers have been known to resent parents who forbid their playing with knives, running in the street, or standing too close to the edge, and who insist instead on eating vegetables, brushing teeth, and getting enough sleep. But parents are expected to know better than children. Parents will lovingly insist on such rules, and discipline infractions, until children are mature enough to recognize that yes, what their parents urged is best after all. It seems hubristic to imagine that we know better than our creator. Although much of what the Buddha urges in both the precepts and the *Dhammapada* is good, perhaps these truths did not require for their discovery six years of asceticism followed by deep thought. Perhaps they could have been more easily and certainly observed in the *torah* and other revelatory writings that antedated him.

A second problem revolves around the phenomenon of personal continuity, a concept difficult to defend in the light of Buddhist anattā. Karma requires that actions result in consequences. As these are not always experienced in this life, Buddhists have proposed future lifetimes in which they might return to the one who performed them. But if there is "no self," then who enjoys or suffers the fruit of what I did? Certainly not I. The skandhas (minus the body) seem an insufficient answer. Yogācāra posits a "storehouse consciousness." This suggestion seems an expedient adopted to allow for continuity while simultaneously holding to no-self. It is not based on empirical evidence. Therefore, neither does a storehouse consciousness solve the problem. The notion of a unified and cohesive soul whose functions include reason, conscience, and will better explains personal continuity. We need not speculate at this point on the precise nature or attributes of the soul beyond these. Certainly the soul need (and must) not be some kind of unchanging, eternal substance like the Hindu ātman (which is Brahman). A soul that is not static but dynamic allows for emergence and development on the one hand, and personal continuation beyond death on the other.

An issue that Kyabgon scarcely mentions but concerns many Asian Buddhists is merit production and transfer. "Meritorious deeds (*puñña*) do not lead to enlightenment, but to (temporary) future happiness in this world or another. This is the usual aim of 'popular' Buddhism."[17] "Both Theravāda and Mahāyāna emphasize the possibility and vitality of merit transfer,"[18] despite the fact that such transfer "appears to contradict the supposed rigidity of the law of karma."[19] The contradiction may run deeper than mere appearance. "[P]ractice of both merit transfer and the afterlife constitute a major part of Buddhist activities in China" and "the practice of transferring merit to the dead in *Petaloka* has been popularly endorsed in society almost since the formation of the Pali canon."[20] This is not the place to consider how consciousness and sensations function and persist without an entity that is conscious and sentient. More germane to this chapter are such questions as:

Who or what defines what "merit" is? Despite Kyabgon's aversion to labeling actions as good or evil, Buddhism considers some at least preferable to others. Sobriety excels drunkenness; truth surpasses lies. But why? Even substituting Kyabgon's preferred "beneficial and non-beneficial" or "wholesome and unwholesome" for "good and evil" does not solve the problem. What does "beneficial" mean, and who is benefitted? As mentioned, Nazism was urged as beneficial in its putative agenda to purify the human race. It was anything but. Even if we do somehow manage to define "beneficial," why and how does the universe recognize and reward it? Why is "beneficial" better than "non-beneficial"? Some people argue that, because of humanity's destructive and polluting ways, eliminating us would be beneficial to the Earth and its surviving creatures. Should we pursue that course? It is not surprising that many have argued that Buddhism, while home to and nurturer of millions of moral people, lacks a firm foundation for ethics, outside of an *ipse dixit* from Siddhartha Gautama. In Christianity, actions are moral when they reflect the character and commands of

---

17. *Long Discourses*, 116.
18. Yu, "Merit Transfer," 48.
19. Williams, *The Unexpected Way*, 205.
20. Yu, "Merit Transfer," 30, 32.

God, whose character is good, and whose commands are neither arbitrary nor self-serving, but issued in the interest of his creation.

Who or what sees invisible intentions and assigns greater merit to noble ones? Who or what sees that alms were given to an arhant rather than to a novice, and assigns far greater merit for the gift to the fortunate but unknowing giver? By what mechanism would karmic consequences be transferred from one individual to another? It may appear noble and altruistic for one person to assign merit to another individual or to all sentient beings. But who or what hears that request and has power to achieve the transfer? This question may be asked when the benefit is dedicated to all, but perhaps more so when designated to one individual. How does an impersonal universe hear such a request, locate the appropriate person (whether living or deceased)—particularly when hundreds or thousands have the same name—and apply it? The Buddhism that eschews God appears to require gods in his stead, and such events as "review in the court of Yama."[21] This is another area in which "Buddhism has an 'explanatory gap.'"[22]

Because so much production and transfer of merit is done in connection with the sangha,

> [m]erit practice in Buddhism ... is sometimes suspected of being a Buddhist device that aims at exacting donations and offerings from lay-society by promising magnanimous rewards for their generosity.... After receiving the bail in terms of merit from their living relatives, Yama releases the dead so that they can gain a better rebirth in the next life. It is, therefore, undeniable that the idea of an intermediate state and the practice of merit transfer are Buddhist programs to gain financial support.[23]

One is tempted to think of memorial masses to release the dead from purgatory as a Christian parallel.

How may an individual calm his queasy conscience and assure that all is well? Buddhist schools and literature differ on whether and how much bad karma can be undone. Any derailment that is accomplished might prove to be only a temporary deferral, not a permanent disposal. In Christianity, because the consequences of one's unwholesome deeds have been paid for

---

21. Yu, "Merit Transfer," 43.
22. Williams, *The Unexpected Way*, 19.
23. Yu, "Merit Transfer," 46.

in full by Christ (transferred to him), the believer's conscience is cleansed fully and permanently from any sense of further debt (Heb 9:13–14).

Although Kyabgon disavows ascribing all of life's circumstances to karma, many Buddhists do. For them, if a cause of one's suffering or success cannot be identified in the present life, its root must be something done in a previous existence. Little or no consideration is given to other options. The Bible, by contrast, is less reductionistic. The actions of others (e.g., parents or society); the fallen world around us; or the nature of one's era, environment, or genetic make-up may also lie at the root. Or, as Qoheleth observed, "The race is not to the swift or the battle to the strong, nor does food come to the wise or wealth to the brilliant or favor to the learned; but time and chance happen to them all" (Eccl 9:11). For the Christian, God may ordain something for his own purposes (Exod 4:11; John 9:3). No, not all stems from karma. Invoking unknown past lives to explain present circumstances is merely an expedient, a faith position adopted out of uncritical commitment to karma. No evidence supports this stratagem. Innocent victims often wrongly blame themselves—children whose parents divorce, spouses who suffer abuse, victims of kidnapping or hostage-taking.

Kyabgon made clear that rebirth does not bring back the same person who returns, but someone who is the same yet different, a "usurper." For Paul Williams, this end of personal existence contributed significantly to his conversion to Catholicism after decades as an academic and practicing Buddhist.

> I began to think that if Buddhism were correct then unless I attained enlightenment or something like it in this life, *I*—Williams, the person I am—would have no hope. For the rebirth of Williams that follows from my not attaining enlightenment would not be the same person as Williams. Clearly I was not going to attain enlightenment in this life. So I (and I suspect all my friends and family) must have in themselves finally no hope. Not only that. Actually, from a Buddhist perspective in the scale of infinite time and infinite rebirths, the significance of each of us as such, as the person we actually are now, converges on nothing. Thus Buddhism for me appeared to be *hope-less* . . . Christianity at least offers *hope*.[24]

Bhasakorn Bhavilai proposes the idea of a neuron functioning within a body and developing a proto-mind. It dies and comes back as a different

---

24. 2002:15.

cell. In time it has gained enough experience to warrant rebirth as an independent, single-celled organism, then a multi-celled organism, then a human. After innumerable re-becomings, in both the human and other realms, this evolved mind can finally opt "to continue in a state of complete freedom, independent of physical form, beyond this world of opposites, beyond happiness and suffering, beyond birth and death."[25] That is, it can attain nirvana. Such a scenario is pure conjecture based on a pre-commitment to Buddhist ideas, supported by no empirical evidence. Even if such a sequence did occur, it is not the same individual who returns. Where is the justice of forcing what is essentially someone else to suffer for my misdeeds? Or why should I deprive myself now to store up good karma for the next guy who happens to come along? To adapt Paul's "words of despair about a life with nothing beyond the dissolution of personal existence as the end,"[26] "If in this life only we have personal existence, let us eat and drink, for tomorrow we die" (1 Cor 15:19, 32).

What would be the point of all this emergence and evolution and escape *ad infinitum*, were it true? The bodhisattva vow to save all sentient beings could never be fulfilled, because new cells are constantly being formed. If countless new cells constantly emerge and begin to evolve through untold lifetimes, with the final incarnation alone attaining nirvana, where is there any meaning? If this is the way things truly are, then existence has no significance. In Christianity, history displays the glory of God, and Hinduism at least posits the *līlā* of Brahman. But what is the point in Buddhism? The answer cannot be the bliss of nirvana, since there cannot be bliss (or any other emotion or sensation) without someone or something to experience it.

Moving on From Here

There are ways, then, that the Christian can use karma to explain the gospel. We often do reap what we sow. It helps no one to deny that fact. The phenomenon is arguably more understandable if behind it stands one who causes people to reap what they sow. Who other than God could see and judge the intangibles, such as intention, which are said to be more important than the deeds themselves? The best hope for freedom from inexorable karma is the God who stands above it. Particularly this is so if this God has

---

25. Bhavilai, *Karma for Today's Traveler*, 75–82.
26. Thiselton, *The First Epistle to the Corinthians*, 1252.

taken on himself in the person of Christ the painful consequences of our evil thoughts and deeds.

If God sees each person's hidden heart, and knows it better than does the person himself, then God is able to recompense most accurately and fairly. If he is wise and just, then his judgments will not err. As the righteous judge Christ will give to each "according to what he has done" (2 Cor 5:10; Rev 22:12 NAS), having pierced through pretense and appearance. A personal, perceptive, righteous God explains appropriate payback better than does a mindless universe operating though impersonal laws. How would such a universe hold together disembodied skandhas of consciousness, perception, etc., and assure that these strangely conglomerated and persisting functions, which continue to function without an entity in which they inhere, inherit conditions appropriate to what they practiced long ago?

With some audiences it may be better to defer debating the logical problems of merit transfer. Instead, we can use this widely-held idea as an analogy, arguing *a fortiori*:

> If human beings who are laden with evil and are also unenlightened are believed to be capable of transferring merit, it is not incomprehensible at all that the Lord Jesus Christ would be able to transfer his merit to others.... The use of this bridge has resulted in many Buddhists coming to Christianity.[27]

The logical advantages of a system of sowing and reaping that includes God vs. one that excludes him are complemented by existential advantages. The freedom that Christ gives from guilt and fear is primary. Late missionary statesman George Peters describes a conversation with evangelist and Bible teacher Bakht Singh:

> As we talked about evangelism and a message for India, I asked him: "When you preach in India, what do you emphasize?" "Do you preach to them the love of God?"
>
> "No," he said, "not particularly. The Indian mind is so polluted that if you talk to them about love they think mainly of sex life. You do not talk to them much about the love of God."
>
> "Well," I said, "do you talk to them about the wrath of God and the judgment of God?"

---

27. Weerasingha, "Karma and Christ," 104.

"No, this is not my emphasis," he remarked, "they are used to that. All the gods are mad anyway. It makes no difference to them if there is one more who is angry!"

"What do you talk to them about? Do you preach Christ and Him crucified?" I guessed.

"No, he replied. "They would think of Him as a poor martyr who helplessly died."

"What then is your emphasis? Do you talk to them about eternal life?"

"Not so," he said. "If you talk about eternal life, the Indian thinks of transmigration. He wants to get away from it. Don't emphasize eternal life."

"What then is your message?"

"I have never yet failed to get a hearing if I talk to them about forgiveness of sins and peace and rest in your heart. That's the product that sells well. Soon they ask me how they can get it. Having won their hearing I lead them on to the Savior who alone can meet their deepest needs."[28]

Christian evangelists address many different people who start from a vast variety of backgrounds and understandings. Some need their whole worldviews inverted, while others are "not far from the kingdom of God." We can use those parts of their beliefs that are good, and lead them from there to what is best.

Bibliography

Abhidharmakośabhāṣyam of Vasubandhu. Translated by Leo M. Pruden. Berkeley: Asian Humanities, 1991.
Bacher, Wilhelm, and Jacob Zallel Lauterbach. "Rahab." In *Jewish Encyclopedia*. jewishencyclopedia.com/articles/12534-rahab, 1906.
Berlin, Adele, and Marc Zvi Brettler, eds. *The Jewish Study Bible*. Oxford: Oxford University Press, 2004.
The Bhagavad Gita. Translated by Eknath Easwaran. Tomales, CA: Nilgiri, 1985.
Bhavilai, Bhasakorn, with David Freyer. *Karma for Today's Traveler*. Chiang Mai, Thailand: Nuntapun, 2005.
The Buddha Speaks of: The Cause and Effect Sutra. N.d. Johor Bahru: Liang Enterprise.

---

28. Peters, "Issues," 167.

Part I: Religious Foundations

Day, John N. "God and Leviathan in Isaiah 27:1." *Bibliotheca Sacra* 155 (October–December 1998) 423–36.

Gordon, Cyrus H. "Leviathan: Symbol of Evil." In *Biblical Motifs: Origins and Transformations*, Vol III, edited by Alexander Altmann, 1–10. Cambridge: Harvard University Press, 1966.

Hodge, Charles. *Systematic Theology*, Vol. 2. Grand Rapids: Eerdmans, 1986.

The Long Discourses of the Buddha: A Translation of the Digha Nikāya. Translated by Maurice Walshe. Boston: Wisdom, 1995.

Parsons, Gregory W. "Literary Features of the Book of Job." *Bibliotheca Sacra* 138 (July–September 1981) 213–229.

Peters, George W. "Issues Confronting Evangelical Missions." In *Evangelical Missions Tomorrow*, edited by Wade T. Coggins and E. L. Frizen. South Pasadena: William Carey Library, 1977. Cited in *Communicating Christ Cross-Culturally: An Introduction to Missionary Communication*, by David J. Hesselgrave, 248–249. Grand Rapids: Zondervan, 1991.

Thiselton, A. C. *The First Epistle to the Corinthians: A Commentary on the Greek Text*. Grand Rapids: Eerdmans, 2000.

Traleg Kyabgon. *Karma: What It Is, What It Isn't, Why It Matters*. Boston: Shambhala, 2015.

Wakeman, Mary K. *God's Battle with the Monster: A Study in Biblical Imagery*. Leiden: Brill, 1973.

Waltke, Bruce K. "The Creation Account in Genesis 1:1–3. Part I: Introduction to Biblical Cosmogony." *Bibliotheca Sacra* 132 (January–March 1975) 25–36.

Weerasingha, Tissa. "Karma and Christ: Opening Our Eyes to the Buddhist World." *International Journal of Frontier Missions* 10/3 (1993) 103–4.

Whatham, A. E. "The Yahweh-Tehom Myth." *Biblical World* 36/5 (1910) 290, 329–33.

Williams, Paul. *The Unexpected Way: On Converting from Buddhism to Catholicism*. London: T & T Clark, 2002.

Yu, Xue. "Merit Transfer and Life after Death in Buddhism." *Ching Feng* n.s., 4/1 (2003) 29–50.

2

An Adaptational Dialogue in Reading Luke 16:19–31 for Thai Buddhists Followers of Jesus

C-S Abraham Cheong

ANY CULTURAL FORM OR system in and of itself is essentially value neutral. It is how it is used that matters. Languages, cultures and social systems are simply instrumental and contingent because every culture is formulated as a coping mechanism, a strategy for survival, belonging to and operated by a society. The same principle can be adapted to gospel communication. Indeed, theologizing as well as biblical interpretation offer relevant windows into human culture showing where God's mission may already be at work in individuals and groups. In this chapter, I explore some Buddhist concepts useful as functional substitutes for Thai Buddhist followers of Jesus in the communication and practice of a contextualized good news. Doing so, I argue in favor of adaptation to the karmic worldview over changing it. I also argue that Thai Buddhist merit-making efforts support and strengthen their allegiance to Jesus Christ, rather than otherwise. Meritorious deeds enacted in Buddhist contexts are not different from the good works of Christ followers, as it relates to my parable interpretation. It is necessary to promote better communication of the gospel within indigenous communities and to ensure that expatriate missionaries avoid cultural misunderstandings and meaning discrepancies. In my exploration of such adaptational dialogue, I attempt to delineate the meaning of the parable of

PART I: RELIGIOUS FOUNDATIONS

the Rich Man and Lazarus (16:19–31) from the perspectives and belief systems of non-western communities. Intercultural exploration of scripture expands everyone's understanding of the text, ourselves and others. The gift of others' insights into theology and scriptural application directs and corrects the wider global church.

For cross-cultural missionaries, two fundamental questions may inevitably arise in their work, according to Paul G. Hiebert. First, "What shall we do with the existing cultural practices, particularly those related to the people's religion?" Second, "How can we best express the gospel in the new culture?" He continues, "Can we use the people's words for God when these are deeply tied to their existing religious beliefs, or should we introduce foreign terms which they do not understand?"[1]

Hiebert's questions are intimately related to the contextualization of the gospel, wherein he explored various relationships of form and meaning, and defined the nature of symbols in human cultures. Building upon his work, I would raise two additional questions, specifically, how can the gospel of Jesus be best communicated with Buddhists who desire to follow Jesus in Thailand? And, to what extent can cross-cultural missionaries adapt local religious language and belief systems and still insure faithful communication? Finally, based on the insights gained from others, what do I (and my sending church) need to change to better align myself with God's direction in mission? Before answering these questions, I will take a brief look at the nature of culture and language as a starting point for this discussion.

As a result of western colonialism and modern scientific achievement from the mid-nineteenth century, western populations had absolutized western cultural superiority and consequently rejected other systems of belief as primitive, superstitious and pagan, holding that such beliefs would result in dangerous and fearful syncretism. Consequently, indigenous heritage and cultural practices like native music, arts, marriage and funeral rites were entirely rejected, to such an extent that believing in Christ meant not only following him, but also adopting western culture.[2] Indeed, western populations believed that it was possible to transfer meaning to the native, only by "sending bits of encoded information."[3] As a consequence, local

---

1. Hiebert, "Form and Meaning," 101.

2. See Kraft, *Anthropology*, 88; Hiebert, "Form and Meaning," 102–3, and Smith "Apply Cultural Contexts," 98–99.

3. Smith, "Apply Cultural Contexts," 103.

believers were forced to face unnecessary barriers in gospel communication with relatives and neighbors.

With the advent of anthropological discoveries in the twentieth century, however, people began to realize that men and women in different cultures see the world in different ways and that all systems of knowledge had to be understood within their cultural contexts, not least because each culture had "its own characteristics and unique texture."[4] As a result, there was a turning away from the west's dominant epistemology. Now, there is acknowledgement that language shapes the way "people see the world," so that local languages as "cultural scripts (patterns)" should be adopted to communicate the gospel effectively.[5] Without such adoption, when missionaries simply seek to avoid syncretism and instead introduce new western forms or symbols, the gospel remains "foreign" and does "not take root at the core of people's lives," creating the problem of "nominality."[6] Smith likewise raises an even stronger alarm against such failures in adaption, "Things may look quite contextual inside, but not be functioning adequately to impact the community outside."[7]

In sum, any cultural form or system in itself is essentially "value free."[8] No universal or ideal language and cultural system faultlessly underlies human thoughts and truths, but instead understanding moves fluidly in different contexts. Language and cultures, as previously stated, are simply instrumental and contingent, because every culture is formulated as "a coping mechanism, a strategy for survival, belonging to and operated by a society."[9] The same principle can be adapted to gospel communication or missiological dialogue. Surely, theologizing as well as Biblical interpretation is a relevant window for "intrusion into a human culture."[10]

In seeking an adequate adaptation of the gospel for Thai Buddhist followers of Jesus, I will explore the possible use of some Buddhist concepts and terms as "functional substitutes."[11] An understanding of these concepts is necessary to promote better communication of the gospel within

---

4. Ibid., 93.
5. See Hiebert, "Form and Meaning," 103; Kraft, *Anthropology*, 38.
6. Gibbs, "Contextual Considerations," 239.
7. Smith, "Apply Cultural Contexts," 113.
8. Hiebert, "Form and Meaning," 10.
9. Kraft, *Anthropology*, 38–39.
10. Conn, *Eternal Word*, 235.
11. Smith, "Apply Cultural Contexts," 110–113.

indigenous communities and ensure that missionaries avoid cultural misunderstandings and "meaning discrepancy."[12] In my exploration of these concepts, I will attempt to delineate the meaning of the parable of the Rich Man and Lazarus (16:19–31) from the perspectives and belief systems of non-western communities. I am following Harvie Conn's assertion that "[w]e do not know what scripture says until we know how it relates to our world."[13] Therefore, this chapter does not attempt a critical research on the text, but rather intends to offer a method of interpretation.

Adaptational Dialogue for Communication

Adaptational dialogue is a reading strategy that places relative importance upon the worldview context surrounding an encounter of a biblical text. This means dealing with the flesh and blood reader, bringing his or her realities into the reading process. These realities would include unique presuppositions, personal and societal experiences, and educational and cultural background. Just as the author assimilates, internalizes, and synthesizes his or her own worldview and cultural experiences into the text with individual expressions and evaluations, the reader likewise plays a similar role when reading. In the reading process, the reader is ultimately responsible for making decisions about what the text delivers, not least because meaning is created within the context of the reader.[14] Meaning does not ultimately reside in the text itself but within those who read it.[15]

Significantly, the adaptational needs of each community are validated by the existence of a fourfold gospel in the New Testament through which theological diversity is kept intact. Together the various gospels communicate one Jesus, the Christ, but with a different emphasis in each in order to address unique and diverse contextual questions, issues, and problems. The diversity of messages appears to address the diversity of needs existent in their respective recipients. Hence, gospel writers themselves were no doubt context-sensitive practitioners giving priority to their readers. This is a lesson we need in mission today.

The receptor-oriented nature of the gospel writers is culminated in no other than Paul the apostle himself, particularly in his letters to the

---

12. Ibid., 103,112.
13. Conn, *Eternal Word*, 220.
14. Søgaard, "Dimensions," 166.
15. Kraft, *Jesus, God's Model*, 92–93.

Corinthians (1 Cor 9:19–23). Firmly declaring his purpose for winning different people, he willingly identifies himself with slaves, Jews, people under the law as well as people without the law, and the weak, although he is not like any of these people. Although the Corinthian audience, blindly following wisdom teachers, denigrated and ridiculed Paul's authority as foolish, he fearlessly marched forward to his recipients to form a relationship, not simply through words but with his life. His concern was not the message but the messenger, just as Jesus himself was God's letter (2 Cor 3:2–3). Indeed, Jesus and Paul both chose to adapt themselves to people's needs and contexts.[16]

Words inform, but relationships communicate. Gospel communication starts with the sender's adaptation to the recipient and his or her specific need. For example, in John 3 Jesus started his conversation with Nicodemus by first entering into his frame of reference and understanding.[17] Adoption works well for the sender; adaptation for recipient; in the same way, gospel communication is not for God but for people. That is why God's revelation in both Testaments had been understandably limited by the recipient's frame of reference. According to Kraft, God's revelation maintains threefold relativity: "in the endowment and opportunities of people," "in the extent of revelation," and "in cultural patterns."[18] It is in God's incarnation that the relativity of God's revelation culminates as it entirely accommodates the "receptor's cognitive environment."[19]

Notably, Jesus loved to teach people in parables, which involved adapting to people's everyday language. Jesus intimately and vulnerably identified himself with his recipients.[20] According to an ancient teaching of Buddhism, "if one truly wants to understand a certain person, he must truly identify himself with that person." Thus, for adaptational dialogue, we should deduce adequate strategies for Thai Buddhist recipients who have long committed to and are deeply embedded in their religious culture. Such approaches must acknowledge and facilitate the fact that God allowed "inherent bridges" for the gospel to be resident within them, already "pregnant

---

16. Kraft, "Contextualizing," 123.
17. Søgaard, "Dimensions," 168.
18. Kraft, *Anthropology*, 80.
19. See Johnson, "Context-Sensitive Evangelism," 69 and Kraft, *Jesus, God's* Model, 30.
20. Kraft, *Anthropology*, 38.

with potential possibilities to know Creator God."²¹ However, adaptational communicators become jeopardized when both Christians and Buddhists, blame and rebuke those who attempt such adaptation as "amphibians" or wobblers staying suspiciously in grey areas.²²

Buddhists Followers of Jesus in Thailand

My question is conveyed in a decisive and straight-forward manner by Paul de Neui, "Is it possible for Thai Buddhists to remain within their cultural context and faithfully follow Jesus Christ?"²³ His question itself is a powerful answer in imperative form. His assertion is based on an observation that, "[i]n a Buddhist country such as Thailand, national identity is closely linked with religious identity; good citizenship is equated with being Buddhist." Accordingly, religious patriotism is, as he strongly contends, "problematic for the cause of the gospel of Christ," so that those cross-cultural workers have often viewed Buddhism as the "enemy of evangelism." The result is people's social alienation and a misunderstanding that Jesus is a foreigner (i.e., Western), "the leader of the foreigner's religion."²⁴ That is why the greatest hindrance to the evangelism of the church is none other than the "church itself," particularly within the Buddhist world.²⁵

Adopting John Travis' typologies, which differentiate Christ-centered communities from the C1 to C6 spectrum, de Neui delineates in detail how to apply the six different models to the Thai folk Buddhist context. Among them, the C5 community is categorized as "Buddhist followers of Jesus" who remain socially "within the context of popular Buddhism" and celebrate their Christian life "in ways that are familiar and meaningful to them." This would include "location and forms of gatherings, communication styles, organizational structures, and methods of leadership and discipleship."²⁶ It is also notable that Thai Buddhism comes from the Theravada tradition, different from the Mahayana tradition found in China, Korea, and Japan, though similarities exist. For many in the Thai C5 community however, Buddhism corresponds primarily to national identity. Hence, it is not nec-

---

21. Smith, "Apply Cultural Contexts," 112.
22. Johnson, "Context-Sensitive Evangelism," 66.
23. de Neui, "Appropriate Typologies," 187.
24. Ibid., 187.
25. Conn, *Eternal Word*, 220.
26. de Neui, "Appropriate Typologies," 204.

essary for the C5 community to change their karmic worldview as far as their merit-making efforts support and strengthen their allegiance to Jesus. For C5 followers, their meritorious deeds which are enacted in Buddhist contexts are very similar to the good works of Christ followers.

In general, members of C5 groups as Buddhist followers of Jesus are not known to refer to themselves as Christians, as they do not accept, follow, or practice western Christianity, but instead refer to themselves as "children of God," claiming an "allegiance to the one true God" and viewing themselves as Buddhists at the same time. This is how C5 members avoid building barriers between themselves and their families and neighbors. Through this "they could follow Jesus and still remain a Thai."[27] In this way, they are better positioned to reach out to their communities by using local culture as a bridge rather than focusing on issues that separate. Biblical examples of this can be seen in the scripture. After his miraculous healing, Naaman makes a request that would appear to compromise the loyalty he professes to YHWH, yet Elisha gives tacit approval (2 Kgs 5:15–19). In the same way, "Gentile believers" in the book of Acts were accepted into the family of God without first converting to Judaism and without erasing their various ethnic distinctions.

Therefore, Thai Buddhists Followers of Jesus, who embody biblical doctrines in cultural forms that are acceptable to their society, are contextualized believers. Some of them are found in the house church in the home of Banpote Wetchgama in Udon Thani, Thailand, as well as in other house churches in Chiang Mai, Roi Et and Bangkok. Paul de Neui reports that C5 models are also found in some villages in Det Udom district of Ubol Ratchatani, Thailand.[28] Of course, there are also potential weaknesses and pitfalls in the C5 model such as isolationism, excessive self-pride, and syncretism, as pointed out by de Neui.[29]

Purpose of Luke's Gospel

A Greek by birth, Luke, wrote two volumes in the NT, probably right after the destruction of the temple, in the early seventies of the first-century. Most biblical scholars agree that both volumes are targeting the Gentile Christian church that was endangered by hostile Jews during Luke's time,

---

27. Ibid., 206–7.
28. Ibid., 206–7.
29. Ibid., 207.

to provide "legitimation" and assurance.[30] The first volume is more theologically apologetic in "responding to Jewish polemic against the Christian movement,"[31] whereas the second is more politically apologetic "to present as defense for Paul" on trial.[32]

It is understood that Luke's readers, first-century Gentile Christians designated as God-fearers, were troubled by the polemics of the Jews. They urgently needed "an objective verification and theological justification of facts" which they had received,[33] mainly in relation to their Gentile identity. They had clearly experienced ambiguity and bewilderment in their situation during this transitional period, a period that retained strong influence by Jews who considered Christianity "a dangerous perversion of Jewish heritage" and urged those God-fearers to "break and to abandon Gentile identity."[34] God-fearers in the gospel may have felt that they were "welcomed, but at the crucial divide still considered to be outsiders to the promises of God." Accordingly, Luke's gospel responds to those who stood at the crossroads, persuading them not to give up but to hold dear their Gentile identity, since regardless of their ethnic mark and cultural distinctiveness, the Christian church is the "completion and fulfillment of Judaism" or the "reconstituted people of God."[35]

However, by compiling the central section of his writing (Luke 9:51–19:44) with Jesus' travels into Jerusalem, Luke adopted into his Gentile-oriented gospel the theological spirit of the Jewish law, that is, the two greatest commandments: love of God and love of neighbor (Matt 22:40; Luke 10:27). Luke's central section, in which Jesus' parables are mainly adopted for communicating these two commandments, is compiled from Deuteronomist teachings by *haggadic* (non-legal) midrash, and adapted for to his Gentile readers.[36] In that moment, it brought Jewish tradition home for Gentile readers. It concerned what Jesus' teachings mean rather than what they meant.

---

30. See Bovon, *Luke 1*, 9; Esler, *Community and Gospel*, 201–219; Tuckett, *Luke*, 66–67.

31. Nolland, *Luke*, xxxii.

32. Jervell, *Luke and the People of God*, 176.

33. Bovon, *Luke 1*, 6.

34. Nolland, *Luke*, xxxii.

35. Fitzmyer 1985:59

36. Cheong, *A Dialogic Reading*, 65–66.

Luke's gospel is best adapted to God-fearers. At the time of the writing many predominantly Jewish traditions were being almost completely eliminated. Most of the Jewish Palestinian tradition was "redactionally modified" to the changing situation (Matt 7:24–27; Mark 2:4, Luke 5:19, 6:48–49). Luke's creativity and freedom in writing and compiling his gospel from the oral tradition is striking, not to mention his OT quotations taken solely from the LXX. Luke adopted Greek substitutes for Hebrew or Aramaic words such as "Lord" (*kyrios*) or "teacher" (*epistatēs*) for rabbi (Mark 9:5, 10:51; Luke 9:33, 18:41;), and "lawyer" (*nomikos*) for "scribe" (*grammateus*) (Mk 12:28, 23:13; Luke 10:25, 11:52).[37] Luke's gospel, therefore, was adapted to target readers in different contexts for better communication.

Parabolic Context of Luke 15:1–17:10

The wider context of these parables in Luke embraces three distinctive motifs. First, the six consecutive parables in Luke 15:1–17:10 (i.e., Lost Sheep, Lost Coins, Lost Sons, Shrewd Steward, Rich Man and Lazarus, and Servant's Duty), build an apologetic crescendo for Jesus' messianic mission towards social outcasts mentioned in 15:1.[38] Second, the two parenesis in 16:10–13 (concerning misuse of resources), and 16:14–18, (the abiding nature of the law even in Jesus' kingdom), sit between the shrewd steward parable and that of the Rich Man and Lazarus.[39] Third, Jesus' didactic teaching on the problems of *scandalon*, causing the little ones to sin, and of forgiveness (17:1–4). In this, Luke separates the original audience into two main groups. On the one hand, Pharisees and scribes (15:2; 16:14), and on the other, disciples and the socially marginalized such as tax-collectors and sinners (15:1; 16:2; 17:1). These parables emphasize to the reader how the recalcitrant former kept rejecting Jesus' call to repentance.

In this portrayal, Luke highlights contemporary Judaism's (and Jewish Christian's) hostility and opposition to Gentile Christians.[40] In this milieu of Jewish animosity, second generation Gentile believers struggled to determine who they were in this new faith community. Jesus' call to repentance in Luke did not, therefore, simply voice the Jewish preoccupation with moral and religious purification. Rather, it required a drastic turning away

---

37. Fitzmyer, *The Gospel According to Luke*, 58.
38. Cheong, "John the Baptizer and Jesus," 178.
39. Ibid., 180–182.
40. Bosch, *Transforming Mission*, 85.

from self-righteous privileges (3:8; 16:15; 18:9), in which they might have to tolerate and accept Gentile believers within their community without insisting upon the latter's conversion to Judaism. Assuredly, Jesus' parables and reversal messages in Luke correspond to his boundary-breaking mission between Gentile believers and Jewish ones.

By this scheme, Luke's first and foremost purpose is to urge reconciliation between those two groups. This is exemplified in Jesus' messianic mission of looking for the lost, and is demonstrated through the main figures in these consecutive parables. The purpose is for the reconciliation, gathering, and establishment of one new family of God. For this, Luke frequently employs the reversal theme (6:20–21, 24–25), focusing on the marginalized who had long been neglected and rejected by the Pharisees but were now recognized by Jesus. Luke's reconciliation strategy exerts great effort to highlight Jesus' practices of border-breaking and reversals. Particularly, as demonstrated through many parables in Luke 15–17, the reconciliation process requires appropriate use of wealth.

In this broader context (Luke 15:1–17:10), note that the parable of the Rich Man and Lazarus is located near the climactic conclusion of Jesus' apologetic argument for his messianic mission.[41] It gives a final warning to the Pharisee audience who are rejecting Jesus' call to repentance.[42] In the parable, the Rich Man is portrayed as a negative example, that is, in the form of obdurate Pharisees, and accordingly rebuked in Jesus' time, whereas the steward in the preceding parable (16:1–9) is characterized as a repentant Pharisee.[43] The two parables in Luke 16 are closely related to the theme of "making friends" and its many corollaries in God's mission. The steward ultimately passes this test by making friends and is successfully accepted into "eternal habitation" (v.9). The Rich Man, however, fails and is rejected from the eternal habitation, just like the rich fool in Luke 12:13–21. The parable of the Rich Man and Lazarus also highlights Luke's ongoing disclosure of the reversal theme with Jesus' kingdom advent,[44] along with the parable of the shrewd steward. The "abomination (*bdelugma*) in the sight of God" in v.15 is "graphically substantiated by the Rich Man's fate."[45] Perhaps, these contrasting deeds of the two figures in Luke 16, the steward

---

41. Nolland, *Luke*, 831.
42. Snodgrass, *Stories with Intent*, 426.
43. Cheong, *A Dialogic Reading of The Steward Parable*, 120–21.
44. Carroll, *Luke*, 335.
45. Cheong, *A Dialogic Reading of The Steward Parable*, 120.

lived self-indulgently (v.19), neglecting the ulcerous and famished Lazarus by leaving him outside the gate (v.20).

Taken within the Lukan context, however, such a suspicion is fairly convincing since his mammon is still "mammon of unrighteousness" (vv. 9,11), which could have gone to the most destitute.[50] His self-indulgence in pleasure that caused him to be in pain is brought by his *tanha* (obsession), according to the Buddhists' Four Noble Truths. Particularly for the karmic audience, his extreme pursuits of pleasure would probably be judged as foolish behavior resulting from an ignorance of *anicca* (vanity), though Christians often judge such actions as wicked or evil. He is the man of "flesh" not the "Spirit" (Rom 8:6) in Paul's language. According to the Buddhist karmic law, therefore, the Rich Man as an example of "money-lovers" (16:14) proved his fate resulting from his foolish obsession,[51] contrary to the life of Schweitzer. It was not, therefore, without reason.

The reader's puzzlement is worsened by the fact that the Rich Man in Hades called Abraham father three times (vv. 24,27,30) and that Abraham intimately called him child (v.25). The reader will question how such familial communication could be possible, to a degree that one called the other family. This puzzlement is natural because only those Jews who were circumcised as descendants of Abraham by the law could call Abraham father (Luke 3:8). If so, how could it be possible for someone who called Abraham his father to fall to Hades? In this context, the Rich Man's thought seems to be like that of the Christians: assurance or election? Is it possible that Luke is trying to shake the Christian doctrine of justification or assurance of salvation, by rigorously putting them at a crossroads?

To a great extent, Luke felt the need to regulate or correct some aspects of doctrinal confusion that had dangerously misled the mission, particularly after the Pauline mission was established (e.g., "mouth confession for salvation" in Rom 10:10). More probably, Luke saw worrying corollaries that not a few believers, who had seriously misunderstood the concept of Christian grace, might have equated it with libertinism or antinomianism; that is, doing nothing or doing anything. Due to unexpected consequences, Luke pursues adaptation for his audience, inculcating rather the individual's responsibility: "Salvation involves a reaction of faith."[52] That

---

50. Cheong, *A Dialogic Reading of The Steward Parable*, 120.
51. Carroll, *Luke*, 338.
52. Fitzmyer, *The Gospel According to Luke*, 1129.

is why John's baptismal preaching overarches the entirety of Luke's gospel,[53] John rebuked the multitudes not to say to themselves, "We have Abraham as our father" (3:8), and warned against their "futile reliance on covenant privilege."[54] Such an accusation by "a kingdom-preacher,"[55] particularly relating to the Abrahamic motif, is not sparse in Luke (3:8; 13:16; 19:9).

Likewise, echoing Abraham's voice, Jesus taught his disciples: "Not everyone who says to me, 'Lord! Lord!' will enter the kingdom of heaven, but only he who does the will of my Father who is in heaven" (Matt 7:21). From the beginning, Jesus' kingdom gospel never overrides the validity of the law, rather it intensifies the responsibility of the individuals for their lives.[56] Paul, who had already founded his theological foundation on Romans 10:10 did not hesitate to teach, "[f]or we must all appear before the judgment seat of Christ, each one may receive what is due him for the things done while in the body, whether good or bad" (2 Cor 5:10). As to the Corinthian audience, such a negative voice by Paul was never surprising because he also felt that they had gone seriously astray as a result of extremely hedonistic teachings of some leaders.

Assuredly, all of Moses and the prophets are clear about issues of justice and assistance for the poor.[57] This is the trumpet sound in Luke's parable, which similarly reverberates in the Matthean parable of the sheep and goats (25:31–46), in which Jesus warns against the latter's neglect of the destitute and those in need at present. In Luke, the presence of the kingdom of God, which never supersedes the Law and the Prophets,[58] heightens the need for bearing fruit here and now, signaling repentance in the appropriate use of wealth, and repudiating exploitation and injustice (Luke 3:7–14). From the perspective of Luke, the gospel of the kingdom of God "affirms and makes yet more radical the demands of the law and the prophets."[59] Accordingly, shown as the summary of the law and the prophets, the two greatest commandments of "love of God and neighbors" failed to be

---

53. Carroll, *Luke*, 338.

54. Cheong, "Lukan Endeavour to Reconstruct John," 673.

55. See Cheong, "John the Baptizer and Jesus," 181; Fitzmyer *The Gospel According to Luke*, 1118.

56. Nolland, *Luke*, 820.

57. Snodgrass, *Stories with Intent*, 433.

58. See Matt 5:18; Luke 16:14; Cheong "Lukan Endeavour to Reconstruct John," 691–93.

59. Nolland, *Luke*, 833.

PART I: RELIGIOUS FOUNDATIONS

upheld by the Pharisee audience that is the concern of Luke's parable in context. More specifically, the Pharisee's "love of God" that was expressed by the Rich Man's assurance, to the extent that he called Abraham father, proved practically invalid in that he had never observed the law of "love of neighbor" towards Lazarus. For the Buddhists, who do not know the concept of God, the Rich Man's "love of God" will be better understood by their similar or equivalent concepts, such as nirvana (awakening) or wisdom of *anatta* (non-self) or even *sunyata* (emptiness), which will naturally lead to embracing others (*bodhi citta*). Only the practice of love of neighbor by appropriate use of wealth will testify to the Christian "love of God" or the Buddhist "no self." Expatriate missionaries coming with great disparity of wealth and support should take heed.

Significantly enough, however, the failure of the Pharisee audience is not yet final in the Lukan context. As grim as the picture of the parable is, the following episodes (Luke 17:1–10) project a glimmering hope for change. Luke seems to assume that the terror-stricken Rich Man in Hades is still asked to accept the "little ones" and forgive (17:1–4), and that he needs "faith" enough to work submissively as an unworthy servant (vv. 5–10). Those little ones in the Lukan context are the objects of God's special attention to be lovingly usher into the community. The same urge is applied simultaneously to the Rich Man; now under severe indictment, though he seems to be contextually viewed in the same way as the disciples who need more faith (vv. 1,5). This contextual bridge has meaning especially when considering Jesus' woeful pronouncement to those who are causing the little ones to sin (17:1). Accordingly, the parable does not give a systematic doctrine for preparing for an afterlife, but rather a vignette that warns what humans must do in the present, and that "humans will be judged for the way they lived."[60]

For the Buddhist reader, they will remember an old teaching that *Ksitigarbha* had vowed not to achieve Buddhahood until the last person in hell was liberated. The concern of Buddhism is to help people solve the problem of *dukkha*, pain and sorrow. Hence, the angel who carried Lazarus into Abraham's side (v. 22) can be viewed as the future Buddha known as *Pra Siarn* in Thailand or *Maitreya*, the "Compassionate One." Interestingly, the fact that the Rich Man's two persistent and desperate pleas are decisively rejected (vv. 27,30) echoes differently as in Nicos Kazantzakis' novel,

---

60. See Lehtipuu, *The Afterlife Imagery in Luke's Story*, 187; Snodgrass *Stories with Intent*, 432.

"Last Temptation of Jesus," which fulfills the Rich Man's petition allowing Lazarus to go down to Hades and bring him back. Such a Ksitigarbha-like scheme would be convincing for the Buddhist reader.

Mediatory Maitreya appears convincing with Luke's portrayal of the angel (v.22), since for Buddhists there is no finality and all existence in the universe is in solidarity (*Pratityasamutpada*, that is "Not-two"). For example, as in the parable of the sheep and the goats in Matt 25, for the Buddhist reader, solidarity is expected for those who have suffered, which is manifest in *Bodhisattva*. Such an experience of "Not-two" is not foreign to Jesus' teaching, as in John 15:13, "Greater love has no one than this, that he lay down his life for his friends." In the Lukan context, the Buddhist reader may find the same problem in the Rich Man who did not recognize his own solidarity with the poor, that is, "Not-two" and likewise that he did not see himself to be co-reliant on others. Could expatriate missionaries fall under the same accusation? True spirituality, whether in Christianity or Buddhism, is an awakening that realizes how deeply we all depend on others as well as on God. This recognition leads to wisdom, acts of compassion and the pursuit of justice.

The Rich Man had never thought or tried to "make friends" with the destitute nor did he ever demonstrate mercy (*maitri*) towards the latter. Rather than pursuing pleasures of the flesh, he was supposed to live by the spirit (Rom 8:6) that would have led him to be a man of "vast openness," that is truthful, generous, and merciful towards others.[61] In fact, identification with those in pain is the meaning and core of Jesus' bearing the cross, which is nowadays called "kenosis Christology." From the perspective of *Mahayana* Buddhists, Jesus' cross can be translated as "emptiness" (*sunyata*) and "non-self" (*anatta*), by way of identification and solidarity with those who suffered, which was the mission of Bodhisattva. According to Thich Nhat Hanh, "emptiness" (*sunyata*) is interpreted as "inter-being" that emphasizes a co-relationship with the universe.[62] For the Buddhists readers, the Rich Man is well understood as the exemplary figure who broke the truth of *sunyata* as inter-being.

Interestingly, no judge or divine arbiter overtly appears in this parable. Abraham is never portrayed as a final judge, although he answers the Rich Man by explaining the cause of the reversal and rejecting his supplication (vv. 25–31). Naturally, Christians think final judgment is executed only by

---

61. Knitter, *Without Buddha I Could Not Be a Christian*, 21.
62. Ibid., 12.

divine God. But Buddhists do not recognize such divine existence. Instead they believe that *karma*, as the "matter of course," simply works in the same way as the law of nature, like gravity.[63] It is no different from the apostle Paul's teaching in Gal 6:7, "People reap what they sow." Hence, according to Buddhists' thought, the Rich Man's fate in the afterlife is envisaged to have brought in karma.

Along with the karmic reading, it is also probable that contextual significance of "the Law (or Moses) and the Prophets" corresponds for Buddhists with the *Dharmakaya*, the body of truth, that provides them with standards and norms to hang on to (Matt 22:40) particularly for the present life. Abraham's hypothetical statement on "rising from the dead" (Luke 16:30–31) which might have postulated a serious inefficacy of grace towards him, is a strong request to the audience to concentrate on Moses and the Prophets in the here and now, abiding in the truth at present. In Buddhists' terms, if one is abiding in the dharma no other supernatural sign of the future is necessary. According to Dharmakaya or the justice of God, a dreadful reversal in the afterlife for the Rich Man is well deserved.

Christians who hold to justification may be shocked that Jesus looked to collaborate with meritorious deeds rather than grace in the parable. Buddhists readers, however, may answer it by the Middle Way. Originally, the middle way in Buddhism avoids two extremes: pursuits of pleasures, i.e., hedonism, on the one hand, and ascetic pursuit of self-mortification, i.e., asceticism, on the other."[64] The middle way mentality seeks a way not just for deeds or grace alone, but a balanced combination of the two; one without the other is unthinkable. In reality merit and grace are marked by "not-two" though they are not one. They participate in each other. Indeed, this suggests a way of overcoming Christian dualism. In certain situations, it sounds valid to say that everything results from our good or our bad deeds. In other situations, it is clear that grace alone has worked. However, in most cases grace does and must blossom into good deeds.

Summary and Conclusion

As for the two questions posed by Hiebert, I have sought to answer them through exploring possible applications of cultural forms of biblical interpretation that could be acceptable for Thai Buddhist followers of Jesus in

---

63. Strong, *Buddhism*, 116.
64. Ibid., 114.

the karmic community. As Paul de Neui responded, "[i]t was not required of early believers that they attend 'Jewish' classes in order to become full-fledged church members. Why are we requiring the same thing from people coming from other religious and cultural backgrounds?"[65] Indeed, his ideas for a cross-cultural mission may have to include followers' freedom and creativity, not only toward their critical decisions on inclusion or exclusion, and adoption or alteration of their old religious and social forms, but also for their process for forming equally valid communication patterns instead of simply insisting on the Christian mode.

In this paper, I have argued in favor of adaptation to the karmic worldview over changing it, and in applying this to the C5 communities (i.e., Buddhist followers of Jesus). In these case merit-making efforts will support and reinforce allegiance to Jesus. Their meritorious deeds enacted in Buddhist contexts are not different from the meaning, if not the form, of the good works of Christ followers, as far as my parable interpretation is concerned. Though there may still be some discrepancies between them, the Buddhist karmic concept can nevertheless be useful for embodying Christian good works. This should be freeing good news, even opportunities for grace, for expatriate missionaries as well.

Here, I have used an interpretation of Luke's parable of the Rich Man and Lazarus for Thai Buddhist followers of Jesus to associate it with "functional substitutes," including some Mahayana concepts. The Rich Man's lack of meritorious action (i.e., mercy) towards Lazarus as depicted in Luke's parable, can communicate the genuine meaning of Christian grace and paradise to the Buddhist worldview. Through this, I have affirmed that karmic culture in itself is not a problem or enemy of evangelism, but rather should be employed as an opportunity by missionaries and Thai believers themselves, for adaptation, akin to the "Egyptian plunder" of the Exodus people in the OT. By doing so, I hope Thai Buddhists of the C5 model can follow Jesus more effectively while remaining fully Thai.

Here are some final suggested substitutes for Thai Buddhist Followers of Jesus:

- *Bodhisattva*: In Luke's parable, the Rich Man's fundamental problem was that he did not recognize in himself any need for solidarity with the poor, that is, "Not-two." In fact, identification with those in pain is the meaning and core of Jesus' bearing the cross, a way of solidarity

---

65. de Neui, "Appropriate Typologies," 191–92.

with those who suffered in the form of "emptiness" and "non-self." For the Buddhist reader, the person and work of Bodhisattva will be helpful to acknowledge and experience Jesus as Christ, though not perfectly overlapped to each other. Even for missionaries this will mean greater sacrifice and acts of compassion into the complex lives of new brothers and sisters than is generally anticipated for foreigners.

- *Maitreya*: Called *Pra Siarn* in Thailand, the angel who carried Lazarus into Abraham's side (16:22) can also be explained by the future Bodhisattva Maitreya, who fulfilled mediatory work for dukka. Jesus' cross as substitution of propitiation can be understood better by the mission of Maitreya.

- *Dharmakaya*: The parabolic point is that only the present decision is valid. In fact, the presence of Jesus' kingdom of God had a similar connotation with the "body of truth," Dharmakaya, as an abiding nature of the law, focusing on the importance of present time. Hence, Luke's adoption of Jewish terminology, "Moses (or the Law) and the Prophets," can be translated by Dharmakaya for Thai Buddhist followers of Jesus in the karmic community. According to Dharmakaya, the Rich Man deserved the dreadful reversal in his afterlife.

- Middle Way: Pauline emphasis on justification by faith alone is a contextual polemic against Jewish legalism in missiological settings arguing that all Gentile believers must desert their ethnic marks according to Jewish law, whereas the gospels and general epistles seem to focus more on the individuals' responsibility for change in their secular lives. So, it would be better for Buddhists' understanding (and missionaries) to adopt the Middle Way, balancing both merit and grace and avoiding the two extremes, an approach that is easily grasped in Luke's parable. Grace and merit participate in each other; grace must be followed by adequate actions. Likewise, it is also necessary for Thai Buddhists and missionaries to actually live into the reality of the grace of God, making them free from the fears of failure.

Bibliography

Bosch, David, J. *Transforming Mission: Paradigm Shifts in Theology of Mission*. Maryknoll, NY: Orbis, 1991.
Bovon, François. 2002. *Luke 1*. Minneapolis: Fortress, 2002.

Carroll, John T. *Luke*. Louisville, KY: Westminster/John Knox, 2012.
Cheong, C-S Abraham. *A Dialogic Reading of The Steward Parable (Luke 16:1–9)*. Studies in Biblical Literature 28. New York: Peter Lang, 2001.
———. "John the Baptizer and Jesus in Luke 16:16." *Scripture and Interpretation* 3/2 (2009) 175–190.
———. "Lukan Endeavour to Reconstruct John the Baptizer in Conjunction with Jesus," *KNTS* 22/3 (2015) 667–710.
Conn, Harvie M. *Eternal Word and Changing World: Theology, Anthropology, and Mission in Trialogue*. Grand Rapids, MI: Academie, 1984.
———. *Evangelism: Doing Justice and Preaching Grace*. Grand Rapids: Zondervan, 1982.
de Neui, Paul H. "Appropriate Typologies for Thai Folk Buddhists." In *Becoming the People of God*, edited by Paul H. de Neui. Pp. 187–216. Pasadena, CA: William Carey, 2015.
Esler, Philip F. *Community and Gospel in Luke-Acts*. Cambridge, UK: Cambridge University, 1987.
Fitzmyer, Joseph A. *The Gospel According to Luke I–IX, X–XXIV*. New York: Anchor Bible/Doubleday, 1985.
Gibbs, Eddie. "Contextual Considerations in Responding to Nominality." In *The Word Among Us: Contextualizing Theology for Mission Today*, edited by Dean S. Gilliland. Pp. 239–261. Dallas: Word, 1989.
Hiebert, G. Paul. "Form and Meaning in the Contextualization of the Gospel," in *The Word Among Us: Contextualizing Theology for Mission Today* edited by Dean S. Gilliland. Pp. 101–120. Dallas: Word, 1989.
Jervell, Jacob. *Luke and the People of God: A New Look at Luke-Acts*. Minneapolis: Augsburg, 1972.
Johnson, Alan R. "Context-Sensitive Evangelism in the Thai Setting: Building Capacity to Share Good News," In *Becoming the People of God* edited by Paul H. de Neui ed. Pp. 63–92. Pasadena, CA: William Carey, 2015.
Knitter, Paul F. *Without Buddha I Could not be a Christian*. Oxford, UK: Oneworld, 2009.
Kraft, Charles H. *Anthropology for Christian Witness*. Maryknoll: Orbis, 1996.
———. "Contextualizing Communication," in *The Word Among Us: Contextualizing Theology for Mission Today* edited by Dean S. Gilliland. P. 121–138. Dallas: Word, 1989.
———. *Jesus, God's Model for Christian Communication*. Seoul: InterVarsity. 1991.
Lehtipuu, Outie. *The Afterlife Imagery in Luke's story of the Rich Man and Lazarus*. Supplements to Novum Testamentum. Leiden/Boston: Brill, 2007.
Nolland, John. *Luke*. Dallas: Word, 1993.
Smith, Alexander G. "Apply Cultural Contexts to Generate Multiple Christ-Centered Communities." In *Becoming the People of God* edited by Paul H. de Neui. Pp. 93–115. Pasadena, CA: William Carey Library, 2015.
Snodgrass, Klyne. *Stories with Intent: A Comprehensive Guide to the Parables of Jesus*. Grand Rapids, MI: Eerdmans, 2008.
Søgaard, Viggo. "Dimensions of Approach to Contextual Communication," In *The Word Among Us: Contextualizing Theology for Mission Today*, edited by Dean S. Gilliland. Pp. 160–182. Dallas: Word, 1989.
Strong, John S. *Buddhism: An Introduction*. Pgw: Oneworld, 2015.
Tuckett, Christopher M. *Luke*. Sheffield, UK: Sheffield Academic, 1996.

3

The 'Karma' of the Old Testament as a Bridge to Communicate Grace to Karmic Communities

Cristian Dumitrescu

Evangelical Christianity focuses primarily on the New Testament as the Scripture of the New Covenant or new dispensation, paying less attention to the Old Testament. However, many non-Christian religions often present beliefs and statements similar to the ones in the Old Testament. For example, Christians are quick to dismiss the idea that there is any parallel between the karmic concept in Buddhism and the "eye for eye" or "life for life" texts in the Old Testament. Although the Bible does not support the Buddhist concept of retribution in a future life, it does teach about the consequences of our deeds in this life with effects in the afterlife. This paper will explore the possible connections between the mentioned Old Testament statements and the Buddhist concept of karma, comparing similarities and dissimilarities, and attempting to present bridges to the biblical concept of grace.

The Meaning of Karma

The law of karma informs many Asian cultures, especially the ones that embrace the Hindu or Buddhist philosophy. Karma is widely understood as the principle of retribution, one receiving exactly what one deserves.

But in reality, the karmic concept is more complex and varies with each philosophy embraced by a particular community. Karma may be positive or negative. If one performs bad deeds, judgment comes in the form of consequences, either in this life or in the next lives. But if one performs good deeds, acquiring merit, the law of karma promises positive rewards and a higher reincarnation status in the next life.

The life of a Buddhist, for example, is filled with prescriptions and taboos. Vows must be fulfilled, especially vows made to the spirits, and every human inhabited place includes a shrine for the spirits. Certain foods need to be avoided, while other human activities should not be abused, such as sexuality. This type of legalistic way of life creates dependency, and at the same time a desire for freedom. Buddhist monks are supposed to follow a stricter lifestyle, while lay Buddhists have less restrictions. But all live under the spectrum of inevitable consequences as a result of the law of karma. The outcome is a very pessimistic view of life.

The general understanding of karmic philosophy is popularly expressed through statements such as, "You get what you deserve," "What goes around comes around," or "You reap what you sow." Although the law of cause and effect or the principle of retribution is a good general principle, karmic communities transform it into a rigid, unique law. Everything is explained based on this principle. People are poor due to a cause in a past life (usually a wrong deed), tragedies are considered consequences of past faults, and when bad things happen to good people it is attributed to unavoidable penalties for deeds or decisions of a previous life. A karmic worldview is based on the assumption that one deserves everything that happens to him or her.

Although the popular understanding of karma is of a rigid, inflexible law of cause and effect, Buddhists entertain a more nuanced view of the concept. For example, Johannes Bronkhorst describes the historical orthodox view of karma and also variants of this concept.[1] He shows how the concept was highly contested over the centuries between the different schools of Indian or Buddhist philosophy, and this debate was reflected in the multitude of meanings offered for the term in Sanskrit reference works. Bronkhorst, however, contends that karma was generally used with two basic meanings: rebirth and retribution, and that the two meanings were not always identical or even overlapping. He concludes,

---

1. See Bronkhorst, *Karma*.

> These issues cannot be discussed without taking into consideration the question that our textual sources very frequently discuss along with them, the question as to how individuals can free themselves from the karmic consequences of their deeds . . . This question is not only inseparable from the belief in rebirth and karmic retribution, it also has an effect on the shape this belief takes in different religious movements.[2]

The diversity of positions regarding the meaning of karma and the required solution is evident in the originating religions of India. For example, early Jainism developed the idea that one's future was decided by one's actions, and the solution offered to break karma was asceticism. Both body and mind had to be immobilized, going as far as not only controlling but suppressing breathing, and denying thinking because thoughts and emotions were seen as having karmic consequences. Physical death was comprehended as liberation from the karmic cycle. But Jains became aware that before becoming inactive every person has been active in this or previous lives and those deeds require retribution. They concluded later that the suffering of hunger, thirst, pain from standing for days, the heat of the sun, and being attacked by insects produced "suffering . . . that destroyed the trace of earlier [mis]deeds."[3] As a result, death was postponed as long as possible, allowing suffering to destroy the retributive consequences of previous lives before the moment of liberation. The longer the suffering, the greater the assurance of breaking the karmic effect.

Early Buddhism rejected Jainist asceticism, with its immobility of body and mind, or the attached salvific suffering. Their understanding of the cause of rebirth focused on the roots of desire, not of deeds. Suffering was not to be sought, in fact, just the opposite. Liberation of the karmic consequences was sought in the annihilation of desire, not only in its restraint. This was not achieved through cessation of activity or of thought, but through the use of thought to purify it and by doing good deeds. Hence the apparition of merit. "The meditator knows that he has succeeded, that he is liberated, that he has arrived at the end of suffering."[4] However, the whole construct was reduced to a psychological process. For Buddhists, deeds are mental and leave traces in the mind that are permanent. Karmic

---

2. Bronkhorst, *Karma*, 4–5.
3. Ibid., 12.
4. Ibid., 27.

retribution for them comes from the state of mind in which deeds are carried out.

The merit and demerit notions (*dharma* and *adharma*) were developed by Vaisheshika thinkers who attributed them karmic retribution powers. Dharma and adharma were considered qualities of the self, bringing pleasure and suffering in one's self. However, philosophers realized that these qualities had no intelligence of their own, and that intelligence comes from consciousness. Dharma and adharma had no consciousness of their own, and could not impact future lives. To the surprise of many, Vaisheshika thinkers "postulated the existence of a creator God who would arrange things in accordance with the past deeds of living beings."[5] His task would be that of an accountant, recording the deeds and assigning retribution for them. One of the Upanishads even calls God the "supervisor of karma." This God's role was limited only to karmic retribution, since he was not the one who established the rules, he was only an enforcer. Although this admission of God is not widespread in Buddhism, it still remains a useful development that Christians may bridge in order to dialogue with believers in karma.

Brahmanism and Jainism, in time, moved further and accepted several new concepts and practices. The first new concept and practice was the transfer of merit from one person to another. This development later impacted Buddhism. Bad deeds from others can attach to someone else and the result is demerit. The same is true for merit. Although not officially accepted as a Buddhist or Jainist philosophy, transfer of merit is practiced by living people in relation to the dead. Respect and veneration of ancestors often requires that one renounces the merits in favor of the deceased parents. Monetary donations are often made so the deceased can benefit from such good deeds. Brahmanical practice allows for *Shraddha* rituals where one can feed the ancestors. This suggests that karmic results can be altered and merit and demerit assigned. Brahmanical tradition also admits rituals of expiation which can help one avoid karmic consequences. In the same vein, curses can void one's merit. "Curses and karmic retribution . . . come to work in tandem, the former giving concrete shape to the just deserts of the person cursed."[6]

The karmic concept presupposes justice and honor, based on a set of moral values. Good deeds and bad deeds, by definition, require a certain

---

5. Ibid., 86.
6. Ibid., 99.

moral standard. But moral standards cannot be abstract and impersonal. Reflecting on this reality, Bronkhorst debated whether the inclusion of a god in the karmic retribution system was useful or not.

> One could say that the belief in rebirth and karmic retribution presupposes that morality is part of the structure of the universe. All those who accept this belief in one form or another are convinced that good deeds will be rewarded and bad deeds punished. This conviction did not need a god, even though the supervision of karmic retribution came to be attributed to an accountant God by some in the Brahmanical tradition. The acceptance of a supreme God sometimes had the opposite effect: rather than explaining and strengthening the process of karmic retribution, God might provide shortcuts, preferably to those who were devoted to Him.[7]

As Alex Smith states, "to Buddhists there is no accountability to any higher power, or to a Creator God. One is only accountable to oneself and one's own *karma*, which will affect future existences through any infractions of *Sila* or other laws."[8] If the rejection of a god as part of the karmic retributive system was preferable, the question of morality and justice still remained. Although an interesting idea, even only as an arbiter of deeds, this god was a creation of human minds, with humanly assigned attributes. Preference for individual moral responsibility was preserved. But individual moralities often clashed, and karmic communities were often in conflict.

> Belief in karmic retribution implies a moral order that governs the universe . . . Everyone agrees that good deeds lead to good results, but not everyone agreed in all cases on what is a good deed. Various beliefs about the ideal form of life, or of society, have to be taken into consideration, and the resulting differences can be striking . . . Belief in karmic retribution implies a moral order, but which moral order?[9]

In time, the concept of karma was enlarged to accept not only the transfer of merit or the existence of an accountant god, but to provide ways for repentance, forgiveness, and grace. The case of *Won*-Buddhism, a reformed and modernized version of Buddhism, is illustrative. Jang Eun-cheol, known as the Prime Dharma Master Kyongsan, introduced the process

---

7. Ibid., 118.
8. Smith, *Missiological Implications*, 46.
9. Bronkhorst, *Karma*, 119.

of forgiveness as the solution to obtain freedom from transgressive karma. He illustrates karma as the principle of *yin* and *yang*.

> If I enjoy a great deal of grace from someone, I develop gratitude toward him, and that mind of gratitude takes the form of the corresponding lifegiving karmic cause for that person—a karma seed of grace ... If someone plants a seed of gratitude, this inevitably manifests itself as grace.[10]

Referring to the teaching of the Sakyamuni Buddha, Kyongsan states that repentance can be achieved only if one believes that "our own mind is the creator that determines our happiness and unhappiness. Only when we understand for certain that our minds are our creators can we engage in true repentance practice."[11] Kyongsan concludes that "the person engaged in repentance practice must have a clear awareness that his mind is his creator before he can engage in sincere repentance."[12] This corresponds to Mahayana Buddhism's self-reliant repentance.

Theravada Buddhism, in response, proposes dependent repentance, by action, "in which we achieve deliverance by confessing our misdeeds before the Three Jewels—the Buddha, the Dharma, and the Sanga—and repenting of them."[13] This method of repentance by action must be matched with repentance by principle where

> One internally removes all defilements and idle thoughts ... They must continue to practice all types of good karma while, internally, they must simultaneously remove their own greed, hatred, and delusion.[14]

Repentance by action includes confession, compensation, service to the public, and requital of grace by bringing offerings through Buddha to the fourfold Graces: the Grace of parents, the Grace of fellow beings, the Grace of heaven and earth, and the Grace of law.

Kyongsan emphasizes the need for repentance. According to him, repentance is "something we do to escape the cycle of good and evil and to live a life of freedom from samsara."[15] Repentance is further described as,

---

10. Kyongsan, *Freedom from Transgressive Karma*, 31.
11. Ibid., 39.
12. Ibid., 39.
13. Ibid., 59.
14. Ibid., 132.
15. Ibid., 68.

> ... the first step in abandoning one's old life and opening oneself to cultivating a new life, and the initial gateway for setting aside unwholesome paths and entering into wholesome paths. For people who repent from past mistakes and continue practicing wholesome paths day by day, past karma will gradually disappear and no karma will be made anew ... Karma is originally ignorance; it perforce will vanish in accord with the light of wisdom of one's self-nature."[16]

Since transgression comes out of ignorance, repentance from transgressions implies illumination and enlightenment. As *samana* Narada explained to Pandu, the jeweler, "ignorance is the source of sin."[17]

This brief survey of the understanding of karma revealed that, in spite of a general view of an inflexible retributive principle, there are interesting variations and nuances of this concept. From a total immobilization of body and mind, to suffering that erases the past karma, to indelible traces in the mind, to the possibility of transferring merit, and to the inclusion of an accountant god who supervises the enforcement of karmic retribution, all the way to repentance and forgiveness, the concept of karma remains the fundamental principle on which Hindu and Buddhist religions are built.

Biblical "Karma"?

The law of cause and effect is believed by Christians, too. Many Christians inherited a retributive view of the consequences of their own deeds. It is very common within traditional Christian churches to hear about the fear one has to live under because of one's actions. Although Christianity identifies disobedience and sin as the main problem leading to shame and fear, the Bible offers an optimistic perspective on life. The Bible goes beyond the rigid karmic understanding. All through the Scripture one may hear God's desire to redeem humankind.

It is also common for Christians to dismiss the Old Testament as legalistic, because it contains scores of laws sometimes associated with negative consequences in case of disobedience. Some use dispensationalism today to distance themselves from the unbearable responsibility God reveals in the First Testament. The New Covenant is often made to look like a worry-free life, regardless of the choices of an individual. This distorted picture, called

---

16. Ibid., 62.
17. Carus, *Karma/Nirvana*, 18.

cheap grace, removes the consequences of sin and apparently discards the retribution principle. It is no wonder why karmic communities have a hard time understanding this popular version of Christianity.

However, a careful look at the Old Testament reveals a potential parallel with the karmic understanding. In Paul Wagner's words, "religious law, as given in the Old Testament, teaches that it is not able to bring salvation but rather brings people into an understanding that sin is bondage and that there is a need for a Savior."[18] God not only provided laws and announced consequences for breaking the laws, but also delivered hope in many forms. From the gates of the Garden of Eden, altars reminded people that God provided a solution to the problem. Noah, Abraham, and all the patriarchs continued to announce God's solution for breaking the retribution circle.

The sanctuary, for example was designed as a pedagogical model to teach Israel and the surrounding nations about the way God will take care of sin and its consequences. The very architecture of the Tabernacle combined the holiness and righteousness of God with his mercy and grace. The whole message of love that Christians like to see in Jesus was displayed at the Sanctuary. In the Holy Room, there was not only the altar for sacrifices, but the chandelier that provided light, suggesting the enlightenment provided by God. The bread reminded the Jews that God was not only interested in implementing the consequences on the law breakers, but he was in the business of providing the source of life for them. He was interested not only in punishing but rather in sustaining and providing. Jesus claimed all these symbols later for himself (John 9:5; 6:48). Blood together with bread and light represented God's character.

At the heart of the Tabernacle, in the Holy of Holies, rested the Ark of the Covenant that contained not only the tablets with the law written by God—the Ten commandments—but also the Seat of mercy, the cover made of gold with two angels pointing to heaven. Once a year, the High priest ministered for the entire people of Israel before the Ark with blood, indicating the substitutionary solution God provided for sinners. Although the retribution for sin was still in effect, the sacrifice pointed to the mediator equal to the law condemning the sinner, a mediator who would bear the consequences. The presence of manna and Aaron's miracle staff inside the Ark reminded Israel that God is a god of mercy and second chances, providing for the needs of people in spite of natural circumstances.

---

18. Wagner, *Beyond Karma*, 211.

Part I: Religious Foundations

The constant presence of sacrifices reminded the Hebrew people about God's solution for sin and shame: blood. This symbol, as well as the prophetic oracles, pointed forward to the Messiah who was the key for the whole salvation system and offered to make his own blood available to anyone who desired freedom from the oppression of sin. Confession of sin was shameful and costly, and people were constantly reminded about the consequences and price of sin; but the very symbols reminding them of retribution for sin assured them of God's grace and mercy. Every year, the Day of Atonement was followed by a celebration and party where people rejoiced in God's love which was equally reflected in the balance between justice and mercy.

Another example where justice was supposed to be balanced by grace was the cities of refuge (Num 35:6, 11–15; Josh 20:2–6). Retributive justice was to be done in cases of murder. But justice was not supposed to be done indiscriminately. Not every death required capital punishment. God instructed Moses and Joshua to set aside six cities where people who unintentionally killed someone could flee and wait there for a fair trial. If the person was found not guilty, they were allowed to live in the city of refuge until the death of the high priest, and only then return home. Avengers were prohibited to enter these selected cities. However, if the person was found guilty, avengers were allowed to kill the person, but limit the revenge to only the guilty individual. No other member of the family was to be touched, or any of the family's wealth. This was God's provision to limit the retribution to an equal measure. "Life for life," "eye for eye," and "foot for foot" were part of God's instructions, known today as *lex talionis*, intended to limit retribution and damage.

Commenting on biblical passages that dealt with this principle (Deut 19:18–20; 25:1–3), Christopher Wright recognized five roles of such laws.[19] First, it had to deal with *retribution*. "The offender was to suffer his just legal deserts which should be appropriate to the offense. That is the significance and justification of the lex talionis ("an eye for an eye," etc.) principle. It was a very limiting law, preventing excessive or vengeful punishment."[20] Second, it had a *purging* role. "Guilt had to be 'wiped away' from God's sight."[21] Third, it helped assure *deterrence*. "'All Israel shall hear and *fear*,' i.e.

---

19. See Wright, *An Eye for an Eye*.
20. Ibid., 166.
21. See Wright, *An Eye for an Eye*.

be afraid to do the same."²² Fourth, it provided *restoration*. "The offender remained a brother and was not to be degraded."²³ Finally, *compensation* was guaranteed. "Restitution was made to the injured party – not to the state as a fine."²⁴ Roy Gane emphasizes that God gave these laws for ensuring fairness of punishment and protection of life. The talion stressed "the importance of respecting the sanctity of another person's body, facing the consequences of one's physical violence, treating everyone equally before the law, and protecting the rights of the victims."²⁵

Looking at the book of Psalms, David Firth notices that even prayers for retribution acted by God were limited by grace.

> The right of retributive violence belongs to Yahweh alone, but also that it is limited by the *lex talionis*. That is to say, the retribution that may be sought from Yahweh does not exceed the harm that has been inflicted by the enemy, or that may be inflicted were an accusation to be proved. How Yahweh is to act is not stated, but the limitation on retributive violence is clear.²⁶

Justice and fairness were meant to guide retribution and protect the integrity of the community. As W. H. Bellinger noticed, "The law of retaliation here seeks order and justice in the community, harmony between act and consequence."²⁷ In John Hartley's words, "commitment to this principle has the potential of promoting retaliation under the guise of righteous indignation."²⁸ Peter Craigie concludes calling this principle "proportionate compensation."²⁹

Karmic communities, especially Buddhists, believe that the good spirits may reward them, and good luck may come from amulets, charms, or from astrological fate. This may be their equivalent of biblical grace. The difference between Buddhism and Christianity is that in Buddhism people are responsible for their own liberation while in Christianity Jesus Christ bears this responsibility. If in Buddhism people try to escape the oppression of past lives, Christians are forgiven when accepting Christ's sacrifice on

---

22. Ibid., 166.
23. Ibid., 166.
24. Ibid., 166.
25. Gane, Roy. *Leviticus, Numbers*, 428.
26. Firth, David G., *Surrendering Retribution in the Psalms*, 4.
27. Bellinger, W. H. *Leviticus, Numbers*, 147.
28. Hartley, *Leviticus*, 413.
29. Craigie, *The Book of Deuteronomy*, 270.

their behalf. The fear of Buddhists comes from the retributive uncertainty of their past and future, and from the unending efforts to replenish the good karma. A repentant Christian learns that his past is forgiven and that Jesus offers eternal life as the way for the future. Reincarnation has no meaning for Christians because the consequences for sin have been transferred onto the divine intermediary.

If a Buddhist seeks liberation from the law of karma, a Christian seeks Christ and his power to live a life according to his holy law. If a Buddhist or Hindu believes he gets what he deserves, a Christian, by grace, receives what he does not deserve, but retribution still takes place through the blood of Jesus.

Merits and Demerits

The concept of merit and karma influenced major events in history. Rape and genocide in hospitable and graceful Asian cultures are difficult to understand, unless one looks at the implications of the concept of karma. Cambodians, for example, raped women, killed them, and smashed children's skulls against the trees during Pol Pot's regime because they believed this was what these women and children must have deserved. Describing this view, Russell H. Bowers relates the case of a woman "who lost many family members to the Khmer rouge . . . she could not hate those who killed them—they were fated to act that way, just as she was fated to suffer this loss."[30] Similar views may be found behind conflicts between Japan, Korea, China, Thailand, and Myanmar. Christianity is not free from a history of genocide either.

Whenever grace was removed from justice, people killed others in the name of retributive punishment. Too often the biblical understanding of retribution was distorted under the name of Christian theology. The Crusades or the Holocaust are painful historical records of times when God's character has been grossly misrepresented. Jews, Gypsies, and other minorities were given what Arian Christians considered were only retributive consequences these unfortunate people deserved. Christian mission was, at times [mis]understood to be the means of purification of a chosen race rather than salvation of all ethnic groups. Retribution without grace leads to concepts of superiority based on presupposed merits and to the elimination of inferiors.

---

30. Bowers, *Folk Buddhism in Southeast Asia*, 62.

Merit in Buddhism (*Kusala*) comes from obeying the rules and precepts, serving the monks, becoming a monk, and building holy shrines and pagodas. But Buddhists also believe in demerits (*Akusala*), which are greater than the merits acquired through good deeds. One's demerits cannot be overcome in one life only. S. Tenzing describes this hopeless conundrum karmic believers go through: "Many people work hard at doing good deeds for years and years but never have any peace that they have paid for their bad deeds. How much is enough? Their conscience gives them no peace and they eventually die in anxiety and uncertainty."[31] Alan Johnson notes that "people are so accustomed to the merit/demerit system and the law of karma paying them back good for good and evil for evil, that the idea of being freed from the weight of our evil deeds without doing anything seems very foreign."[32]

Although merit is not enough to compensate for all the demerit, people transfer their merit to their parents, dead or alive. It is common for sons to become monks in order to make merit for their parents. Elaborate ceremonies are also followed to transfer merit to dead ancestors. Daniëlle Koning notices that simply

> Being religious includes the important responsibilities one has towards one's parents and ancestors . . . This explains the importance of practices like *buat* (becoming a monk) or *taakbaat* (offering food to monks), the merit of which is devoted to deceased loved ones, though participants in such events may lead otherwise largely secular lives.[33]

Smith points to the double entendre of transferring merit to ancestors: "The merit maker in these instances is not deprived of the merit originally gained by the good deeds. In fact, the 'act of transference,' being a good deed in itself, enhances the merit already acquired."[34]

In an excerpt from Buddha's prophecies about the Compassionate One, Wagner makes known Buddha's view of the value of merits in the deliverance from sin.

> "Even though you all would do alms-giving such as in the ceremony of presenting new robes to the Buddhist priests, follow the

---

31. Tenzing, *Freedom from Karma*, 8.
32. Johnson, *Context-Sensitive Evangelism in the Thai setting*, 80.
33. Koning, *I Believe For 50%*, 150.
34. Smith, *Transferring Merit in Folk Buddhism*, 109.

five moral precepts, the eight moral precepts, two hundred twenty-seven, nine million or nine thousand to the highest point; raise your hand in homage, give your body to be burned as an offering, or meditate five times a day, you are still not likely to be delivered. If you did all of the above every day you would gain merit only to the extent of a strand of hair on the head of an unborn baby eight months in his mother's womb; and if all of the above would be multiplied countless numbers of times, it would not bring you into the door of heaven."[35]

Throughout the Bible, humans have no merit, all their righteousness and good deeds are described as rags (Isa 64:6). Sin, which may be interpreted as the equivalent of the demerits in Buddhism, cannot be overcome by good deeds only. Sin is not only a bad action, or the result of it, although breaking the law is a sin. The Bible teaches that human nature is corrupted by sin, and regardless of how many deeds one may perform, human nature remains sinful. There is nothing good in humans but the image of God (Rom 3:8–10), the core of human nature is corrupted. Only Jesus, who offers his merits and has no sin, can solve the problem. He wants to restore the relationship through which the power to overcome sin is available. This is grace.

For Buddhists, spirits are an important factor in making merit and interpreting karma. The problem is that spirits are moody. They need to be appeased, hence the multitude of spirit houses or shrines where fresh food, drinks, and nice smelling incense are almost always present. All these offerings provide opportunities to make merit. In contrast, the Bible offers the picture of a loving God who is always just and merciful at the same time. God does not have to be appeased. The solution to the human predicament resides in different places. For Buddhists, the solution is seen inside the karma enslaved person, while in Christianity it is the sovereign God who is outside of the law of karma and enters the world to offer the solution by redeeming the sinful human nature.

In Buddhism, one seeks to enter Nirvana, while the Bible teaches that God's kingdom ("Nirvana") penetrates humanity's space and time. Nirvana, when re-interpreted, can be viewed by some as an equivalent concept of eternal life in the Christian faith. But Nirvana is only about peace and tranquility; hell seems to be the lives lived before joining nirvana. The spirits that karmic communities believe in do not offer salvation, forgiveness, or

---

35. Chantavongsouk, *Buddha's Prophecy of the Messiah*, 24–25; Wagner, *Beyond Karma*, 113–115.

mercy, although mercy and compassion are part of Buddhist teaching. The Bible presents the Good (Holy) Spirit who is part of the divine Trinity as one who brings freedom from bondage and fear. It is the Holy Spirit's merit to change lives, not human merit. For Buddhists, there is little hope after death because of the huge demerit accumulated. Those living a Christian life have hope because of Jesus' sacrifice on their behalf that promises better consequences after death.

Rituals, such as prayers, are an important part of Buddhist spirituality and daily life. Buddhists understand forgiveness as sympathy for others (empathy). Since karma is unpredictable and inescapable, empathizing with others in suffering may help the needy and acquire merit for the helper at the same time. Prayers are often not for freedom, but are mantras intended to obtain merit. The desire for freedom is often expressed in other areas of life but not in the area of spirituality, where the fate of karma is believed to be inescapable. Christians may use prayers and other rituals in order to communicate grace. In the case of monks or nuns, the barrier for empathy may be their understanding of close relationships that are considered unhealthy because relationships require attachment, resulting in suffering, trouble, and demerit.

One of the Buddhist virtues is compromise. The biblical equivalent for compromise may be grace. In the parable of the Prodigal Son (Luke 15), Jesus describes the father as willing to personally accept the shame of his errant offspring in order that the son might be honored by the villagers. Karma requires that the son should be killed, and Kenneth Bailey implies that the villagers most probably enacted *kezazah*, the ceremony through which the son was cut off, excluded from the community, and thereby his merit erased.[36] But the father takes upon himself the shame and the guilt and breaks the power of karmic law. Stories of broken karma such as Adam and Eve, Abraham and Sarah, Jacob and his wives, Joseph and his brothers, or David the king of Israel should be heard by Buddhists in order to correctly understand the God described in the Bible. If karma requires that the wayward lost sheep suffer the consequences, the good shepherd inversely leaves all other sheep in the safety of the pen and rushes to search for the lost one before predatory animals attack it. Similarly, the woman of the house does not abandon the coin that was lost but searches diligently because there is a close relationship between the woman and the coin. Without the coin, her karma would mean honor lost forever, indelible demerit.

---

36. See Bailey, *Finding the Lost Cultural Keys of Luke 15*.

PART I: RELIGIOUS FOUNDATIONS

The God of the Bible is different than the angry and vengeful Hindu gods, such as Shiva. It is not that the God of the Bible rejects just retribution, there are plenty of biblical passages and Psalms that talk about God's justice and righteousness. God is interested in securing the pardon of a person by providing Godself as the means for restitution and takes upon himself the consequences of the wrong actions of the entire world. The only appropriate sacrifice for the sin of humanity was someone who was outside of the karmic principle and was equal to the law that required the just consequences. This shows that the God of the Bible does not treat lightly his own issued law, but makes sure that each breaking of the law receives the appropriate response and consequence. However, God's character goes beyond rigid retribution, God is also merciful without lowering the requirements of justice. In Wagner's words, "God's grace is more powerful than any moral law. It can accomplish in people's lives what they could never do by their own efforts, namely to live a life that fulfills the demands of any moral code of law."[37]

Building Bridges

Although between karma and grace there seem to be major differences, there is also much common ground. Both worldviews agree that the core human problem is spiritual. As Stephen Davis noted, "both systems of salvation agree that the deepest human problems are spiritual in nature . . . What is wrong in human life is, at its deepest level, religious or spiritual."[38] None of these religions claims moral relativism. For both views, intentions and actions can be morally evaluated. And each worldview acknowledges that good and evil should be rewarded accordingly.

Evidently, the differences are problematic. The dissimilarities between Buddhism and Christianity range from terminology and forms to meanings and interpretations. Although both philosophies recognize the possibility of spiritual growth, the assumptions behind the processes are different. Both promise liberation from the core problem affecting humanity, but the way to achieve it is different. Is there a way to build bridges of understanding between those enslaved under the law of karma to the good news of freedom in Jesus Christ?

---

37. Wagner, *Beyond Karma*, 81.
38. Davis, *After We Die*, 33.

For example, the concept of ransom is difficult for karmic communities. Karma negates the chance for an intermediary or payment for demerits. The only accepted "ransom" is individual merit. In a very individualistic karmic philosophy or religion, substitution and atonement as described in the Old Testament are missing concepts. However, in Buddhist practice, substitution is often present. A son can make merit for his parents by becoming, even temporarily, a monk. Although merit is personal, bridges between Christian and karmic views in this case may be made using the common practices of karmic communities.

For karma believers, history is based on cyclical thinking. Buddhism, for example, embraces a repetitive cycle. Although describing cyclical events, the Bible projects history as a spiral moving forward. For example, the book of Judges may seem to describe a cyclical karma, but there is no indication that the men and women God raised up as judges were actually reincarnations of one person into subsequent new lives. God created seasons that are cyclic, but they never return to the same departure point in time. People organize festivals, ceremonies, and holidays during a lifetime, but it should be noted that these rituals are not repeated. A person goes through birth, adulthood, and death rituals only once, and time moves forward. The lunar cycle, although it looks similar every month, never returns to the same spot in the sky every month. References to natural processes may help build bridges between Christian freedom and those in karmic communities.

A discussion with a Buddhist about what is right or wrong does not lead him to a different understanding of retribution. Even regeneration has a different meaning than the biblical term. Christian terms and concepts such as "new birth" often confuse karmic believers because of the similarity to the Buddhist notion of reincarnation. However, this very concept may become a bridge if it is explained as the original Greek text translates, being born "from above" (John 3:3–8), not in a lower or inferior state. It must be pointed out that a spiritual change should happen in this life in order for the better life to happen. That life should begin and happen here and now.

The problematic Old Testament statements, "eye for an eye" or "tooth for a tooth," as previously noted, were not given by God as mandatory retribution law, but as a limit to the damage often caused by people who were looking for revenge taking the life of a person for a simple tooth. Indeed, life was required for taking life, but God was not in the business of encouraging people to take revenge under emotional impulses. The refuge cities were intended to protect the criminals in cases where the damage or killing happened unintentionally. Many other laws (i.e. laws regarding rape and sexual shaming situations) were given for the same reason: to limit the damage, and to make sure mercy joins justice. Karmic believers understand that consequences are unavoidable, but they have a hard time accepting that someone else may take care of the consequences of your deeds. Buddhism, for example, is an extremely individualistic religion, in spite of the fact that people live in communal societies and monks live in *sangha*. A clarification of such biblical passages in their context may become a bridge for karmic believers to understand how grace works side by side even within justice. The books of Ecclesiastes and Proverbs may also facilitate communicating grace to Buddhists through wisdom and riddles.

The Bible describes a God who invaded the karmic world of cause and effect. If karma concludes that we get what we deserve, God by his grace offers what we do not deserve. Grace goes beyond karma. It provides the picture of a Cosmic Conflict which we are part of. It talks about a divine friend who is involved with us against the enemy. We do not deserve diseases and death, whether they are due to our failings or not. In the biblical worldview, merits have impact upon the process of salvation. The human internal condition has been affected by sin, but God in his grace provided a solution. In the light of the Bible, karma becomes an incomplete explanation of why things happen. Although it may provide order and control in an otherwise chaotic world, karma isolates and restricts people in their search for a better life. God's grace brings unmerited forgiveness, and teaches us to forgive others. Grace brings down barriers and empowers us to treat others better than they deserve.

Our own experience of discovering grace is an excellent bridge. One can explain how grace enables us to do good deeds, without fear of retribution for failures. Christians share high ethical and moral standards with karmic believers: do not kill, lie, steal, or be sexually immoral (Ten Commandments). The importance of emphasizing these similarities is expressed by Wagner:

> These laws, when practiced by Christian people, might lead some Buddhists to conclude that the Gospel is not different from their own teachings about good values. It is vitally important at this stage of communication to affirm how the Gospel upholds the high standards and values that the Buddhists take as their ideal. Many people who try to communicate the Gospel make the mistake of disregarding these similarities. This only alienates the Buddhist by

leading him/her to believe that Christians do not value the family or the good, ethical behavior to which they aspire. What is then left of the Gospel message is too strange for them to be able to appreciate it at all.[39]

Finally, a potential bridge is eschatology. Karmic believers are looking forward to the coming of Maitreya, the only compassionate savior who may come in an indefinite future to bring peace and harmony to planet earth. In Buddha's prophecies, he is described as the "sacred person who will be so kind as to come to the world, to help you all in the future."[40] His name is *Phrasii ariya mettrai* which translates as "the three-fold merciful one." Buddha instructs an old Brahmin that Phrasii ariya mettrai "is the one that will take you past regeneration to reach heaven, the end of suffering, and to see the face of three special ones, as you are hoping to do. You will never find it by the old way."[41] Wagner notices that "a vital expectation of Maitreya, or a coming Savior, is found all over Asia."[42] This teaching of Buddha may offer the opportunity to explain to karmic believers the Old Testament references to Messiah who is the Merciful one, the God who desires a relationship with them, a God who is not dependent on karma. A God that is different than Buddha or any other deity karmic communities are used to. A God who is equally just and merciful.

Bibliography

Bailey, Kenneth E. *Finding the Lost Cultural Keys of Luke 15*. St Louis, MO: Concordia, 1992.

———. *The Cross and the Prodigal: Luke 15 Through the Eyes of Middle Eastern Peasants*. Downers Grove, IL: IVP, 2005.

Bellinger, W. H. *Leviticus, Numbers*. New International Biblical Commentary. Peabody, MA: Hendrickson, 2001.

Bowers, Russell H. Jr. *Folk Buddhism in Southeast Asia*. Cambodia: Training of Timothys, 2003.

Bronkhorst, Johannes. *Karma*. Dimensions of Asian Spirituality Series. Honolulu, HI: University of Hawai'i Press, 2011.

Carus, Paul. *Karma/Nirvana*. La Salle, IL: The Open Court, 1973.

Chantavongsouk, Inta. *Buddha's Prophecy of the Messiah*. La Mirada, CA: The Lao Conference of Churches, 1999.

---

39. Wagner, *Beyond Karma*, 76.
40. Ibid., 114.
41. Ibid., 114.
42. Wagner, *Beyond Karma*, 2006, 222.

and the Rich Man, could be vividly portrayed as karmic, particularly by the Thai Buddhist readers.

Parable Reading in Luke 16:19–31

Albert Schweitzer was well known to the world for giving up every "luxurious blessing" he had and going to Africa as a missionary doctor. His decision was also known as a shocking response to this parable, "We are Dives [the Rich Man] . . . Out there in the colonies, however, sits wretched Lazarus."[46] Burdened by receiving gifts of grace as well as by the wrong doings of the west, Schweitzer felt much responsibility for carrying out redeeming actions towards the African populations. His grace found full legitimacy in his actions.

The parable of the Rich Man and Lazarus (16:19–31) is the fifth parable in the Lukan context of 15:1–17:10. This parable is colored by three significant motifs: criticism of Pharisees as money-lovers (16:14), self-justification (v.15), and the abiding nature of the law exemplified by Jesus' "declaratory legal" criticism of Jewish divorce law in vv.16–18.[47] These contextual motifs with three layers are richly and conclusively demonstrated by this parable. Interestingly, Jesus vehemently criticizes the Pharisees, who are considered the backdrop audience, as "money-lovers" (*filarguroi*). It was one of the accusatorial *topos* against the enemy's avarice in the Greco-Roman world,[48] supposedly related to the parable. In addition, the last layer is directly connected with Jesus' final words against the Rich Man (v.31), contending for the law's sufficiency and efficacy to the church era (e.g., Matt 5:17).

For Buddhist readers, a first question may arise: What is the basis for the judgment that sends the Rich Man to Hades and Lazarus to paradise in their afterlives? There are no explicit bad deeds committed by the Rich Man to cause such a reversed fortune,[49] only a brief remark that he "received good things in his life time" (v.25). However, the reader may still be puzzled: Is this a sufficiently decisive reason to result in such fatal judgment? In the parable text, it is only implied that the Rich Man might have

---

46. Snodgrass, *Stories with Intent*, 433.
47. Fitzmyer, *The Gospel According to Luke*, 1120.
48. Cheong, *A Dialogic Reading of The Steward Parable*, 167–71.
49. Fitzmyer, *The Gospel According to Luke*, 1128.

Part I: Religious Foundations

Craigie, Peter C. *The Book of Deuteronomy*. The New International Commentary of the Old Testament. Grand Rapids, MI: Eerdmans, 1976.

Davis, Stephen T. *After We Die: Theology, Philosophy, and the Question of Life after Death*. Waco, TX: Baylor University Press, 2015.

Firth, David G. *Surrendering Retribution in the Psalms: Responses to Violence in the Individual Complaints*. Waynesboro, GA: Paternoster, 2005.

Gane, Roy. *Leviticus, Numbers*. The NIV Application Commentary. Grand Rapids, MI: Zondervan, 2004

Hartley, John E. *Leviticus*. Word Bible Commentary. Grand Rapids, MI: Zondervan, 2015.

Johnson, Alan R. "Context-Sensitive Evangelism in the Thai setting: Building Capacity to Share Good News." In *Becoming the People of God*, edited by Paul H. de Neui. 63–92. Pasadena, CA: William Carey, 2015.

Koning, Daniëlle. "'I Believe for 50%': Negotiating Spiritual and Scientific Realities in Contemporary Thai Cosmologies." In *Seeking the Unseen: Spiritual Realities in the Buddhist World*, edited by Paul H. de Neui. 141–153. Pasadena, CA: William Carey, 2016.

Kyongsan, Dharma. *Freedom from Transgressive Karma: Lecture on the Instruction on Repentance*. Seoul, Korea: Seoul Selection, 2011.

Smith, Alex. "Missiological Implications of the Key Contrasts between Buddhism and Christianity." In *Sharing Jesus in the Buddhist World*, edited by David Lim and Steve Spaulding. 31–55. Pasadena, CA: William Carey, 2003.

Smith, Alex G. "Transferring Merit in Folk Buddhism." In *Sharing Jesus Holistically with the Buddhist World*, edited by David Lim and Steve Spaulding. 99–124. Pasadena, CA: William Carey, 2005.

Tenzing, S. *Freedom from Karma: How to Find Release from the Results of our Bad Deeds*. Chiang Mai, Thailand: Central Asia, 1998.

Wagner, Paul. "Beyond Karma: A Model for Presenting Freedom in Christ in the Buddhist Context." In *Communicating Christ in the Buddhist World*, edited by Paul H. de Neui and David Lim. 210–232. Pasadena, CA: William Carey, 2006.

———. *Beyond Karma: A Model Introducing the Good News of Salvation Through Jesus Christ from an Asian Perspective*. Self-published, 2004.

Wright, Christopher J. H. *An Eye for an Eye: The Place of the Old Testament Ethics Today*. Downers Grove, IL: IVP, 1983.

4

Contextualization of Merit-Making and Grace for Christward Movements in the Karmic World

David S. Lim

How can we effectively produce Christward movements (CM) in the Buddhist and karmic world? This chapter advances that to do so we should use the terms, concepts and teachings (including "merit making"), that Buddhists use in order to lead people to a personal relationship with Jesus Christ. We should encourage these believers to follow Christ together in micro-communities called "house churches networks" (HCN) which adopt this approach to faith. This is "radical contextualization." Diversion from this approach has been one of the main reasons for the failure to effect Christward movements among Buddhists.

"Radical contextualization," means starting with any term, concept, ritual, or artifact from any worldview or religion, including Buddhism which does not even believe in the existence of God. We can use elements in each particular Buddhist's worldview to invite them to follow Jesus Christ, without extracting people from their community and culture. We can join with Buddhists in our common search for truth by using their understandings and interpretations of reality. We are hereby showing we are sharing the journey together.

There are basically two kinds of Christward movements (CM). The first are those who plant churches in religious structures separate from the

Part I: Religious Foundations

Buddhist community. These prefer to be called "Church Planting Movements" (CPM) or "House Church Movements" (HCM) and are classified mainly as C-4 in the C-1 to C-6 spectrum. The other uses the C-5 paradigm and has been called "Insider Movements" (IM) or "Disciple Multiplication Movements" (DMM). This second type avoids extraction evangelism and disciples convert informally in-house church networks (HCNs). It spreads vertically and horizontally seeking to transform Buddhist structures (monks, temples, monasteries) from within. Most CMs in China, Cambodia and Vietnam tend to be of the first kind (C-4), while those in Japan, Myanmar and Thailand to be of the second (C-5). India has a mix of both, though the largest ones are C-5.[1]

IMs are now clearly defined in *Understanding Insider Movements*, edited by H. Talman and J. J. Travis.[2] Sadly this major book contains only two minor chapters on IMs in the Buddhist world. In the Cape Town Commitment of the Third Lausanne Congress 2010, IMs were recognized as a promising way forward, albeit with caution. It states:

> So called 'insider movements' are to be found within several religions. These are groups of people who are now following Jesus as their God and Savior. They meet together in small groups for fellowship, teaching, worship and prayer centered around Jesus and the Bible while continuing to live socially and culturally within their birth communities, including some elements of its religious observance … Some commend such movements. Others warn of the danger of syncretism. Syncretism, however, is a danger found among Christians everywhere as we express our faith within our own cultures. We should avoid the tendency, when we see God at work in unexpected or unfamiliar ways, either (i) hastily to classify it and promote it as a new mission strategy, or (ii) hastily to condemn it without sensitive contextual listening.[3]

IMs catalyze transformation from within (and often from below) through winning to Christ the community leaders (including religious) through DMMs. The aim is not to introduce Christendom/denominational practices and structures (indigenized or not), but to disciple Christ-followers to live for and bear witness to Christ without being extracted from their

---

1. Lim, "Asia's House Church Movements Today."
2. Talman and Travis, *Understanding Insider Movements*.
3. Lausanne, *Cape Town Commitment*, 47–48.

socio-religious situation. This was clearly taught by Paul in 1 Corinthians 7:18–19 and 9:19–23.

As disturbing as it may be, the Holy Spirit is leading people today to become Christ-following Buddhists who pray to God in Jesus' name and seek to do his will as revealed in the Bible (1 Tim 4:4–5) yet still connected with their Buddhist culture. Individually and corporately in their HCNs they seek to share their faith as insiders, aspiring to persuade as many of their relatives, friends and workmates to follow Jesus Christ through obedience to his teachings. This does not exempt any from being persecuted when they are discovered. In fact, in the midst of trials the testimony of these sisters and brothers stands a much better chance of being accepted and embraced by others.

It is best that they avoid being called "Christians." This often turns people off and closes opportunities to share Jesus. For example, in the northeastern region of Thailand *Khris-tee-yen* (Christian) has several negative meanings such as one who follows a foreign religion; one who works for foreigners; one who has sold out national identity to foreigners; one who had leprosy since early Protestant ministries worked among lepers; one whose ancestor had evil spirits and was expelled from the village, or one who cannot go to heaven because their funeral was not led by a Buddhist monk.[4]

Members of IMs should be able to choose how they will be labeled. One group even calls itself "New Buddhists."[5] They explain that while Buddhism requires each one to depend solely upon oneself, New Buddhism is complete dependence on the Creator. It is his grace shown in Jesus Christ that saves from *samsara* and sin and also empowers living the path (dharma) that leads to happiness (nirvana) in this life and in the afterlife.

In my view, it is mainly through major IMs that the Great Commission can realistically be achieved, given the sincere effort but insignificant results of world evangelization in the past three decades since the first Lausanne Congress in 1974. Here are the four distinct marks of CMs, IM-style: simple message, simple manner, simple method and simple mission.

---

4. Wetchgama, "The New Buddhists," 103–104.

5. Ibid., 106–107.

Part I: Religious Foundations

Simple Message: Gospel of Grace

We can simply and effectively share the gospel of Jesus Christ with Buddhists in their karmic worldview: Karma is indeed a reality – good will be rewarded, while evil will be punished. Our lives will be judged according to the merits and demerits accrued in this life (2 Cor 5:10; Rev 22:12). We can use karma and merit-making as bridges and common ground for evangelism. In fact, we can find and should surface many other common elements in the Buddhist worldview.

Karma

Karma is the absolute and ultimate determinant in Buddhism. It is "an impersonal, natural law that operated in accordance with our actions" without any law-giver or external ruling agent.[6] Its classic popular motto is "Do good, receive good; do evil, receive evil." This is similar to the Biblical teaching: "Do not be deceived: God cannot be mocked. People reap what they sow" (Gal 6:7).

The goal in Buddhism is to purify negative karma, to help generate positive karma, and to exhaust all karma ultimately through merit-making. For any negative or positive intention and action done, there will be a commensurate result automatically. The effects of one's actions may be delayed, perhaps in a lifetime, but it will surely come. One arrives at enlightenment (*bodhi*) when all karmas, negative and positive, are exhausted when the sense of ego is totally extinguished, and a state of unending bliss (nirvana) is achieved.

Merit-Making

Perhaps the most basic motivation for most Buddhists today continues to be merit-making (dana). Merit (punna) can be transferred, especially to parents, thereby earning oneself more merit. Dana involves earning merits to improve one's karma (kamma), in the cycle of repeated reincarnations (samsara). Buddhist professor Dhammananda teaches that merit cleanses the mind and purifies it of "evil tendencies of greed, hatred and delusion."[7] Merit is accumulated on behalf of or on account of the maker of the merit.

---

6. Dhammananda, *What Buddhists Believe*, 113–115.
7. Ibid., 202.

Even the motivation and quality of thoughts, words and deed involved in merit-making can influence future karma for good or ill. Merit is generally considered positive and beneficial, but demerits (or negative merit) from evil acts are equally potent and affect karma adversely.

Buddhist scholars identify ten major merit-making deeds:

1. Generosity or giving (*dana*)
2. Morality by keeping the precepts (*sila*)
3. Mental culture through meditation (*bhavana*)
4. Reverence or respect (*apachayana*)
5. Service in helping others (*veyyavaccha*)
6. Transference of merits to others (*pattidana*)
7. Rejoicing in the merits of others (*pattanumodana*)
8. Preaching and teaching the Dharma (*dharma desana*)
9. Listening to the Dharma (*dharma savanna*)
10. Straightening one's views or acting with right views (*ditthijju*).[8]

Several other kinds of good works also gain merit: donating to monks, familiarizing oneself with the religion, or being a leading lay follower.[9] A person can also share material things, behave in a moral way, and train their mind to gain merit. Other examples include having polite modest conduct, doing service for the common good, involving others in good deeds, rejoicing in the good deeds of others, explaining Buddhist teachings to others and correcting others' view to the right (Buddhist) views. Merit may be gained by commissioning the construction of bells, stupas or shrines, copying and reciting scripture, purchasing land for the construction of Buddhist temples, donating calligraphy, praying for monks, painting murals with inscriptions, and constructing images of Buddha in written, spoken or visual forms. Such "good works" are basically understood as the giving or sharing of resources towards ensuring a better rebirth and moving people towards nirvana.[10]

---

8. Ibid., 101–103.

9. Adamek, "Impossibility of the Given," 136.

10. Walsh, "The Economics of Salvation," 355. Cf also Somaratna, "An Evangelical Christian Analysis of Theravada Buddhist Spirituality."

Good deeds have a cumulative effect towards earning merit. The more a person gives or shares, the more they have. The Buddhist thought of karma, action, and deeds can be seen as being very similar to the concept of "good works" in Christian traditions.[11] Though most Christians believe that good works are non-meritorious for salvation (like "filthy rags," Isa 64:6), all traditions consider them as the natural fruit and evidence of salvation (Eph 2:8–10; Heb 11:6; Jas 2:14–26). Based on Romans 2:1–16, some traditions teach that "good works" is also a means of salvation for those who have not heard the gospel.

Grace

Buddhism also has the concept of grace. Merit transference (*pattidana*) concerns the sharing of merits – without expectation of reciprocity or reward. "Acquired merit can be transferred . . . it can be shared vicariously with others" either living or dead.[12] All of these meritorious deeds not only produce benefits for the one making merit, but also give merit to the recipient of its transfer.[13] Sharing merit is believed to contribute to one's improved future karma as well as to help others.[14]

In practice, the three groups that benefit from such benevolence are the monks (*sangha*) or holy people, one's parents, and the needy. Those who transfer merit "also receive the fruits of their deeds ... the act of transference, being a good deed in itself, enhances the merit already acquired. In their state of happiness, the departed ones will reciprocate their blessings on their living relatives."[15] Most Buddhist cultures practice different ways to transfer merit, especially to ancestors. Rites, incantations, ceremonies and good deeds help improve the state of those in the after-life and also ensure one's own future security. Most vivid of such merit-making and merit-sharing may be seen at Chinese funerals where paper money, cars, houses and cell phones are burned symbolically to help their "living dead" in the other world. In Mahayana Buddhism, the departed have continuing knowledge and experience that continue after death, and their presence and powers can affect the lives of their kin still living on earth.

---

11. Adamek, "Impossibility of the Given," 143.
12. Dhammananda, *What Buddhists Believe*, 393.
13. Ibid., 204.
14. Adamek, "Impossibility of the Given," 136.
15. Dhammananda, *What Buddhists Believe*, 393–397.

Most Theravada Buddhists have a folk religious concept of grace based on merit-transference.[16] For this reason many Thai men became monks to transfer merit to parents, especially to mothers.[17] In *dana*, the idea of grace (free gift) is already assumed, as an ideal at least. There's no obligation at all for the receiver to reciprocate the giver. The message of the Christ follower can focus on the uniqueness of God's grace not as spiritual progress or better rebirth but an end in itself that impacts everything.

Just as needed help must come from outside oneself from spirits, bodhisattvas, the Buddha or the merit of others, folk Theravadins join Mahayanan and Tibetan Buddhists in openness to receive outside help from Christ as Savior, liberator and deliverer. As can be seen throughout the history of Christendom, each person, church and community will develop their own soteriology on whether such work of salvific grace is permanent (Calvinist), impermanent (Arminian, semi-Pelagian and Pelagian) or both (Wesleyan). But why should this become an issue? There are more important tasks at hand.

Gospel

Thus we can share Jesus contextually with Buddhists, including using the Buddhist concepts of karma, merit-making and grace in our evangelism. There are many congruencies that overlap between Buddhist and Christian worldviews, especially regarding life in the temporal reality or earthly existence. We can see continuities in the teachings of their founders, in their Scriptures, and in the writings of their contemporaries.

Like all religions, Buddhism has been evolving throughout history as it adjusts to the worldviews and cultures it has encountered. It has been contextualizing ever since its growth within India at the 1st Council of Rajagoha (ca. 483 B.C.) and during its expansion from India to Sri Lanka in the third century B.C.[18] Today the Dalai Lama has taught that theists and Christians can be Buddhists "if they reframe their minds to the Buddhist teachings and practices."[19] He acknowledges that there are varying views on major beliefs within Buddhism itself.[20]

---

16. Smith, "Transfer of Merit in Folk Buddhism," 113–118.
17. Davis, *Poles Apart?*, 92–93.
18. Cf., Burnett "The Challenge of the Globalization of Buddhism."
19. Dalai Lama, *Compassion and Wisdom*, 49–61.
20. Ibid., 54–55.

Part I: Religious Foundations

Each community and every individual may interpret merit-making and grace differently. It is difficult to determine when these are based on classic Buddhist understandings for better karma or on folk religious practices seeking to control the unseen world of spirits and reality. Is the action motivated by love (especially for parents and ancestors) to transfer "grace" or is it motivated by the desire for personal gain of luck, power, position, possessions or prosperity? Is it simply family tradition or cultural custom? Any combination of the above and others are possible.

This diversity opens varied opportunities to introduce Christ according to the spirituality of each person or community. As Buddhists read the Bible, they will find many of its teachings to be good, even similar to their own. The main challenge for all of us is how do we live out the high moral demands of our faith? Christ followers believe we need God's grace in Christ to enable us towards the perfection (nirvana) which God requires (Matt 5:48; 1 Pet 1:16–17). As we walk humbly with God in his path of righteous living (Mic 6:8), we need to constantly abide in Christ repenting whenever we make mistakes and commit sins (1 John 1:9). In Christ, God's grace purifies us and empowers us to live in constant holiness drawing on the power of his Spirit (Phil 2:12–13).

For Buddhists who seek release from their existential sufferings, Jesus Christ is their healer and deliverer from *dukkha* and *samsara*.[21] For those who seek victory over spirits and demons, Jesus Christ is the victor who conquers all forces.[22] And for those who seek a Savior who exemplifies sacrifice for others like any bodhisattva (like *Amida, Guanyin*), Jesus Christ is the unique and all powerful substitute for atonement of sin (1 John 2:2; 4:10; Rom 3:25; Heb 2:17) and for reconciliation with God (2 Cor 5:19, Rom 5:10). For Japanese, Jesus Christ is the Great *Kami* (or Buddha) who is the Head of the cosmos, who rules over the varied gods and blesses us with life-giving power.[23] He is the source of life, karma and all goodness, the *logos* (*dharma, tao*) who enlightens all (John 1:1–9,14,18).

There are many modern forms of Buddhism which have adopted western Christian worldviews and lifestyles which may make bridging easier for westernized witnesses of Jesus Christ. Some are working for political and social reforms (even militantly), such as B. R. Ambedkar's "Neo-Buddhism"

---

21. Cf., Hiebert 1999, 77–79.

22. Col 2:15; cf. Fukuda, *Developing a Contextualized Church*, 71–87; Nyunt, *Missions Amidst Pagodas*, 106.

23. Fukuda, *Developing a Contextualized Church*, 58–66.

in India, A. T. Ariyaratne "engaged Buddhism" in Sri Lanka, Ouyporn Khuankaew's "Feminist engaged Buddhism" in Thailand, Aung San Suu Kyi's "activist Buddhism" in Myanmar, and Thich Nhat Hanh's political "engaged Buddhism" in Vietnam. Some have adopted a rationalist scientific worldview, like the Japanese New Buddhism, which will become more common as science sees psychological and medical benefits in yoga, mindfulness and meditation practices. This has been popularized by Thailand's Buddhadasa and the Dalai Lama. Others have even adopted Christian rituals and practices like relief and development ministry like Taiwan's Tzu Chi Foundation and Thailand's Buddhadasa's Dharmic Society. To them, Jesus Christ may be presented as the embodiment of compassion, justice and non-violent advocacy.

When asked if we believe in Buddha, we can say that he was indeed the Enlightened One who found truths for righteous living, and even a prophet who predicted the coming of *Maitreya* Buddha, whose name is Jesus of Nazareth. Just before he died, Buddha spoke to Ananda about a future Buddha called *Maitreya*,

> I am not the first Buddha to come on earth, nor shall I be the last. In due time, another Buddha will arise in this world, a Holy One, a Supreme Enlightened One, endowed with wisdom, in conduct auspicious, knowing the universe, an incomparable leader of men, a master of *devas* and men. He will reveal to you the same Eternal Truths, which I have taught you. He will proclaim a religious life, wholly perfect and pure; such as I now proclaim.[24]

Dhammananda also teaches that Buddhists who seek to gain merit through the committed religious life "will have a chance to be reborn as human beings in the time of the *Maitreya* Buddha and will obtain *Nibbana* identical with that of Gautama Buddha."[25] Alex Smith notes that this hope was particularly popular in the early 1900s among the Lao of Northern Thailand and Laos.[26]

Very few, if any, Buddhists are willing to say that they have gained enough merit to reach nirvana, the ultimate stage of enlightenment. Jesus Christ brings nirvana (perfection) and completes what is unfulfilled in Buddhism. He is the way (*dharma*) in any cultural forms, because all things

---

24. Dhammananda, *What Buddhists Believe*, 45–46.

25. Ibid., 46.

26. Smith, "Transfer of Merit in Folk Buddhism," 15–18.

come from the Creator.²⁷ Classical Buddhism interprets Christ crucifixion as ignominious, neither voluntary nor heroic, simply the just retribution of karmic causation. Christ's horrific torturous death could only mean one thing: in his previous existence he must have been very wicked to have acquired such bad karma.²⁸ Yet Buddhist cultures have incorporated folk or "secular" understandings of redemptive suffering. Many legends and histories among Buddhist peoples do record the concept of sacrificing for others where one person has voluntarily died in the place of another.

> Buddhism knows much of sacrifice for others, both in the conception of the Bodhi-sat in Northern Buddhism who defers his entry into Nirvana for the sake of men and in the spiritual fables of the Jatakas, the Birth Stories, which picture often in a childlike way, but sometimes with telling maturity, the sacrifices undergone by the Buddha in earlier lives. Neither Bodhi-satts nor Jatakas may be historical, but they are evidence of a conviction within Buddhism that a sacrifice is both right and effective.²⁹

The concept of self-sacrifice for others can be found in many Theravada Buddhist cultures. One famous historical record of a vicarious substitutionary death was that of Queen Srisuriyothai of Siam. In an ancient culture the death of the king in battle would mean the taking over of his country, but this queen sacrificed her life as she received the Burmese general's sword blow instead of her husband King Chakraphat. This heroic deed showed that she willingly sacrificed her life for the King and her country. A memorial *chedi* was built to commemorate her heroic deed.

Merit-making on behalf of another is common to many religions. In fact most religions require the guilty one to transfer their guilt to another by means of a ritual of substitution. The "banana leaf float" ceremony in many countries in the karmic world incorporates this concept. After the "house cleaning ceremony," in the evening the whole village will proceed to the local river with a banana leaf float and each person will vicariously place upon the float all the uncleanness of house and heart and believe that it will be taken away down river as the float disappears. Also the Thai expression, "a goat which 'takes away' sin" suggests sin being taken away through the blood of an animal being shed in place of the person concerned. In Tibetan Buddhism there is an actual "scape-goat ritual," a goat is

---

27. Wetchgama, "The New Buddhists," 106–107; Davis, *Poles Apart?*, 93–97.
28. Davis, *Poles Apart?*, 85.
29. Appleton, *Christian Presence and Buddhism*, 51.

selected and symbolically "loaded with guilt," and then sent out to be killed by whoever finds it.

Modern people consider historical martyrs as national heroes, especially those who gave their lives on behalf of the nation. Their deaths are extolled as the ultimate self-sacrifice and described as substitutionary. Such deaths are not interpreted in the Buddhist understanding of karmic predestination. Instead, these are "heroes" who died sacrificially on behalf of others.[30] Substitution, vicarious suffering, and liberation through intervention are attractive concepts to modern Buddhists directly addressing Theravadan self-determinism, fatalism and samsara.

Common Grace

We can share Jesus Christ contextually and affirm almost all teachings of classic Buddhism: the Four Noble Truths, Eight-fold Path and the various interpretations (traditions) of Buddha's teachings.[31] Buddhists just need to add the call to "remember our Creator" (Eccl 12:1), "Fear God and keep His commandments" (v. 13), and to revere a personal Supreme Being who will judge all things done in history (v. 14).

God has revealed his will in human conscience (Eccl 3:11 "in human hearts"). Romans 2:14–15 explicitly states that God has written his commandments in the hearts of people who do not have the Book of the Law (Torah). God's self-revelation to humanity is called "General Revelation" because of God's "Common Grace." God's existence, many of God's attributes and even God's will are made known to all human beings. Some of these are included in the teachings of Buddha, despite Buddha's non-theistic view. We can point out similarities in the moral teachings of Buddha and those found in the Bible.

This innate knowledge about God's will and ways is based on God's image inherent in human beings (Gen 1:26–27; 9:6, Jas 3:9) and God's self-revelation in creation and in human conscience (Ps 19:1; Rom 1:18–20). Human cultures and religions do have immoral and demonic aspects, but they are due to sin, ignorance, finitude and weakness that are also inherent in human nature. Yet people with all their weaknesses and sins do seek God in response to his gracious revelation. It's our responsibility to recognize this religious instinct, without attributing and condemning everything in

---

30. Davis, *Poles Apart?*, 85–86
31. E.g. Matt 5–7; cf. Vasanthakumar, "An Exploration of the Book of Ecclesiastes."

Buddhism (and other religions) to sin and Satan. Paul's appreciative non-polemical approach (Acts 17) did not endorse idolatry, but shows a respectful recognition of people's spiritual quest.

The "theology of religion" of radical contextualization promotes the common ground instead of just the "point of contact" approach.[32] There are both continuities and discontinuities between the Buddhist and Christian faiths, but in evangelism, we must start and focus on the continuities and allow the discontinuities to be corrected gradually later. Yet we must consider continuities to be real truths. God has left revelations of his truth among all peoples and their cultures (Acts 10:38; 14:17; 17:22–31). We can start with whatever light is already there and introduce Jesus and his teachings from that level of understanding: "While commitment to Christ precludes commitment to the finality of other faiths, it does not rule out acceptance of truths that other faiths may contain."[33] Willingness to learn of truth found in other religions shows our own need to grow in understanding. We can even acknowledge the abuses and failures of Christianity as a religion without feeling that faith in Jesus is threatened.

Getting the simple message right is necessary but not sufficient. Besides presenting the message with the right (contextualized) words and concepts, effective contextualized witness for IMs also requires at least three other dimensions: simple manner, simple method, and simple mission.

Simple Manner: Relationships of Grace

Leading people (including Buddhists) to Christ should be a simple matter. It is akin to excitedly gossiping a piece of good news to a friend. For this reason new believers are usually the best evangelists. The harvest is ready (John 4:35) and plentiful (Matt 9:37); we need to pray for more harvesters (v. 38). The Holy Spirit has been "poured out upon all flesh" (Acts 2:17–18) "to convict the world of sin, righteousness and judgment" (John 16:8–11) and guide people into all truth (16:13–15), for God desires that all will be saved and come to the knowledge of truth (1 Tim 2:3–4; 2 Pet 3:8–9). We can expect spiritual hunger. Our role is to be good witnesses choosing the best way possible to win as many people as possible to God's embodied truth, Jesus Christ (John. 1:1–18).

---

32. Cf. Lim, "Biblical Christianity in the Context of Buddhism," 195–197.

33. Cf. McDermott *Can Evangelicals Learn from World Religions?*; Yong *The Holy Spirit and the Non-Christian Faiths*; Cracknell *In Good and Generous Faith*.

Simplifying our message means simplifying the manner of sharing Jesus in three ways: relational, dialogic and narrative. These will minimize possible conflicts as some worldview and lifestyle changes will arise from differences in worldview.

Relational

Worldview change is tough, but is best done through sincere relationships and informal story-telling.[34] Establishing a friendly or intimate relationship is perhaps the most important factor in effective evangelism. As we share confidently, we must beware of appearing offensive by sending the message, "You're wrong; I'm right," thereby turning our friend off from the opportunity to hear the Gospel. We do not need to attack or condemn others by rejecting or belittling the good in another religion. In fact, all criticism of their religion must be avoided until that person shall have "converted to Christ." There is hardly any use to try to convince someone whose mind is still in the dark (John 3:19–21; Eph 2:1–3; 4:17–18). Corrections can come later, and usually they are the work of the Holy Spirit who guides believers into all truth (John 16:13)!

Buddhist spirituality is attained through the tangible benefits of earning merit through good works. With the goal of Buddhism being to alleviate suffering in life, we can recognize the importance of daily events and look for ways to help. Christ followers can join in daily routines and concerns of our communities. If others recognize God's truth as a reality in the everyday life of believers, they may be drawn to the source of grace itself. Due to the relational focus of Buddhist cultures, ministry to Buddhists should focus not so much on beliefs as on the practical concerns of people and their families. Ministry should attend to the narratives of their lives and be willing to enter into their journeys as well as to share our own journey, thus letting actions speak louder than words.[35] Our outreach should be more about experiencing God's grace in the world together than involving them in our evangelistic activities.

---

34. Hiebert, *Transforming Worldviews*, 84; Strauss & Steffen, "Change the Worldview," 462–463.

35. Yong, *The Holy Spirit and the Non-Christian Faiths*, 15–18.

Part I: Religious Foundations

Dialogical

A gentle and patient attitude evinced by a listening and conversing posture is required (1 Pet 3:15). Evangelism should be in the form of an open invitation to friends to join in your search for truth. The acceptability of our message often largely depends on the credibility of the messenger which has to be earned, especially by outsiders.

Eventually there will need to be at least two major worldview changes: from samsaric (cyclical) to historical (development in space and time), and from impersonal force to personal deity.[36] This should be done dialogically and expectantly. Jesus Christ is the liberator from samsara, breaking the chain of karma.[37] Along with appreciating Buddhism *in toto*, prayer to a personal God in the name of the historical Jesus of Nazareth, and willing obedience in accordance to God's historic word will be added (1 Tim 4:4–5). Upon conversion to Christ, the Holy Spirit will guide Buddhist background believers to the right perspectives and proper behaviors that befit their new faith. New Buddhists can share with their networks that Christ came to fulfill, not destroy, the best of Buddhism, and his coming adds new dimensions to enrich their faith. This "critical appreciation" approach is not leveling down to the lowest common denominator, but leveling up to the highest possible revelation.

Avoiding confrontation or polemics, but showing love and trust correlates with the preferred behavioral pattern of Buddhism called *upaya*: "meekness"[38] and "gentle strength."[39] As we engage each other in a truly dialogic conversation, we acknowledge our common humanity as equally needy, equally sinful and equally dependent on God's grace. We listen attentively and sensitively to understand, and thus divest our evangelism of any stereotypes or fixed formulae which are barriers to true dialogue. In this way, the discipling process actually starts from the beginning. The more time we spend with the disciple before and after the conversion experience, the faster and more effective will be the discipleship to Christ-like thinking and living.

---

36. Cf. Smith "Transfer of Merit in Folk Buddhism," 117–118; Hiebert *Transforming Worldviews*.

37. Song, *The Compassionate God*, 181–191; Yong, *The Holy Spirit and the Non-Christian Faiths*, 115; cf. Bhikkhu *Why Were We Born?*

38. Cf. Mejudhon, "Meekness."

39. Cf. Bowers, "Gentle Strength and Upaya."

Narrative

Finally, for worldview change, it is best to use the narrative approach: stories, proverbs, parables, and songs.[40] Recent examples can be seen in Cambodia[41] as well as dances, drama and rituals in Japan.[42] Most importantly may be the use of Genesis 1–3 to teach God's creation and its fall, as well as John 1–3 to show Jesus Christ's origin and mission, particularly for Buddhists to adopt the historicity of time and the personhood of God.

In the past two decades, Oral Bible Storying has been used to teach the truths of God's Word by simply telling Bible stories and helping the listeners to discover the truth for themselves by asking questions in a discussion or conversation format. Christ-followers in China memorized entire books of the Bible. Those who were imprisoned can quote whole texts while in jail, so they could witness to Christ even when in solitary confinement.

To make our task simpler, we can choose the stories, psalms, proverbs and teachings that are needed in the local context. The use of pictures or visual aids has to be carefully done. They can bring confusion or may distract from the story, unless they are drawn by native artists in local art forms. Though a picture is worth a thousand words, any given picture does not convey the same one thousand words to every person.

Simple Method: Movements of Grace

According to Luke 10:4–8, Jesus trained his disciples by sending them to just simply share their life and faith with a "person of peace" (v. 6). This is the key strategy of disciple multiplication (or making) movements (DMM), which is simply described in 2 Timothy 2:2: "the things that you have heard me say in the presence of many witnesses entrust to reliable people who will also be qualified to teach others." We aim to saturate each community with the gospel through discipling each Christ-follower to disciple their own network of relatives and friends starting with just one person and their household.

---

40. Cf. Evans, "From the Biblical World to the Buddhist Worldview."

41. Cf. Jones, "Moving Towards Oral Communication of the Gospel," Mam, "Communicating the Gospel through Story and Song in Cambodia."

42. Cf. Fukuda, *Developing a Contextualized Church as a Bridge to Christianity in Japan*.

Part I: Religious Foundations

Each Christ-follower is equipped and empowered to make their own disciples as they meet regularly, preferably not more than one year discussing the relevance of God and his word together. Each of them is a priest, a minister blessed to be a blessing to those who come in touch with them, discipling each to confidently have direct access to God and with authority to represent God on earth, including in their karmic contexts. Each Christ-following individual and group simply learns how to hear God through the discipline of set times of devotions and the habit of constantly asking "Lord, what would you have me do to please you?" (1 Cor 10:31; Rom 12:1–2).

In DMMs, each Christ-follower learns how to facilitate Bible sharing by asking three simple questions about a chosen passage: "What does this text teach us about God and humans?" "What does it teach us to do?" and "Who are the two or three people you can share what we've learned?" The objective is that the head of each household (including servants and guests) can lead a weekly Bible sharing time, and thus all members will have also learned how to lead "house churches" (HC) with their respective kin, friends and workmates. Gossiping about Jesus and his teachings will have become a habit or custom in each community across the karmic world and everywhere.

As New Buddhists, they can naturally catalyze DMMs as they remain as good (if not better) neighbors in their community and workplace, and as they participate in community affairs and festivals and excel in community services (read: good works). When they gather, even as "two or three," they encourage each other to love God and their neighbors (Heb 10:24; 1 Cor 14:26). The Holy Spirit will guide them into all truth (John 16:13–15).

Cross-cultural missionaries do not need to do much, as Jesus trained his disciples to do in Luke 10. Strategically they just need to befriend, evangelize and disciple a "person of peace" (v. 4b–7), who is a local resident who will then lead the DMM in his community and networks. The key is to let the first converts to Christ remain in their professions and socio-religious identities (1 Cor 7:17–20) as Christ-following Buddhists.

In 2003, a nurse came to know Christ through another nurse in an IM in Japan. She was a New Age practitioner who wanted to study abroad to become a New Age leader. The Christ-following nurse led her to visualize her past experiences which she had expertise in. She saw herself and her ex-boyfriend in her imagination. Though he had once made her angry and had wounded her, she saw herself hugging him and they were weeping together. She could not understand why she did it, but after a while she understood when she saw Jesus approach them and hugged both of them with his warm hands. Jesus was bathed in tender light and she understood supernaturally that he would never abandon her. For her, conversion and healing occurred at the same moment. The experience was so real that she couldn't help but share it with her friends. Three days after her baptism she shared her experience with a friend who was her partner in reading tarot cards. She led her friend to experience Jesus, and the same thing happened in her friend's life. They began meeting weekly for prayer and accountability, and after three months, they started a HC in one of their homes where they used to read tarots. They had experienced Christ directly and were excited to share their experience with other nurses and friends, many of whom have also become Christ-followers with them and thus launched a DMM. This HCN emerged in a family-like small group of Christ-followers who had a passion for sharing Christ with their friends.[43] DMM should be viewed as a lifestyle rather than just a strategy.

As New Buddhists serve their fellow Buddhists in love, they will naturally rise in recognition and leadership in their communities and professions. Even without being intentional about it, their opinions and recommendations will be seriously considered. They will also be in a position to evangelize and disciple monks and other community leaders. This is how DMMs produce Christ-following communities naturally and take over governance positions and even "turn empires upside down" from the bottom up and from the inside out (1 Cor 1:26–29). This is the incarnational approach of Jesus, the apostles and the early church, as well as CMs in church history up to this day. This is how God intended nations and peoples to be discipled (Matt 28:19; Acts 1:8).

In our age of rapid technical changes (from social media to artificial intelligence and robotics), and its accompanying political and religious disruptions, good ideas and practices can come from anywhere and spread everywhere. Any movement can start from anywhere. Our mission of world evangelization through DMMs become easier and simpler as long as we remain "low tech" to focus on "high touch" (caring and sharing). DMMs follow the same logic as viral multiplication of social media, and work on the same dynamics. People live within extended webs of relationships and spend much time relating to and communicating with people in their social networks; these are the people they trust and learn from the most. Successful viral media spreads through such networks of relationship, and

---

43. Fukuda, "Incarnational Approaches to the Japanese People," 360–361.

PART I: RELIGIOUS FOUNDATIONS

multiplication of faith communities spreads through these networks in much the same way.

Simple Mission: Communities of Grace

The DMMs will gradually result in HCNs whose simple spirituality will have minimal religious practices. Following Christ does not require public displays of religiosity: in fact, Jesus literally discouraged such, including loud praying, fasting and alms-giving (merit-making) (Matt 6:1–18). Christ-following Buddhist leaders will establish shalom where their constituents enjoy life with love and justice (1 Tim 2:1–2). Their spirituality does not need to develop elaborate theologies, ethics, liturgies and hierarchies. As Christ-followers lead inductive Bible sharing regularly, their inherited socio-religious traditions will be reduced and/or transformed into simpler forms having overcome fears and guilt feelings, which are the roots of superstitious practices, lucky charms and elaborate rituals.

Based on 1 Corinthians 7:17–24, their simple faith will evolve in at least three ways: non-clerical (v. 17, 20, 24), contextual (v. 18–19) and developmental (v. 21–23).

Non-Clerical

Above all, each Christ-follower will be discipled to be self-supporting through the means of a livelihood (Eph 4:28; 2 Thess 3:6–12). DMMs are lay movements and HCNs are lay-led, different from the clergy-led structures of historic Christendom. New Buddhists will phase out the need for the monastic order (sangha), as they learn about the "priesthood of every believer." Though the monks will continue to be fed at the start, as they become Christ-followers, they will each learn a trade or become teachers. Those who have leadership qualities will naturally rise into management and governance positions in the community and marketplace.

Contextual

New Buddhists will develop contextualized religious practices, retaining most of them and redefining them as Christ-centered and Christ-ward customs, with historical and personal (non-samsaric) beliefs and values. Most popular Buddhist practices, including ancestral and merit-making practices will be simplified. As members reflect on the word some customs may eventually phase out as they live out the logic of non-samsaric and post-animistic worldviews. They may even become more biblical and Christ-centered than the tradition-laden and event-oriented denominations in today's uncontextualized and westernized churches in the karmic world.

Our mission is an occupation plan, not an evacuation plan (1 Cor 15:24–25; Phil 2:9–11) because Christ is ruler over all things (Col 1:16–17).[44] Jesus Christ entered European pagan cosmologies and transformed them Christward. Christ-followers sanctify the non-Christian (1 Cor 7:14; 10:20–26), because all things can be purified (Titus 1:15) by prayer and the word (1 Tim 4:4–5). New Buddhists can join in Buddhist activities with a clear conscience. When they are confronted and asked about their motivation, then they can explain and witness to Christ, even if it may result in persecution. Meanwhile, they have already been doing DMM already before such conflict arises.

New Buddhists may continue to practice the rituals and ceremonies of their families and communities.[45] Even if their culture assumes these are for merit-making, these practices are "good works" which are never sufficient to reach God or nirvana (perfection). It is Christ who fulfills and completes what is unfulfilled in these Buddhist practices.

Sarun testifies that as a new convert to Christ, he had no qualms to engage in *tom bun* (merit-making) in a Buddhist temple, carrying two joss sticks and a lotus flower, while verbalizing his desires, with the hope of improving his karma.[46] He also prayed to God to bless his family, especially to help his sister-in-law financially. Two days later his sister-in-law called to tell him that her financial problem was solved. She was elated that God answered his prayers.

But previous to that day, he had thought of doing *tom bun* again to ask for financial blessing. But that time, he heard God tell him twice that God would take care of all his needs, so he did not do it. His conclusion: "Both

---

44. Taylor, "Contextualization, Syncretism, and the Demonic," 377

45. Fukuda, *Developing a Contextualized Church*, 219–230; de Neui, "Contextualizing with Thai Folk Buddhists," 132–135; Wetchgama, "The New Buddhists," 106; Davis, *Poles Apart?*, 136–137; cf. Dyrness, *Insider Jesus*.

46. Cf. Sarun, "Avoiding Syncretism."

acts look very similar on the outside, but very different on the inside. What matters is on the inside, which makes the latter act syncretistic."[47]

Many Buddhists are quite nominal, with no habits of regular visits to the temple. Their Buddhism surfaces only in family affairs, especially during festivals and funerals. We should encourage them to become better Buddhists and even grow the best Buddhist sect in their contexts. If any of their behavior disturbs our conscience, we may gently inquire in what way is it Christ-centered or Christ-honoring. As New Buddhists, they can lead in many advocacies: peace movements that resist militarization and advance reconciliation and non-violent change; ecological awareness and activism against climate change and for clean and green/blue programs; as well as vegetarianism and healthy lifestyles. Sundays can return to God's original plan for rest and family.[48] Moreover, in our stress-filled fast-changing world, they can teach some forms of meditation, yoga and mindfulness classes. Depending on the context, they may even use Buddhist names and titles, teaching privately that Jesus Christ is the *Maitreya* Buddha, Savior, liberator and/or dharma to the Creator.

They can join in community festivities and even be part of its leadership team, instead of setting up meetings for "Christian worship." In their annual calendar of festivals, some can be transformed into the Christian equivalent of Christ's birthday (Christmas), his death and resurrection (Good Friday and Easter), "church anniversary" (Pentecost), thanksgiving (Feast of Tabernacles), and others. Funerals can gradually be simplified to honor the dead without the complexities of karmic merit-making.

They will gradually learn how to get rid of anything that is sinful: idolatry, individualism, immorality and injustice. Not all at once, as none of us have been totally rid of such sins ourselves. Elisha permitted Naaman to do ceremonial worship to pagan gods (2 Kgs 5:17–19), and Paul permitted the Corinthians to eat foods offered to idols (1 Cor 8–10).[49] Almost all of our present church practices (in liturgies, weddings, Christmas, Easter, Halloween and more) were adapted from pagan customs of pre-Christian European tribes anyway! Will new believers practice water baptism and Lord's supper, and how? These and others may be discovered as they study the scriptures together.

---

47. Ibid., 386.
48. Gen 2:2; Deut 6:1–11, cf. Lim "Biblical Worship Rediscovered."
49. Cf. Dyrness, *Insider Jesus*.

Developmental

Lastly, the practices of merit-making and merit-sharing will simplify into focusing on "loving our neighbor" as members of one family sacrificially as Christ loves us (John 13:34–35; 1 John 3:16–18). This was once most concretely expressed in the "common purse" of the earliest church's "caring and sharing economy" (Acts 2:42–47; 4:32–37; 6:1–7; cf. 2 Cor 8–9) for socio-economic development. The HCNs that experienced a gospel explosion in six big provinces in China spread among folk Buddhists from village to village through the witnessing lifestyles of ordinary Christ-followers who were known for their serving, caring and hard-working work in their neighborhoods. Even Communist cadres and leaders became "secret believers" in these HCNs.[50]

If the Buddhist temple and community already do community services, join them and aim to become part of the leadership and wherever possible introduce "prayer and the word" into the existing structures. If the community lacks such ministries, New Buddhists can start serving informally and later formally setting up people's organizations or non-government agencies to address particular needs with the blessing of the community leaders.

The best practice in community development today is entrepreneurship,[51] especially social entrepreneurship.[52] Christ-followers should organize "savings and investment clubs" or cooperatives (*kibbutzim*) as social (or community) enterprises that empower the poor to rise economically together, so that no one will remain poor (cf. Acts 4:34; Deut 15:1–11). Temples and monasteries will become multipurpose community centers which will also serve as offices for their coops and social enterprises as well as their marketing hubs. This will keep the HCNs from dependency on external funding, and if they receive outside funds, to be better stewards of such.

---

50. Cf. Hattaway, *Back to Jerusalem*.

51. Cf. Bussau and Mask, *Christian Microenterprise Development*.

52. Cf. Yamamori and Eldred, *On Kingdom Business*; Rundle and Steffen, *Great Commission Companies*.

Part I: Religious Foundations

Conclusion

IMs make Christ look natural and local by avoiding the use of foreign (non-local) forms, except prayer to God through a new name Jesus Christ and following His teachings to do good deeds as revealed in the Bible. Ordinary people can hear God's voice and do extraordinary work of God without the hierarchical system of church order. God will give contextualized answers to the questions that people will ask from their everyday life.

Sociologically, IMs of New Buddhists will look infiltrative (if not subversive), operating in clandestine ways, which will eventually become a major, if not the dominant sect within the majority Buddhist society. If done consistently and competently for ten years (or less) with strategic use of social media, they should be able to transform the socio-religious worldviews, cultures and lifestyles in their karmic contexts!

Buddhist converts to Christ in IMs will remain as Buddhists and can call themselves "New Buddhists"[53] when they give their allegiance to Jesus.[54] They can and should remain in their socio-religious identity as they gradually proceed to change their worldviews and some practices through DMMs. Their decision to follow Christ entails the willingness to redefine the meanings of Buddhist forms into Christ-centeredness, Christ-likeness or simply Christward. If any change in forms (terms, concepts, values, rituals or behavior) is needed, appropriate functional substitutes will have to be developed,[55] preferably discussed first with other insiders especially their community leaders. Whatever good that lies latent in the religious beliefs and practices of Buddhists can be redeemed, ennobled and perfected to the glory of God. Jesus Christ can be incarnated in their social structures so as to inspire change in their values, beliefs and lifestyles as they imbibe the stories and teachings of the word.

I know of an IM that is led by monks. A couple of years ago, a high-ranking Tibetan Buddhist lama became a Christ-follower in the USA through reading and meditating on the gospel of John. He went back to Dharamsala to persuade his fellow monks to follow Christ with him but he was cast out immediately and fled for his life and became a refugee in a southeastern Asian country. There he changed strategy. He put on his robe, identified himself as a lama, and was able to persuade the chief abbots of

---

53. Cf. Wetchgama, "The New Buddhists."
54. John 1:12–13; 1 Cor 2:2; 1 Thess 1:9.
55. Davis, *Poles Apart?*, 86–93.

two Buddhist temples to hold meditation classes with the gospel of John. They were convinced to follow Jesus Christ as the Dharma (Chinese: Tao) and have now introduced such meditation classes to several temples in that country and beyond.

There is really no need for outsiders to stay long to oversee the DMMs led by insiders. Many of us will be alongsiders—as catalysts, advocates and supporters of IMs. Our role will be to preserve the simplicity, purity and indigeneity of the New Buddhist movements in all four aspects: self-governing, self-theologizing, self-propagating and self-supporting. As outsiders our role may be to help westernized churches understand and be patient with IMs and protect IMs from good intentions of so many church aids which will complicate and divert them from focusing on DMMs. We may be involved in facilitating partnerships with and among IM leaders, while also promoting IMs as widely as possible.

We need to focus on IMs to fulfill the Great Commandment to love God by serving our neighbors in the karmic world. Without this Christ will remain marginal, foreign and rejected, not because he is not good news, but because his witnesses will continue to present and represent Him poorly if not wrongly in their contexts. Let's stop perpetuating church growth strategies which result in slow growth or even no growth. There are strategies that result in multiplication, or even in explosive growth – why not humbly copy them? They are not copyrighted anyway. It was Jesus who trained his disciples to do it since the beginning.

God is already at work among unreached people groups (John 16:8–11). Let us evangelize and empower "people of peace" to walk with Jesus with their neighbors and networks but let's not do too much. Let's leave room for the Holy Spirit. Let's be "heretics" (Christ-following Buddhists or their alongsiders) for one year following this paper's suggestions for one year as fully as possible. Perhaps some of us may be called to become Buddhists to catalyze IMs as insiders among them. Then there will be 150 new CMs among Buddhist UPGs in the coming year.

As we hesitate and delay our shifts to CMs and especially IMs, we waste more time, money, talents and sacrifices to very poor harvests. We welcome the inputs of outsiders, especially alongsiders, for we need to learn from Jesus together as one body. Let's prioritize the output of local Christ-followers who depend on the Holy Spirit (not humans) in DMMs to interpret the Bible as they answer their own socio-cultural and socio-religious questions.

Part I: Religious Foundations

May more Christians follow this "radical contextualization" approach, so that combined with the incarnational or friendly approach, many more Buddhist peoples can be brought effectively to accept and follow Jesus Christ as the one who offers them the grace that empowers to walk the path of goodness in this life and in the life to come with thoughts, words and ways that are meaningful for them, yet may be strange for us.

Bibliography

Adamek, Wendi L. "Impossibility of the Given: Representation of Merit and Emptiness in Medieval Chinese Buddhism." In *History of Religions* 45-2 (2005) 135–180.
Ambedkar, B. R. *Dr. Babasaheb Ambedkar: Writings and Speeches, vol. II.* Bombay: Education Department of the Government of Maharashtra, 1992.
Appleton, George. *Christian Presence and Buddhism.* London: SCM, 1961.
Bhikkuk, Buddhadasa. *Why were We born? Essays on Life and Enlightenment.* Bangkok: Amarin, 2008.
Bowers, Russell, Jr. "Gentle Strength and Upaya: Christian and Buddhist Ministry Models." In *Sharing Jesus Effectively in the Buddhist World* edited by. David Lim, Steve Spaulding and Paul de Neui, 109–148. Pasadena: William Carey, 2005.
Burnett, David. "The Challenge of the Globalization of Buddhism." In *Sharing Jesus in the Buddhist World* edited by David Lim and Steve Spaulding, 1–17. Pasadena: William Carey, 2003.
Bussau, David, and Russell Mask. *Christian Microenterprise Development: An Introduction.* Oxford: Regnum, 2003.
The Cape Town Commitment. Peabody, Ma: Hendrickson. http://www.lausanne.org/content/ctc/ctcommitment. 2011.
Cracknell, Kenneth. *In Good and Generous Faith: Christian Responses to Religious Pluralism.* Cleveland: Pilgrim, 2006.
Dalai Lama (Tenzin Gyatso). *Compassion and Wisdom.* Singapore: Amitabha Buddhist Centre, 2001.
Davis, John R. *Poles Apart? Contextualizing the Gospel in Asia.* Bangkok: OMF, 1993.
———. *The Path to Enlightenment.* London: Hodder & Stoughton, 1997.
De Neui, Paul. "Contextualizing with Thai Folk Buddhists." In *Sharing Jesus in the Buddhist World*, edited by David Lim and Steve Spaulding, 121–146. Pasadena: William Carey, 2003.
Dhammananda, K. Sri. *What Buddhists Believe.* Kuala Lumpur: Buddhist Missionary Society, 1998.
Dyrness, William. *Insider Jesus.* Downers Grove: IVP Academic, 2016.
Evans, Steven. 2008. "From the Biblical World to the Buddhist Worldview: Using Bible Narratives to Impact at the Heart Level." In *Communicating Christ through Story and Song: Orality in Buddhist Contexts* edited by Paul H. de Neui, 128–150. Pasadena: William Carey, 2008.
Fukuda, Mitsuo. "Incarnational Approaches to the Japanese People using House Church Strategies. In *Sharing Jesus Effectively in the Buddhist World* edited by. David Lim, Steve Spaulding and Paul H. de Neui, 353–362.Pasadena: William Carey, 2005.

———. *Developing a Contextualized Church as a Bridge to Christianity in Japan.* Gloucester: Wide Margin, 2012.
Hattaway, Paul. *Back to Jerusalem.* Carlisle: Piquant, 2003.
Hiebert, Paul, R. D. Shaw and Tite Tienou. 1999. *Understanding Folk Religion.* Grand Rapids: Baker, 1999.
Hiebert, Paul. *Transforming Worldviews: An Anthropological Understanding of How People Change.* Grand Rapids: Baker Academic, 2008.
Jones, Dale. 2008. "Moving Towards Oral Communication of the Gospel: Experiences from Cambodia." In *Communicating Christ through Story and Song: Orality in Buddhist Contexts"* edited by Paul H. de Neui, 174–202. Pasadena: William Carey, 2008.
Lausanne Congress. *The Cape Town Commitment*, Part IIC, Sec. 4, 2010.
Lim, David. "Biblical Christianity in the Context of Buddhism." In *Sharing Jesus in the Two Thirds World* edited by V. Samuel and C. Sugden, 175–203. Grand Rapids: Eerdmans 1983.
———. "Biblical Worship Rediscovered: A Theology for Communicating Basic Christianity." In *Communicating Christ through Story and Song: Orality in Buddhist Contexts* edited by Paul H. de Neui, 27–59. Pasadena: William Carey, 2008.
———. "Asia's House Church Movements Today." *Asian Missions Advance* 52 (July 2016): 7–12.
Mam, Barnabas. "Communicating the Gospel through Story and Song in Cambodia." In *Communicating Christ through Story and Song: Orality in Buddhist Contexts"* edited by Paul H. de Neui, 174–202. Pasadena: William Carey, 2008.
McDermott, Gerald R. *Can Evangelicals Learn from World Religions? Jesus, Revelation and Religious Traditions.* Downers Grove: InterVarsity, 2000.
Mejudhon, Nantachai. "Meekness: A New Approach to Christian Witness to the Thai people." In *Sharing Jesus Effectively in the Buddhist World* edited by David Lim, Steve Spaulding and Paul H. de Neui, 149–186. Pasadena: William Carey, 2005.
Nyunt, Peter Thein. *Missions Amidst Pagodas: Contextual Communication of the Gospel in the Burmese Buddhist Context.* Carlisle: Langham Monographs, 2014.
Rundle, Steve, and Tom Steffen. *Great Commission Companies.* Downers Grove: InterVarsity, 2003.
Sarun, Taweeporn. "Avoiding Syncretism: The Testimony of a Jesus-Following Buddhist." In *Understanding Insider Movements* edited by H. Talman and J. J. Travis, 385–386. Pasadena: William Carey, 2015.
Smith, Alex. "Transfer of Merit in Folk Buddhism." In *Sharing Jesus Holistically in the Buddhist World* edited by David Lim and Steve Spaulding, 99–124. Pasadena: William Carey, 2005.
Somaratna, G.P.V. "An Evangelical Christian Analysis of Theravada Buddhist Spirituality Expressed in the Almsgiving Ceremony." In *Seeking the Unseen: Spiritual Realities in the Buddhist World* edited by Paul H. de Neui, 173–190. Pasadena: William Carey, 2016.
Song, Choan-seng. *The Compassionate God: An Exercise in the Theology of Transposition.* Maryknoll: Orbis, 1982.
Strauss, Robert, & Tom Steffen. "Change the Worldview… Change the World," *Evangelical Missions Quarterly* 45.4 (October 2009) 458–464.

Part I: Religious Foundations

Taylor, David. "Contextualization, Syncretism, and the Demonic in Indigenous Movements." In *Understanding Insider Movements* edited by H. Talman and J. J. Travis, 375–383. Pasadena: William Carey, 2015.

Thich Nhat Hanh. *Being Peace*. New York: Read How You Want, 2005.

Vasanthakumar, Michal Solomon. "An Exploration of the Book of Ecclesiastes in the Light of Buddha's Four Noble Truths." In *Sharing Jesus Holistically in the Buddhist World* edited by David Lim and Steve Spaulding, 147–177. Pasadena: William Carey, 2005.

Walsh, Michael. "The Economics of Salvation: Toward a Theory of Exchange in Chinese Buddhism." *Journal of the American Academy of Religion* 75 no. 2 (June 2007): 353–382.

Wetchgama, Banpote. "The New Buddhists: How Buddhists can Follow Christ." In *Understanding Insider Movements* edited by H. Talman and J. J. Travis, 103–107. Pasadena: William Carey, 2015.

Yamamori, T., B. Myers and K. Eldred, eds. *On Kingdom Business: Transforming Missions through Entrepreneurial Strategies*. Wheaton: Crossway, 2003.

Yong, Amos. *The Holy Spirit and the Non-Christian Faiths: Towards a Pneumatological Theology of Religions*. Grand Rapids: Baker Academic, 2003.

———. "A Heart Strangely Warmed on the Middle Way: The Wesleyan Witness in a Pluralistic World." *Wesleyan Theological Journal* 48 no. 1 (Spring 2013): 7–27.

5

From Karma To Grace
By Merit Or Mercy?

Alex G. Smith

MAKING MERIT IS THE ubiquitous universal means by which Buddhists hope to counter their karma. By personally accumulating good works they attempt to balance or counteract their entrenched karma. Simply stated, "Do good get good; do bad get bad." But what if one does both good and bad simultaneously? Then folk Buddhists say, "Negative karma (*papa*) must be dealt with first, before positive merit (*punna*) is of any value." Since accumulated past karma affects the present life and karma in this life impacts future cyclical rebirths, how may one fully escape the iron grip of karma? Making much merit is the major hope for Buddhists to become liberated.

What Does It Mean to Be Buddhist?

Usually westerners answer this question with classical Buddhism beliefs and tenets taught in western universities or eastern monasteries. However, the real Buddhism of most devotees of Buddha is often far different than this ideal textbook portrayal of the Buddha's dharma.

One missionary to Thailand wrote: "Recently it was helpful to interview a few people to get to know them better and also to learn about some of their beliefs. It was interesting to learn that though most Thais call themselves Buddhist, what this means in reality can be very different."[1] Observe the reciprocal expectations of those who replied, "It's about doing good to others, so that they'll receive good back." Another person said, "It's about having sacred objects that give protection from evil spirits." Still another said that being a Buddhist is about following Buddha's teachings.[2] Others often respond, "I am a Thai therefore I am a Buddhist, just like you are westerners, therefore you are Christians."

These mixed viewpoints are acceptable understandings of Buddhism as local practicing Asians interpret it. Different perspectives and definitions do not lessen the reality that the Thai are clearly Buddhists, with or without extensive knowledge of the religion. Later discussion will explain how Buddhism incorporated animism and spirit entities. Does merit or worshipping spirits truly counter karma? Are there other ways to freedom through compassion, grace or mercy?

Conundrum of Average Thai Awareness of Buddhism

Many outsiders think Thai lay people don't really know much about Buddhism. I sometimes have concurred. However, my hour's experience with a Thai taxi driver in Bangkok on the way to the international airport at 3 a.m. in April revised my thinking. It reinforced the reality that the Thai's knowledge of Buddhism is considerably deeper than most foreigners expect. Originally from an eastern province, this taxi driver was in his thirties, married and had two young children. Considering intense discussion on merit and karma at SEANET's steering group the previous day, I decided to check this Thai driver's views on those matters. His replies indicated he was lucid on Buddhist issues with a clear depth of understanding. For a layman, his precise perception of Buddha's teaching was so clear it utterly surprised me.

I asked him how was he able to explain so succinctly and knowledgeably? He said the Thai learn Buddhism from birth. Parents teach them from early in life. Tiny babes are helped to bow to honor Buddha images (*wai phra*). It is education from day one. By osmosis Buddhism seeps in and saturates thoughts, values, and behaviors. The religious power of Buddhism is the nerve center of their worldview, interpreting the central map

---

1. Steer, *What Does it Mean to be a Buddhist?*, 1.
2. Ibid., 1.

of reality around them. Buddhism quickly becomes habitual practice and is in the Thai blood stream. Thai idiom says, "It flows in your blood and enters deeply into the marrow of your bones" (*laai pay nai lyat khao lyk pai nai kraduuk dam*).

This taxi driver's lucid knowledge on Buddhism literally astounded me. So much so, I thought he probably served in the monkhood for a long time. But when I asked him he simply said, "I was a monk for three days only." So his Buddhist knowledge came from saturation via his family and surrounding karmic society more than from direct concentration in the temple or contact in the Sangha. Thus, by emic osmosis and social enculturation Buddhism perceptibly seeped into his consciousness and understanding. Why can we not get the biblical equivalent of that kind of depth in the majority of Thai Christians?[3] Karma and merit flow profusely through the brain waves, thought patterns and emotional responses of folk Buddhists.

Multitudes of practicing popular Buddhists are engrossed in managing karma (fate) by making merit (works) and manipulating magic (spirits). Despite energetic efforts to overcome karma, their fears, frustrations and failures to satisfactorily accomplish liberation often required their finding more ways of escape, such as relying on mercy, grace and faith—ways perhaps difficult for them to comprehend. Now note basic definitions surrounding these Buddhist dynamics.

Observations of Buddhist Cultural Contexts

An understanding of key Buddhist terms and their meanings is essential to real discussion and analysis. This includes many animistic accretions that were integrated over time into Buddhism and became accepted as integral parts of it. This mixture is fundamentally folk Buddhism.

Karma: The Core of Buddhism

Webster's Dictionary defines karma (from Sanskrit deed, act, fate) as "the totality of a person's actions in any one of the successive states of his existence, thought of as determining his fate in the next; loosely: fate, destiny."[4]

---

3. Smith, *Smith Snippets*, 2.
4. Guralnik, *Webster's New World Dictionary*, 769.

Herman with Keyes ties karma to merit, who with Babb identifies "a distinctive connection between moral responsibility and destiny."[5] He also sees in Theravada less of a retrospective view and more of an emphasis towards "actions that are believed to enhance one's karmic prospects, that is, to actions that produce "merit."[6] While Keyes recognizes that "karmic legacy is seen as the consequence of actions in a previous existence."[7] He also asserts, in keeping with Buddha's teaching that it is not

> [S]ome previous "self" who performed the actions whose consequences are now being felt; rather the karma that may be invoked to explain suffering or other misfortunes is construed as an impersonal force – the law of karma – over which one has no control.[8]

Furthermore, folk Buddhists "may not immediately invoke karmic destiny to explain" their present suffering or problems.[9] Instead they may identify other possible causes for it, such as "acts of spirits or gods, the unsettledness of one's vital essence, the conjunction of cosmic influences as manifest in astrological codes."[10] This is important news for mission practitioners for here in popular Buddhism are obvious animistic cracks in the seemingly impenetrable wall of religion. Furthermore, Keyes recognizes that folk Buddhists may see human or other causes arising from "the aggressive actions of others expressed directly or through such indirect means as witchcraft and sorcery, and for those exposed to modern scientific knowledge, viruses, infections and other natural forces."[11] For example, whole families of Buddhists, including Khamoo (Tai–Dam) and other Tai–Lao peoples, were expelled from their villages simply because they were accused of *phibop* witchcraft.[12]

When a Buddhist "chooses to explain his or her misfortune in terms of one of these non–karmic theories of causation—particularly if the theory implies belief in a supernatural power" they compromise their belief in

---

5. Herman, *Community*, 117; Keyes, *Karma*, 13.
6. Keyes, *Karma*, 13–14.
7. Ibid., 15.
8. Ibid., 15.
9. Ibid., 16.
10. Ibid., 16.
11. Ibid., 16.
12. Smith, *Siamese Gold*, 111–112; 151–152.

karmic destiny.[13] Referring to the Burmese and their belief in supernatural beings called *Nats,* M.E. Spiro affirms this compromise occurs.

> To attribute ... vicissitudes to the *nats* and to believe that their propitiation (or lack of propitiation) can in any manner influence one's life-fate, is to implicitly deny the omnipotence of karma, a doctrine which constitutes the very core of Buddhist teaching.[14]

In cases where Buddhists perform the proper rituals to safeguard or avert crises and yet their worst fears still occur, Keyes succinctly notes

> It is precisely in such circumstances where one's efforts fail to rectify misfortunes personally caused by forces that are part of ordinary mundane existence (and it should be noted ... spirits are as much part of this existence as germs are) that one turns to an explanation in terms of an ultimate, absolute, irrevocable force, a force that is conceived of as karmic destiny.[15]

Keyes suggests that popular practicing Buddhists think of positive karma as merit.

> Karmic theory defines not only a moral universe within which problems of ultimate meaning can be confronted, but also a mode of action whereby it becomes possible to augment the positive moral element of karma that adheres to one. This moral element of karma has a tangible quality... Buddhists also think of positive karma–that is "merit"–as having a tangible character.[16]

He consequently identifies two sources of karmic qualities which derive "from one's karmic legacy or from merit-making."[17] The first is past action, the second is future effort. Keyes illustrates this using the Thai concept of *tham bun*, meaning to make and accumulate merit.

---

13. Keyes, *Karma*, 16.
14. Spiro, *Burmese Supernaturalism*, 254.
15. Keyes, *Karma*, 17.
16. Ibid., 18.
17. Ibid., 19.

Part I: Religious Foundations

Buddhist Merit is Works Performed

Merit, says Maguire, is "the positivity one develops by performing virtuous actions, which can contribute to future happiness."[18] Specifically, "Merit (Sanskrit: *puṇya*, Pali: *puñña*) is a widely recognized concept in Buddhism. It is a power which accumulates as a result of good deeds, acts, or thoughts."[19] Devotees amass merit as an ever-increasing force to counter karma. This merit produced by good works continues to assist them in future rebirths. Negative and opposing merit is demerit (*papa*). Popular belief argues that increasing merit can weaken demerit. Making-merit is fundamental to Buddhist ethics and virtue (*sila*). Especially in Theravada contexts, the system of making merit functions like a kind of volunteer social tax on devotees. Economically, it acts as a significant contribution to welfare and support in society.

Buddhist scholars identify ten major merit-making deeds: generosity or giving (*dana*), morality by keeping the precepts (*sila*), mental culture through meditation (*bhavana*), reverence or respect (*apachayana*), service in helping others (*veyyavaccha*), transference of merits to others (*pattidana*), rejoicing in the merits of others (*pattanumodana*), preaching and teaching the Dharma (*dharma desana*), listening to the Dharma (*dharma savanna*), straightening one's views or acting with right views (*ditthijju*). All of these meritorious deeds not only produce benefits for the one making merit, but also give benefits or merits to the recipients of its sharing or transfer.[20]

There are manifold ways of making merit. Primarily the Buddhist idea of *dana* is earning merit (*punna*) which affects one's karma (*kamma*), which particularly affects future reincarnations (*samsara*). Basically then merit is the concerted efforts of doing good deeds, which elicit positive effects for the future. Even the quality of thoughts, intention and motives influence one's karma for good or bad, just like deeds, speech and other actions. Thus, merit is accumulated on behalf of the maker of the merit. Merit is generally considered positive and beneficial, but demerit from bad or evil actions is equally potent and affects karma adversely.

Folk Buddhists expend much effort in giving money (*dana*), doing good deeds, distributing alms (*thaan*), and accumulating merit (*punna*)

---

18. Maguire, *Essential Buddhism*, 239.
19. Wikipedia, *Merit*, 1.
20. Dhammanada, *What Buddhists Believe*, 204.

to help counter their karma. The range of activities for establishing merit is broad, including giving food to the monks daily, building new temples, listening to the Dharma, providing robes for monks, participating in devotion, offerings, helping the poor, transferring merit to others, and a host of other acts. Merit is created by offering food, incense, flowers, fruit, drinks, models of animals and dancing troupes before the images of Buddha, or by burning paper money and various items for the deceased. Devotees can also gain merit through meditation, yoga, prayers and acts of worship. These include giving gifts to the temples, using "rosary" prayer beads, glancing at prayer flags, turning dharma wheels, writing prayers on paper placed in front of temples or images, and even glancing at mantras engraved on rocks. Pilgrimages or sacred tours (*dhamma–yatras*) to the sites in Buddha's life are another means to make merit. Tibetan Buddhists practice long harsh journeys of pilgrimage, stopping every few yards to prostrate their bodies, stretched full-length on the ground. Though Buddhist precepts do not affirm it, Buddhists believe accumulating merit helps counteract their karma.

Even having a Thai adopted child (*but boon tham*) indicates an act of making merit. But this child's status is not like biblical adoption, because in the Thai situation *but boon tham* has no right to inheritance. Compare the biblical difference in Romans 8:15–17.

Thus, merit can be accumulated in numerous ways; the most fruitful of which derives from deeds done towards monks and especially the Triple Gems of Buddha, Dharma, and Sangha. Merit is gained through disciplined actions of developing morality or virtue, giving and generosity, and even meditation.

M. A. Wright, a Roman Catholic priest who spent years in the Buddhist monkhood, suggested that Buddhist ordination was making merit as a form of sacrifice, reminiscent of pre-Buddhist blood sacrifices.[21] Some scholars like Keyes suggest that earlier sacrifices were the basis for ancestral cults and consequent Buddhist response through sharing of merits with deceased progenitors so as to diminish their suffering in their next existence.[22] This does not alter their current state or karma. Buddha's inclusion of this unseen world of spirit beings in merit making also opened the door to incorporate other animistic entities and objects.

---

21. Wright, *Some Observations in Thai Animism*, 1–2.
22. Keyes, *Millennialism*, 287.

Part I: Religious Foundations

Prevalence of Magic Manipulation Among Buddhists

In anthropological terms magic is the way of dealing with many daily crises in life. Hiebert writes, "When the right chant is recited or the right sign is used, the supernatural power will respond in the expected way."[23] Hiebert's three-tiered worldview model of high Religion (ultimates and destiny), middle Magic (crises of life), and low Science (practical experience and knowhow) fits well here. A bevy of specialized spirit mediators and occult practitioners, including some monks, employ their arts and skills to assist Buddhists in managing the mysterious spirit world. These spirit mediums often manipulate and propitiate spirits and gods. During Buddhism's global expansion, its syncretistic penchant to assimilate local beliefs resulted in many forms of animistic folk religion. Thus, these primitive forms were submerged under the mantle of Buddhism. Here are four examples.

At Rajagaha, Buddha endorsed King Bimbisara's desire to transfer merit to his wailing, upset ancestral *petas* (hungry ghosts), likely because of the prevalence of ancestral cults of that era.[24] Buddha's teaching contains "a lot of stories about peta beings" and "there are a lot of petas with dreadful, fearful and disgusting shapes."[25] Buddha set up specific rules by which transfer of merit could be accomplished.[26] Worshipping ancestral manes (spirits of the dead) facilitated Buddhist merit sharing. Consequently, in time the cloak of etic Buddhism covered the essence of emic animism and spirit beliefs of the people. Merit later became more focused on virtue, ethics and morality, simultaneous with merit sharing.

Another example was King Asoka's son, Mahindra, who initiated a mission to Anuradhapura (Sri Lanka). Senerath Paranavitana, former Archeological Commissioner affirms

> When the missionaries of Asoka preached the doctrine of the Buddha, it became clear that the great majority of the people worshipped nature spirits, called the yakkas (demons), who were supposed to dwell in rivers, lakes, mountains, trees etc. The worship of sacred trees and groves was also connected with the primitive forms of worship. The heavenly bodies received the adoration of the people, and to a great extent influenced their everyday life.[27]

---

23. Hiebert, *Cultural Anthropology*, 377.
24. Smith, *The Struggle*, 167–169; TBCM, *Sharing of Merits Pattidana*, 3–6.
25. Sumana, *Sharing of Merits*, pt. 4.
26. Smith, *The Struggle*, 167–168.
27. Cf. Ratnasinghe, *Buddhism in Sri Lanka*.

Virtual Library-Sri Lanka confirms that pre-Buddhist people experienced pervasive animism and prevailing ancestor worship "in which supernatural being and Yaksas & Yaksinis played an important role. Yaksas called Kalavela and Cittaja were the two most important Yaksas worshipped by the pre-Aryan aborigines."[28] Besides giving obeisance to these two Yaksas, early peoples of the island worshipped another eight important deities, some of whom "were actual ancestors of the people."[29] Furthermore, "It is only natural to expect that Mahinda overcame and converted some superhuman beings in Sri Lanka. Mahinda appears to have converted at least one such superhuman being called 'rakus' (demon) who later served Buddhism quite well."[30] The same article above also claimed by legend that

> God Sumana of Samantakuta (Adam's Peak) was also a pre-Buddhist deity. He was, perhaps, originally a Yaksa, and later-on was elevated to the position of a deva after his conversion to Buddhism by the Buddha during the latter's first visit to Sri Lanka. Even after the Sri Lankans were converted to Buddhist they desired to continue to venerate their friendly deities. But being Buddhists, they did not like to worship a non-Buddhist deity. They, therefore, converted these deities to Buddhism and elevated them to a higher plane, as in the case of Sumana. Such is also the case with most of the other local gods . . . almost all the important deities who survived the introduction of Buddhism became Buddhist sooner or later.[31]

Thus, by conquest and subjugation these Sri Lankan demons and ancestral spirits were incorporated into Buddhism, under its mantle and influence.

A third example of Buddhism's integrating animism overtly, occurred in Tibet in the 7th and 8th centuries. Similarly, Guru Rinpoche (Padmasambhava), an Indian master of tantra, conquered the existing Tibetan Bon demon-spirits and at their request allowed them to remain in Vajrayana Buddhism as spirit protectors of the Dharma. Frequent ceremonial propitiation of demons is currently practiced in Tibetan monasteries. Furthermore, the high magic ceremony (tantra) producing the powerful protective

---

28. Virtual, *Religious Conditions*, 1.
29. Ibid., 1.
30. Ibid., 1.
31. Ibid., 1–2.

Part I: Religious Foundations

symbol, Kalachakra, invites 722 of these demon spirits to enter and reside in it.

Fourth, during the eleventh century A.D. in a dynamic action King Anawrahta formally inducted into Buddhism the animistic Nats of Burmese indigenous tradition. In *Folk Elements in Burmese Buddhism*, Dr. Maung Htin Aung expertly details this process of Buddhist incorporation.

> When the great king Anawrahta of Pagan united the whole of Burma into a single kingdom in the eleventh century and made Theravada Buddhism the national religion. There were already in existence a number of primitive religious cults. The most important and the most popular of which were the worship of Nat spirits, astrology, and alchemy. In addition, although the Theravada Buddhism which had flourished in the earlier kingdom of Prome had died out long before, there also existed Mahayana Buddhism and Tantric (or magical) Buddhism; according to the Chronicles, however, these were debased and distorted, bearing strange fruit from the fertile soil of native cults of magic and sorcery. All the different cults were given an artificial unity by the fact that they were all under the patronage of the Ari monks. These Ari monks had some acquaintance with the Buddhist scriptures, gloried in the name of the Buddha, and wore dark-brown robes and conical hats. But they also presided over the *Nat* spirit festivals, at which hundreds of animals were sacrificed.[32]

Aung clearly describes the king's actual ceremonial installation and integration of the Burmese Nats into Buddhism, whereby they worshipped the Buddha.

> As for Nat worship, the people, in spite of the king's edicts, went on worshipping the Nats, and Anawrahta finally decided to bring them over into Buddhism. The figures of the thirty-six Lords were taken from their shrines and placed in the king's great pagoda in an attitude of worship; he declared that the number was now thirty-seven, because Sakra, the king of the gods and guardian of Buddhism, was at the head of the pantheon. The Cult of the Thirty-Six Lords therefore, became The Cult of the Thirty-Seven Lords, and Anawrahta replaced some of the earlier lords with the Nat spirits of some of his dead heroes.[33]

---

32. Aung, *Folk Elements in Burmese Buddhism*, 1.
33. Ibid., 4.

Aung succinctly summarizes the climactic effect and consequence of the Nat spirits and their images being formally inducted into the worship of Buddha in 1056 A.D.

> All this was possible mainly because the Burmese concept of the Nat was a very comprehensive one and took in under its wing Hindu gods as well as Buddhist figures. As the Nats themselves were now shown to be worshippers of the Buddha it was deemed proper for Buddhists to worship the Nats. The feasts of the full moon became festivals of the full moon being given a coating of Buddhism.[34]

Biblical Views and Discussion

Turning now to Christian perspectives from Scripture might add some confusion as well as clarity to various subjects related to our topic of concentration. Over-simplification often causes confusion.

Karmic Communities Hope to Contribute Merit Together

Though Buddhism primarily centers on the individual, some writers like Herman and J. S. Walters, refer to karmic community. The Mahayana concept of bodhisattvas being members of society whose merit assists in the progress of the group towards nirvana developed as karmic community.[35] Classical Buddhism taught that the long journey to nirvana is primarily individualistic, certainly it is self, if not, selfish-oriented. One must depend only on oneself.[36] No one can assist another to reach liberation. Even Buddha can't help. Accumulated karma is also individual and personal. Making merit is essentially for the benefit of the individual in relation to bettering future rebirths. In contradiction to this, Buddha also taught that transfer of shared merit was possible.

Furthermore, according to Buddha, humans have no enduring soul or eternal spirit. From his birth religion he faced a dilemma regarding eternal soul, taught in Hinduism as "transmigration of the soul." Because the Buddha believed nothing was permanent or had eternal reality, he rejected

---

34. Ibid., 4.
35. Herman, *Community*, 117.
36. Ibid., 116

the ego-soul concept as impermanent non-entity experiencing constant change. Nonetheless, many popular practicing Buddhists believe they do have some permanent essence of being (soul, spirit, ego, or personage) which continues into future rebirths in the cycle of life. Hence, they make merit avidly, hoping for better rebirths in the future. This soul doctrine (*anatta*) continues to be debated among some monks. If no soul–spirit essence of being human is true then Buddhist transfer of merit to living ancestral ghosts (*peta*) must also be questioned.[37] How can ancestors, the supposed recipients of merit sharing, be non–ego–beings? Scholars suggest that pre-Buddhist ancestral cults of India were the basis for Buddha's endorsing transfer of merit, which was for the good of deceased relatives primarily.[38]

During 2500 years of its historical global journey, many Buddhist rites, rituals, ceremonies and festivals, including some assimilated animistic ones, developed as merit–making practices. While all merit activities primarily affect individuals, some also involve the broader karmic community. This is particularly true of many pre-Buddhist festivals related to the seasons or ancient beliefs in the world of spirits, ancestors and gods. Certain festivals are clearly Buddhist in origin such as celebrating the birth–enlightenment–death of the Buddha (*Vesakha*), commemorating Buddha's first sermon (*Asalha*), the beginning of their Lent (*Vassa*), the end of Lent (*Kathina*) and the sending out of the first Buddhist missionaries (*Kattika*). However, others of earlier origin were adopted and integrated into Buddhism and now are seen as Buddhist. Among these are honoring the Mother of Waters (*Loy kratong*) and the New Year (*Songkran*) for Theravadans; Hungry Ghost Festival of Mahayanans, and the Great Prayer Festival (*Modlam Chenmo*) in Tibetan tradition. While ordinations and funerals are mostly Buddhist in focus, naming ceremonies, house warmings, weddings, and completion of vows are largely animistic or Brahmin. Often at each life cycle marker point appropriate Rites of Passage were initiated and became normal Buddhist social customs.

The karmic community is unified when rituals or ceremonies involving the whole social group are usually activated together. Non-participation usually warrants censure from the community. Some examples of this required involvement are annual offerings to the village spirits or tribal ancestors and installation of a new town pillar (*lak myang*). Also, when crises

---

37. Ibid., 116.
38. Keyes, *Millennialism*, 287; Pye and Strong, *Merit*, 5874.

like natural disasters, plague, or catastrophes descends upon the group or the whole village, the karmic community comes together to make merit in an attempt to dispel causes of the disasters. Where clan identification is a strong social factor, communal worship offered to common ancestors is frequently done in concert with the whole karmic group. During such times the cooperation of the community of animistic-karmic spirits is invoked. The Hungry Ghost Festival is a case in point.

This festival is not directly a Buddhist one, but is commonly practiced among Mahayana Buddhists of Chinese, Taiwanese, Tibetan, Japanese, Korean, and Vietnamese backgrounds. They celebrate Hungry Ghost Festivals in connection with their Buddhist beliefs. The lowest of the six primary worlds of Buddhism is *naraka*, the abode of hell-beings and hungry ghosts (*petas*). Hungry Ghost Festivals are closely allied to ancestral veneration and worship. Generally, these festivals are held in July or August, depending on the lunar cycle. Activities like the giving of offerings and concentrated chanting are believed to help calm the unsettled spirits of the living dead enabling them to pass peacefully into the next world or incarnation. During this season, Buddhists commonly clean up the ancestral gravesites and then worship the ancestors at family graves or shrines. While this is usually a family event, the whole society consequently celebrates in pacifying the ancestral *petas* simultaneously as karmic communities. Usually around July, the Japanese also celebrate the additional Festival of O-bon, during which families reunite and get together to remember and honor their ancestors. Offerings are made to Buddha and the monks usually visit at family home shrines to read the Sutras. In this sense, the karmic community of the spirit–animistic world of Asia is syncretized into Buddhism and may be considered as making group merit.

These festivals meet deep needs in the hearts of Mahayana Buddhists, so Christians should not easily dismiss them. Instead, the Church must understand why these ceremonies are communally necessary to folk Buddhists and then find ways to meet those heart-felt deep needs in appropriate biblical and cultural ways using acceptable functional substitutes.

Textual Similarities to Karma in Scripture

In the Bible are hints of a concept like karma. For instance, "The heart is deceitful above all things and beyond cure. Who can understand it? I the Lord search the heart and examine the mind, to reward each person according to what their deeds deserve" (Jer 17:9–10). The first verse is comparable in some ways to karma, which Buddha considered the bane of every life form in the world. The Bible describes all humans as having a similar curse, namely sin. So karma and sin are respective universals. The second verse's phrase, "according to what their deeds deserve" seems at first to mirror karma's cause and effect, except that God is the one in control (not karma) and God is personally monitoring the acts, intents and thoughts of all humans. So there is inescapable accountability to a personal Creator God. But since Buddhist karma is impersonal, no definite responsibility is required of anyone, except possibly one's self.

Note a few other examples of karma-like retribution. The men of Korah who disrespected and rebelled against Moses and Aaron were swallowed up by the earth opening up beneath them (Num 16). Cain murdered his brother Abel and so was cursed (Gen 4). Achan's sin violated God's explicit holy commands given at Jericho so consequently he brought swift judgment on himself and his family (Josh 7). In Acts 28, Paul, who survived a shipwreck on Malta on the way to Rome, is bitten by a viper while he gathered sticks for the fire. The local Maltese immediately declared "He escaped drowning in the sea, but justice (fate) has caught up with him." They believed he must be a murderer because of his perceived bad karma. So they expected him to drop dead from snake poison instantly. When he did not die, they changed their view and considered him to be a god.

Christ clearly questioned karma as a principle. In Luke 13, he indicated that all humans were in the same universal fallen condition of sin, depravity and judgment. All were equally sinners, not chained in various graded levels of karma. To sin in one point of the law is to be guilty of all (Jas 2:10). Jesus explained that the "Galileans, whose blood Pilate had mingled with their sacrifices" were "no greater sinners than all other Galileans, because they suffered this fate" and "those eighteen on whom the tower in Siloam fell and killed them" were no worse than all those in Jerusalem (13:1–5).

Furthermore, Jesus healed the man blind from birth (John 9). The disciples asked, "Who sinned, this man or his parents that he should be born blind?" Theirs was a karmic question about cause and effect. But categorically rejecting karma, Jesus answered, "It was neither that this man sinned, nor his parents; but it was in order that the works of God might be displayed in him" (v3). Therefore, neither did the man's blindness come from karma in a former life nor from his or his parents' sin.

Paul declares "God will repay each person according to what they have done" (Rom 2:6). The cause is clearly because they have contempt for his great "kindness, forbearance and patience" through responses of their stubbornness and unrepentant hearts (2:4–5). Thus, they reject the truth of God's grace and mercy, continuing to do evil rather than seek God (2:7–11). Still, Paul, using a pattern similar to karma affirmed in Galatians 6:7 "Do not be deceived: God cannot be mocked. A man reaps what he sows" (Also see Job 4:8, Ps 126:5, Prov 22:8). But this is not the same as impersonal unremitting karma of Buddhism. Some miss the prior phrase connected to this injunction, "Do not be deceived: God cannot be mocked." So the emphasis here is on the supreme, personal, living Creator God who is watching and evaluating. Therefore, be careful because none can escape his omniscience or his holy judgment. Furthermore, Paul is speaking here to church believers (v1–2) and consequently is not declaring how the Galatians became sinners or how sinful humans may become more righteous. In Paul's theology, good deeds (works) follow faith after repentance, for he declared to the Gentiles that "they should repent and turn to God, performing deeds appropriate to repentance" (Acts 26:19–20). Therefore, notice what merit is in biblical terms.

Debatable Meaning of Merit in Scripture

Some illustrations in scripture stir thoughtful reflection on what might seem to be making-merit. For instance, Enoch walked with God in such virtue that he did not die, but was taken up into heaven (Gen 5:22–24).

Dorcas, a disciple, "was always doing good and helping the poor." Still she died, but Peter raised her to life again (Acts 9:36–42). Each of these examples indicates an already established right relationship with God. The strength and quality of their good works were not adequate to gain access to God's favor, but their faith relationship with him did. In his human form Christ himself went about doing good (Acts 10:38). But these actions issued out of his holy essence as God, not in order to accumulate merit. Technically, Jesus as God does not make merit because he is already perfectly replete and complete from eternity. He is essentially always full of goodness, mercy and grace (John 1:14).

In Second Samuel 24, King David takes a census of Israel and Judah. Commander Joab tries unsuccessfully to dissuade him. Later David is troubled over doing this. He feels guilty and comes repentant before God. The

Part I: Religious Foundations

Lord gives him three choices of judgment. Believing God is merciful and may shorten judgment, David chooses to fall into God's hand of grace. God sends a pestilence for three days. Seventy thousand men die in the plague. At God's command, the avenging angel finally stops the slaughter near a threshing floor. Then through the prophet Gad, God gave David orders. He obeys, buys the threshing floor, and builds an altar to the Lord. He offers burnt sacrifices and peace offerings on the altar. "Then the LORD answered his prayer in behalf of the land, and the plague on Israel was stopped" (2 Sam 24:25). David's actions did not cause God, as if propitiated, to stop the plague. David simply obeyed God, who sovereignly and graciously responded in mercy, compassion and grace.

One specific case that appears to challenge the biblical mode in favor of earned merit seeming to move God occurs in Acts 10. Scripture records that Roman Centurion Cornelius's "prayers and gifts to the poor have come up as a memorial offering before God" (v4). At first glance this appears to be by merit, especially because this Gentile "gave many alms" and "prayed to God continually." But crucial words in this text identify Cornelius as a devout "Godfearer" (v2, 22). This indicates he was a true believer in Jehovah already. He likely attended the synagogue, although he stopped short of ceremonially becoming a Jewish proselyte. Affirming his clear relationship to the Almighty, God speaks to both Cornelius the Gentile seeker and to Peter the Jewish Apostle. He tells Cornelius to send men to seek out Peter. God shows Peter that no humans, even non-Jews, are outside his care, mercy and salvation. God sends him to Cornelius to proclaim the message essential to his full salvation by faith alone in Jesus Christ, and not because of human merit or good works. Peter clearly tells the gospel, concluding his witness with "everyone who believes in him receives forgiveness of sins through his name" (v43). There and then like another Pentecost, the Holy Spirit came upon the whole household and baptized Cornelius, these Gentiles and friends (v34–48).

Generally, Buddhists tend to relate well to three biblical books which seem to fit their particular worldview: Job (suffering), Ecclesiastes (wisdom), and James (merit/doing). Some of the themes they identify with in James are impermanence (1:10), equality of all—no caste (1:9, 2:1–4), desire—lust (1:14–15;4:1–3), wisdom (3:13–14), peacemaker (3:17), and especially doers of works (1:22–27; 2:16–26; 4:17). But it is James' emphasis that "faith without works is dead" and "I will show you my faith by my works" that resonate most with self-dependent Buddhists. James seems to elevate merit and works above faith and believing. However, in this context James is not denying or denigrating faith, but affirming it as a necessary priority. He questions the quality of faith in those who believe lightly. At the same time, he correctly reinforces the need for faith to be productive, not dormant or inactive. If one's faith in God is genuine, then good works must follow to bring glory to the Lord. He is not saying works produce or generate true faith in God. On the contrary, works issue from real faith. Jesus asserted this in answer to the crowd's question, "What must we do to do the works God requires?" Jesus replied believe in me (John 6:28–29).

Making merit or doing good works cannot change the sinner nor relieve the karmic person, any more than the prophet's relevant rhetorical question: "Can an Ethiopian change his skin or the leopard its spots? Neither can you do good who are accustomed to doing evil" (Jer 13:23). Or as Jesus similarly questioned, "Who of you by worrying can add a single hour to your life?" (Luke 12:25). No amount of effort can change the ultimate future one iota. It is true that Jesus put an emphasis on transformed "being" as well as the resultant "doing" of good, in that order. He called for obedient action, not just hearing his word (Matt 7:21–27). But these active good works came from changed hearts converted through faith in him and his substitutionary sacrifice for humankind, not vice versa, since works without faith are also dead.

Magic: Connecting with the Spirit World

From earliest time, humans by their own efforts made merit apart from faith, attempting to justify themselves and clear their failures before the gods. The first example in scripture occurred in Genesis 3. Adam and Eve, the first human pair that God created encountered the spirit world of Satan in the Garden of Eden, God's perfect sinless setting. We might say it was a pristine "karma free" zone then. Satan tempted them to go against God's command. Succumbing to the Devil's trap, they disobeyed God. Then they reverted to use human works by sewing fig leaves together in order to cover their nakedness and exposure of sin, shame, and failure from Creator God (Gen 3:7).

Later, God commanded Israel, "Do not make any gods to be alongside me; do not make for yourselves gods of silver or gods of gold. If you make an altar of stones for me, do not build it with dressed stones, for you will defile it if you use a tool on it" (Exod 20:23, 25). Acts chapter seven describes

Part I: Religious Foundations

God's view of human energy and effort used to produce merit, as "what their own hands had made" (v. 41).

Note the progressive downward spiral: Israel repudiated God, made idols and images of gods, gave sacrifices to their idols, and rejoiced in the works of their own hands (vv. 39–41). So God turned away, gave them up to worship the host of heaven in the wilderness and the images in the tabernacle of Molek—"the idols you made to worship" (vv. 42–43). Human merit and works as well as pseudo-worship are inadequate means to restore broken relationship with God. Humanity became enmeshed with the deceptive spirit world, one that produces great fear and paralyzing bondage in all religions. To placate them humans resort to a stratagem—idolatry.

Human nature retreats from the spiritual unseen realm to the observable tangible one of physical images. They make idols in their own forms using their own efforts—images representing their gods. The Buddha did not desire his followers to make images of him, but they did. Ambedkar did not want his Neo-Buddhist disciples to build images of him to worship, but they did. Jehovah commanded the Jews not to make idols, but they stubbornly did. "John Calvin spoke of our human hearts as an idol-making factory."[39] The works of human hands usually taints any pure worship of the Creator.

Isaiah describes how idolatry is the epitome of human work, merit and folly. Idols are made by the work of humans. A person selects a tree, part of which he builds into an idol to worship and pray before and part of it he burns to cook food to eat and to warm himself (44:9–20). Mind you there are other kinds of idols humans build that are not always visible, but are nonetheless idolatry. This is true of Christians as well.

The Bible is replete with examples of "magic" used in Israel and the surrounding nations, mostly in connection with idolatry: sorcery, witchcraft, soothsaying, divining, and so forth. Malinowski suggests "Magic is the bridge between the golden age of primeval craft and the wonder-working power of today."[40] Humans flirt with idolatry like bees take to honey.

Various kinds of mediums facilitated interaction with the spirits, ancestors, powers and angels using ephods, Urim and Thummin, as well as through oracles, dreams, visions, and prophecies. Magical objects like the pillar of fire, the burning bush, the brazen serpent, Paul's handkerchief, Peter's shadow and others were instruments of God's communication often

---

39. Guinness, *Fool's Talk*, 88.
40. Malinowski, *Magic, science and religion*, 83.

used in warnings or in miraculous healings.[41] Some items like the golden calf and the brazen serpent later became object of idolatrous worship and had to be destroyed. Idolatry and demonic control were devastating to Israel as well as all humanity. It enslaves them under evil oppression and prohibits expressing genuine worship of their Creator. Furthermore, it fractures relationships with one another. However, its pervasive spiritual slavery sometimes unifies forms of communal togetherness in adverse socio-religious reaction, such as persecution of non-conformists, opposition to innovation, or rejection of Creator God. Religious and mission history is replete with examples of this in whole villages, tribes, and people groups.

Mercy and Grace—
A Biblical Response to Merit and Karma

Faith in the living God with his supreme power, protection and provision prove superior to the operations of magic in all its variegated forms. Nevertheless, human nature's natural penchant for "doing" continues to rely upon their own good works for salvation and liberation.

Observe the language of the Philippian jailer in Acts 16 who asked the Apostle Paul, "What must I do to be saved?" (by works-merit). Note Paul's response, "Believe in the Lord Jesus, and you will be saved...." (by faith in God's grace). Faith is possible and practical because God's gift of superlative mercy and grace flow from his completed work in Christ as propitiating sacrifice. In Ephesians 2:8, the Apostle Paul succinctly sums up the dynamics of spiritual reconciliation, "For it is by grace you have been saved, through faith—and this is not from yourselves, it is the gift of God . . . "

Mercy is "a refraining from harming or punishing offenders, enemies, persons in one's power; kindness in excess of what may be expected or demanded by fairness, forbearance and compassion."[42] Grace, a related term is, in theological jargon, "the unmerited love and favor of God toward man; divine influence acting in man to make him pure and morally strong."[43] Let us review scripture on the Lord's mercy and grace, which define conditions by which fallen humanity are acceptably reconciled to God.

Grace issues from God's immaculate righteous character expressed in his patient longsuffering, immense lovingkindness, constant compassion,

---

41. Smith, *Buddhist Spiritual Realities*, 51–54.
42. Guralnik, *Webster's New World Dictionary*, 889.
43. Ibid., 605.

Part I: Religious Foundations

unending love, and forgiving predisposition. So David can boldly plead, "Have mercy on me, O God, according to your unfailing love; according to your great compassion blot out my transgressions. Wash away all my iniquity and cleanse me from my sin. For I know my transgressions, and my sin is always before me" (Ps 51:1–3).

Perfect beings obviously do not need grace or mercy or to make merit. By the above definition, grace with mercy and compassion operate on behalf of offenders and sinners or for those under the pressing stress of karma. The Bible reveals that God disburses his grace freely to those in need; to those who call upon him. Mercy and compassion are also distributed primarily to the undeserving. In Romans 5, the Apostle Paul affirms that God distributes his grace and love to humans classed as helpless, ungodly, sinners, and enemies (vv. 6–10). His grace and favor are poured out freely by the Holy Spirit into their hearts on condition of their contrite confession, genuine repentance, and believing faith in Christ who died to reconcile sinful humankind to himself (vv. 5–10).

Paul boldly declares, "And if by grace, then it cannot be based on works; if it were, grace would no longer be grace" (Rom 11:6). His Epistle to Titus also affirms "He saved us, not because of righteous things we had done, but because of his mercy . . . through Jesus Christ our Savior, so that, having been justified by his grace, we might become heirs having the hope of eternal life" (3:5–7). This abundant grace truly is good news to people of every country and environs.

In Romans 5:12–20, Paul contrasts two men: the first, Adam; the second, Christ. Sin entered the world through the first, passing death and judgment on all for all humankind has sinned. (In a sense this is not unlike universal karma.) The gift of God's grace came in or through the second, bringing justification and life for humanity through the sacrifice of Christ on the cross. (No equivalent substitutionary gift of grace that the writer can identify is taught in Buddhism.) These two types represent sinning man who tries to be God but fails miserably causing death, and God who became incarnated as the only perfect holy man who fulfilled his purpose to reconcile fallen creation and grant forgiveness and eternal life (Rom. 6:22–23; 8:19–25). In the end, nothing can separate his redeemed children from the love of God that is in Christ Jesus (Rom. 8:37–38).

Paul's long argument in Romans 9, on Abraham concludes that he received God's promises through faith alone and that this was not based on the Law or works for "It does not, therefore, depend on human desire or effort, but on God's mercy" (vv. 12, 16, 30–32). Ephesians gives Paul's conclusion, "For it is by grace you have been saved, through faith—and this is not from yourselves, it is the gift of God—not by works, so that no one can boast" (2:8–9).

Buddhists tend to reject grace and faith in favor of making merit and producing works towards gaining their liberation by self-energized efforts. Biblical grace is quite foreign to their thinking. However, one Buddhist sect seems to have an uncharacteristic hint of grace. Amitabha (Sanskrit) a bodhisattva who accumulated significant merit from good works over multiple past lives, is worshipped alongside Buddha. Amitabha, called Pure Land Buddhism among Chinese (Emituo Fo) is known as Amida Butsu in Japan, Amit'a Bul in Korea, and A di dà Phât in Vietnam. It emphasizes simple faith in Amitabha Buddha, whose grace and compassion alone, so it is believed, can save the Amidist. Basic salvation is accomplished by repeating a mantra Nà mó Āmítuó fó (Chinese), Namu Amida Butsu (Japanese), 'Om ami dhewa hri' (Tibetan). Repetition of this formula assures the believer an entry into the Pure Land of the "Western paradise" at death. In contradiction to classical Buddhism, one's release cannot be gained by one's own efforts alone, but only through calling on Amitabha and having faith in his name. This form of Buddhism is most popular among the masses in China, Japan, Korea and Vietnam, but is not accepted by many of the other stricter Buddhist sects. Strangely, despite the potential, the church has not been able to adequately connect with this "faith in the name" and pseudo grace concept in building bridges towards Christ's Gospel of pure grace.

Missiological Applications

In southwest China in the most ethnically, linguistically diverse, mountainous region of the world live the Bulong. A worker serving these beautiful people described their context.

> Year after year, the Bulong toil in their steep fields along the mountainsides, harvesting enough rice to feed their families and growing tea as their main source of income. They deal with the same hardships as other remote ethnic groups in the area: lack of education, lack of good medical care, poor infrastructure. They also face the same struggles and life issues as people around the world – love, family, relationships, neighbors. And year after year, the Bulong carry out rituals at the Buddhist temples in their villages,

Part I: Religious Foundations

bowing before idols and trying to earn merit by their works. Over and over again, they consult shamans for help in times of trouble and seek to keep evil spirits at bay by making blood sacrifices or offering food.[44]

This portrait of the Bulong fits similar contexts of folk Buddhists. It aptly describes the profile of Hiebert's anthropological three-tiered worldview model: High—Buddhist rituals connecting them with ultimate issues, Middle—magic with shamans manipulating the spirit world and propitiating it through sacrifices, and Low—practical science dealing with knowledge in their daily struggle for physical survival of their families. First, intercultural workers do well to apply this model to any people group they work with in Asia. One key in serving them is to focus on alleviating their fear of the spirit world through strategies like emphasizing a message of Christ's power, using power encounter approaches, and exercising spirit exorcism.

Second, focus on their animistic underpinnings, rather than confront entrenched religious traditions. In April 1867, Daniel McGilvary arrived as a pioneer missionary in Chiang Mai. His first convert was an elderly well-respected Buddhist monk, named Nan Inta, who was baptized on January 3, 1869. Initially he came to McGilvary seeking medical help for a serious cough. Missionaries lovingly served the monk with medicines. As Nan Inta raised sincere questions on science and philosophy, months of interaction and serious discussions followed. McGilvary did not argue much about Buddhism with him, but saw an opportunity to stimulate debate through Inta's use of animistic astrology. This was based on old Buddhist sacred books and charts. Using these texts to calculate a major astrological event, Nan Inta projected an incorrect date for the imminent great eclipse of August 17, 1868. McGilvary challenged him with a more precise date his western science predicted. McGilvary proved right. Inta's belief in old Buddhist cosmology was shaken. McGilvary used an animistic contact point to win over Nan Inta, who became a true faithful and valued member of the church, influencing many future generations.[45]

Third, clearly proclaim and teach a strong theology of God the Creator of all things. The growing atheistic atmosphere of our twenty-first century requires fresh, creative and innovative ways to emphasize God's greatness and grace. In modern times, many including nominal Christians have little

---

44. Durston, *Durston's Digest*, 1.
45. Smith, *Siamese Gold*, 66.

or no concept of the Almighty, although creation all around them gives witness to his power and glory (Rom 1:19–22). Emphasize his limitless might; his providence in caring for all - including those who do not believe he exists (Acts 14:15–17); his protection from and subjugation of demons (Mark 5:1–16); and his redemption of humankind by grace through Christ's death and resurrection. This God is able to help because he is still alive today, and ever lives to make intercession for us (Heb 7:25). Assist people to become connected with God intellectually, emotionally and experientially.

Fourth, Christians are to exemplify doing good works, not in order to gain salvation, but because they have received salvation. Often believers from Buddhist backgrounds do less good works than when they formerly made merit. As faithful Christians, they should outshine their friends in doing good, but now from a new motivation of thankfulness to God. Be assured that doing good, helping the poor, caring for the sick, looking after widows and orphans, providing for the homeless and so forth are always commendable, whether done by Buddhists, Christians or others. So teach Asian churches that God's grace in Christ frees us from the burden of sin and karma. They represent Christ working through redemptive centers to the community. He gives human beings new hope. While they need to repudiate reliance on self in favor of dependence on God, they ought also to increase their selfless efforts to produce good works worthy of glory to Christ Jesus, "For we are God's handiwork, created in Christ Jesus to do good works, which God prepared in advance for us to do" (Eph 2:10). Believers are to "spur one another on toward love and good deeds" (Heb 10:24). Paul charges Christians to engage in, be zealous for, and be examples of good deeds (Titus 2:7, 14; 3:8). All are to be equipped for every good work (2 Tim 3:17). Because God richly supplies our needs, Paul told Timothy to "Command them to do good, to be rich in good deeds, and to be generous and willing to share" (1 Tim 6:17–18).

Fifth, crucial functional substitutes could be developed for appropriate festivals, ceremonies and rituals, such as New Years, harvest thanksgiving, house warming, and others. Once a church elder asked me if we could do a Christian ceremony for cutting off the topnotch of a youth, at the completion of a vow he and his wife made years before becoming Christian. After listening to the whole story we agreed to do so, using Thai elders to perform the ritual, and implementing some biblical reinterpretation. Instead of thanking the spirits for their protection, we agreed to dedicate the youth to the care and keeping of God's Holy Spirit. Three stages in Van Gennep's "rites of passage" are separation from the old state, transition through ritual reorientation, and incorporation by acceptance into the new state. These stages were implemented in the above case. When instituting functional substitutes or other rites and rituals, leaders need to carefully follow this pattern. The Rites of Passage formula is also vital to the conversion process of separation, transition and incorporation. Paul indicates this repeatedly. He called for the Gentiles to turn from dead works, idols, darkness, and Satan to the living Creator, light, God, and forgiveness (Acts 14:15; 26:18; 1 Thess 1:9; Col 1:13–14). The transitional rite between the two was baptism, declaring faith in Jesus. Being changed from the old sin-karmic state into new grace-creation in Christ resulted in good works, genuine expressions of mercy, love and compassion towards others (2 Cor 5:17).

Conclusion

We conclude appropriately with the true story of a Thai who, despite his debilitating disease, by the grace of God served as a missionary pastor and church planter for years. His experience of walking from karma to grace involved his Buddhist background, family, Thai Christians and foreign missionaries. They impacted his life through good works using medical, educational, spiritual and agricultural skills. The miracle of wholeness was the product of holistic approaches applying God's grace and love.

Aging Thong Yu of Central Thailand had advanced Hansen's disease (leprosy). The disfiguring effects sadly showed on his body - no fingers, no toes, the bony bridge of his nose eaten away, and ugly infected ulcers on his extremities. He was a Thai Buddhist and believed his disease was the result of karma. After all, in childhood he stole food items and fruit from local shopkeepers in town. So karma played out causing his leprosy which destroyed the fingers that stole. Over the years, he was careful to make as much merit as possible. But he had no joy, no peace, and no relief from his disease. His deteriorating condition left him hopelessly depressed. In his forties, he set up a makeshift shack on the side of the mountain below a prominent Buddhist monastery on the edge of town. Yu was waiting and wanting to die. His karma was too much to bear in this life, so maybe the next rebirth might raise him to a better status.

Then one day he heard some western missionary nurses of OMF had arrived in the town to treat leprosy patients, but he was not interested. How could they possibly alleviate his advanced condition caused by karma?

After months of cajoling from his leprous associates he finally came down off his hillside hut to attend a leprosy clinic on the outskirts of the city. Missionary nurses lovingly treated his smelly ulcers, cleansed his gaping sores, and gave him special medicines. They visited him in his shack, gave advice and shared the gospel. During several months of attending clinics he was surprised to see others like himself. He noticed some exhibited joyful changes in their lives. He observed that they believed in this Jesus of some new religion. Yu began to show interest in this God proclaimed at the clinic. Surprised to learn that God loved him in spite of his karma and disfigurations, he listened intently to the story of God's grace. Christ's merciful, free offer of salvation from sin and liberation from karma interested him. No longer did he have to work and make merit over multiple lifetimes to escape karma. In time, he personally accepted God's grace in Christ. He experienced a new peace of heart, change of life and fresh perspectives on living. He immediately began to witness fervently to everyone in the clinic. He also became an avid student of the Bible. He experienced a combination of physical healing, spiritual renewal and social inclusion in a new group, the church. He no longer felt isolated, ignored, or despised.

He remembered that his affluent sister and her husband lived nearby. They were farmers and had considerable land. One day grabbing his Bible, Thong Yu walked to where his brother-in-law was plowing his fields with water buffalo. He shared his testimony and witness of Christ's love. As the brother went down one furrow, Yu followed him, stumbling along with Bible in hand declaring the gospel of God's mercy and power. When the brother turned back to cut another furrow, Yu turned and followed him, proclaiming persistently. Soon the brother accepted Christ, accompanied by his wife and children, and later their spouses too. A house church was started in their home.

Tong Yu was baptized and became a faithful member of the small church of a dozen or so mostly leprosy believers, who met in the open walled clinic. He heard about a Leprosy Bible School in Northeast Thailand (Isaan). Yu desired to know more of the Bible and decided to study there for a couple of years.

Returning to Central Thailand he spent considerable time at OMF's Manorom Christian Hospital across the river from his home. At their Leprosy Rehabilitation wing he learned how to manage practical life better, and despite his handicaps, how to use tools including saw, hammer and chisel to make things, so he could support himself. How could he do this with no fingers? Staff trained him to grip tools tightly between his stumped hands. In time he became quite skillful, building cupboards and other furniture. He built wooden rifles with strong rubber bands, which he sold to the lads who herded the water buffalo in their fields. They used them to shoot stone pellets ahead of the animals so they would turn in the right direction, without having to chase the animals down.

In time, Tong Yu sensed that God was calling him to be a local missionary in the north of his home province. He desired to share God's grace and start churches among many leprous patients there. He approached the small mother church and offered to be their missionary. Would they send him out, pray for him and partly assist in his expenses? The elders and church agreed and sent him out. One of the European missionaries assisted Yu to get established in the northern district and encouraged him to be self-supporting. He helped him to raise chickens and pigs for food, and start a home garden. Things went well for a while until some local ruffians stole the produce he depended on to survive. Thievery occurred frequently. Yu was not discouraged, but trusting in God, started afresh each time.

As he walked miles visiting and teaching the gospel, his sore feet got seriously infected requiring hospitalization. Doctors advised him to stop walking so much. Our local team decided he needed a bicycle. But Yu had never ridden before and how could he do so without fingers or toes? The Christian hospital staff remembered a new miracle material called Velcro, so mittens with Velcro were created for him. We also put Velcro strips on the handlebars of the bike so he could grip them. Another problem was hand brakes. How could he use them without fingers? From my youth biking days, I remembered the Perry hub with reverse peddle brake. We obtained one from Australia and had it fitted in the local Thai bike shop. Tong Yu had strong motivation and equal adamant determination. He dug a stake into the ground in front of his home attaching a rope from it to the bike. For hours he practiced riding, falling down often, until he mastered the needed skill.

Tong Yu faithfully continued to serve the local monthly leprosy clinic and ride his bike to establish church groups in the surrounding region. Within a few years he married one of the Christian leprous women. For decades, he persistently spread the news of God's grace in Christ. The provincial mother church kept supporting and praying for him. When he came to retirement age he and his wife returned to the city, from which he had been sent out. He reported to the members the blessed fruit God had produced through grace and announced he was retiring. Since he had been faithful, the Thai believers offered and agreed to continue supporting him. After a year or so, Tong Yu in typical entrepreneurial fashion started his own tricycle-taxi (*sam lo*) business. He hired local youth to ferry passengers around town. He then told the church that since he was self-supporting, they could stop their financial help and use that money to fund new outreach projects. Several years went by, and after losing his wife and becoming frail Tong Yu moved to a rest home for leprosy patients in North Thailand. There he died. But the power of God's grace overcame karma and produced through Yu fruitful good works which remain in many transformed lives to this day. What a victorious portrait of grace and mercy, producing glorious transformation in individuals and society.

Postscript: OMF's leprosy treatment program in Central Thailand was so successful that within thirty years the World Health Organization recognized that leprosy was controlled in that region. The clinics were closed. Currently, teams of mobile Thai medics riding motorbikes disburse leprosy medicines and prophylactics to the homes of all infected families. Today, as a result of God's sending dedicated missionary personnel from around the world to do good among them, leprosy is contained in Central Thailand. God moved people like Tong Yu "from karma to grace."

Bibliography

Aung, Maung Htin. *Folk Elements in Burmese Buddhism*. Rangoon, Burma: Religious Affairs Dept, 1959.

Dhammananda, K. Sri. *What Buddhists Believe*. Kuala Lumpur, Malaysia: Buddhist Missionary Society Malaysia, 2002.

Durston, Dick. "Durston's Digest," April newsletter. 2016.

Guinness, Os. *Fool's Talk: Recovering the Art of Christian Persuasion*. Downers Grove, IL: IVP, 2015.

Guralnik, David B., editor. *Webster's New World Dictionary*. New York: Simon and Schuster, 1984.

Herman, A.L. "Community: Violence, Peace and the Ways of Community." In *Buddhism and Peace: Theory and Practice*. Chanju Mun, editor. 107–124. Honolulu, HI: Blue Pine, 2006.

Hiebert, Paul G. *Cultural Anthropology*. Grand Rapids, MI, 1983.

Keyes, Charles F. "Millennialism, Theravada Buddhism, and Thai Society." *The Journal of Asian Studies* 36-2 (1977) 283–302.

Keyes, Charles F. and Daniel E. Valentine. *Karma: An Anthropological Inquiry*. Berkeley: University of California Press, 1983.

Maguire, Jack. *Essential Buddhism: A Complete Guide to Beliefs and Practices*. NewYork: Pocket, 2001.

Part I: Religious Foundations

Malinowski, Bronislaw. *Magic, Science and Religion*. New York: Doubleday Anchor, 1954.

Pye, Michael and John S. Strong. "Merit" In *Encyclopedia of Religion,* Lindsay Jones, editor. Detroit: Thomson Gale, (1987) 5870–5873.

Ratnasinghe, Aryadasa. "Buddhism in Sri Lanka." In The Urban Dharma Newsletter, February 3, 2004. http://www.urbandharma.org/udnl2/nl020304.html accessed Dec. 24, 2016.

Smith, Alex G. "Buddhist Spiritual Realities: Divining and Discerning the Future." In *Seeking the Unseen: Spiritual Realities in the Buddhist World.* Paul H. de Neui, editor. 43–68. Pasadena: William Carey, 2016.

———. *Smith Snippets.* May 2016, Newsletter.

———. *Siamese Gold: The Church in Thailand.* Bangkok: Kanok Bannasan, 1982.

———. "The Struggle of Asian Ancestor Veneration." In *Communicating Christ in the Buddhist World,* Paul de Neui and David Lim, editors. 149–176. Pasadena, William Carey, 2006.

Spiro, Melford E. *Burmese Supernaturalism*. Philadelphia: Institute for the Study of Human Issues, 1978.

Steer, J and C. "What does it mean to be a Buddhist?" In *Thai Tempo* Feb 2014 email.

Sumana, Sayadaw U. "Sharing of Merits." Buddhist Hermitage, Lunas. http://www.abuddhistlibrary.com/Buddhism/B%20%20Theravada/Teachers/Sayadaw%20U%20Sumana/The%20Sharing%20of%20Merit/SharingofMerits.html.

TBCM, Theravada Buddhist Council of Malaysia. "Sharing of Merits Pattidana," Aug. 15, 2013. http://tbcm.org.my/sharing-of-merits-pattidana/.

Virtual Library—Sri Lanka. "Religious Conditions in Pre-Buddhist Sri Lanka." http://www.lankalibrary.com/rit/pre%20buddhist.htm.

Walters, Jonathan S. "Communal Karma and Karmic Community in Theravada Buddhist History." In *Constituting Communities: Theravada Buddhism and the Religious Cultures of South and Southeast Asia.* J C Holt, J N Kinnard, and J S Walters, editors. New York: State University of New York Press, 2003.

Wikipedia. "Merit" http://en.wikipedia.org/wiki/Merit_Buddhism.

Wright, M. A. "Some Observations in Thai Animism." *Practical Anthropology.* 15 (1968) 1–7.

Part II

Cultural Perspectives

'Are not you Israelites
the same to me as the Cushites?'
declares the Lord.
'Did I not bring Israel up from Egypt,
the Philistines from Caphtor
and the Arameans from Kir?'
AMOS 9:7

6

The Nature of Merit-Making of Pure-Land Buddhism and Zen (Shang) Buddhism within Chinese Naturalism

Tae-Yun Timothy Hwang

This chapter aims to give insights on the acculturated doctrine of Chinese Buddhism, particularly on the merit-related doctrine of the Pure-Land School and the Zen School in China. For as has been rightly put by Jung Jin Hong, the religious life of the believers is not restricted within doctrinal codes alone, but instead it breathes within the interpretation and appropriation of the given original tradition.[1] Thus, this kind of Buddhism is the object of this study.

Christian mission, although grounded in the authority of the Bible, has been sadly conditioned with little flexibility in the task of acculturation as it moves to a new setting in the mission field. In fact, the Bible is characterized by openness and generosity but Christian mission carriers are often inflexible in their own orthodoxy. In contrast, Buddhism, which takes her scriptures as a mere means of finding the true self, has been quite loose and free even in relation to its imported interpretation. It is nevertheless interesting to observe that the reinterpreted doctrine for a newly given setting appears different from the former one. Its new form and shape, however, is well accepted and popularized. Hence, I bring this case to bear for a better

---

1. Jung, *Yeollikwa Datchim*, 187.

PART II: CULTURAL PERSPECTIVES

contextualized theology for Christian mission in China, and similar contexts like Korea, Japan, and Northern Vietnam.

To begin with, the idea of merit in Hinduism and Buddhism originated from the karmic-community where it is understood as a sort of ritual or means. It is rooted in the concept of cause and effect at work in the world.

Buddhism that originated from India had to change in order to adapt to a different context when it entered into China. The Chinese cultural soil was completely different from that of Indian Buddhism from which it was transplanted. The doctrine of merit-making was appropriated within the larger philosophical framework that was distinctly Chinese. Among the various Buddhist branches, the Pure-Land School and the Zen School proved particularly adaptable, and as a result their branches stretched out all over China, spreading farther towards the neighboring countries.

East Asian countries share a common cultural heritage known as Chinese Naturalism. This naturalism is also known as the foundational philosophy of China. According to Callicott, Baird and Ames, this philosophy may be characterized by three principles: (1) the principle of holistic unity, (2) the principle of internal-movement, and (3) the principle of organic balance.[2] This understanding of the universe became the base from which Confucianism and Taoism grew. These three principles were also maintained within the Chinese expression of Buddhism.[3]

This acculturation occurred over many centuries and impacted how Chinese Buddhism eventually become a united whole. Due to the broad nature of the topic, this chapter does not claim to be comprehensive or detailed in scope. Instead, it only focuses on the main topic, namely, merit-making or *guna*. The findings of the study on this topic will be used for Christian missiological reflection.

Chinese Naturalism as the Seedbed of Chinese Buddhism

China and India both have a monsoon season with heavy rain and wind. Because of this shared characteristic, their ecological world became diverse and abundant. This constant and regular change of weather transformed the environment where people lived. One theory of cultural development

---

2. Callicott, *Nature in Asian Traditions of Thought*, 10–11.

3. Li Ze Hou, *Is This the Time for Chinese Philosophy?* 51, Nakamura, *Ways of Thinking of Eastern Peoples*, 175-76.

suggests that physical environments impacted the development of specific cultural worldviews. Following this line of thought, it can be posited that the worldviews of India and China are the outcome of their own way of distinct interpretations of their physical environments. Over time distinctives developed. Today, whilst India views the natural world as an illusion, China views the natural world as real and dynamic.

For the Chinese worldview, the world in which they live is very concrete. Spring, summer, fall, and winter are tangible. What is bona fide in the lives of the Chinese is found in the natural world. This world is the very source of human life. The Chinese poet Li (Tai) Bai 李太白 wrote in his poem "On the Way to the Capital after Departing Children" about the world as follows:

> I return home when the rice wine is fermented.
> The chickens in the yard are well fed with yellow corn.
> My wife and I with our two children laugh with joyous smiles
> Around the table with rich and abundant chicken soup.

Another poet Du Fu 杜甫 saw the world in his poem "Toward Spring 春望" thus:

> The mountains and rivers remain.
> Though the king and his family I serve are gone,
> Another spring comes back
> And gives new green branches in the streets of the ruined city.

Both of these Chinese poets viewed the world as a real place that can be trusted. The natural world, according to this worldview, has long life and is being renewed again and again. Human life, by contrast, is rather fleeting and has no hope for its own renewal. Thus, human life itself is a blessing but there is a sadness too. Humans may enjoy this life with what nature bestows. We must enjoy this life within the realistic world. The given time is too short and constrained with countless limitations. Du Fu 杜甫 described the human life in the same poem "Toward Spring" as follows:

> The white hair of mine fell out even by scratching.
> Now no more hair is left to hold my silver-made hairpin.

Note that the Chinese mind longs for a world that allows for a happy and long life. This ideal, which is embodied in Taoism, was depicted in paintings of well-known Chinese gardens such as Yi He Yuan, Zho Zhen Yuan, Cang shi Yuan.

To view the natural environment as real in this way requires perceiving the world through the creative eyes of a poet. From the human perspective, this material world is full of movement and events. Yet the Chinese view is that these movements are not merely the inevitable results of past events; they are actually the world's own movements. The living of all forms of life occurs in this heartfelt but temporal world. Yet the world also operates on its own. Humanity is viewed as one small stream within the much larger stream. Mankind does not live in separate isolation from the rest of the natural world, but rather as an integral part within the cosmic process and within the world's movements. This world cannot merely be reduced to purely scientific or philosophical concepts of modernity because it has its own realistic meaning. Hence, it is humanity's obligation to perceive the meaning of this world as a poet would, with sensitive understanding and imagination.

It is within this Chinese worldview of the natural order that the standard for human life is to be found. The desire to live is assumed to be a right of any living being on this earth. This instinct is the very essence of human nature too. This is the reason that Chinese religions contain moral and socio-political codes reinforcing and preserving this distinctly human craving. Simply put, the length and breadth of a person's life is not understood to be outside of the individual as if dictated by external forces but actually abides within.

To take this one step further internally, every living human being in this world is given its own subsistence by his or her own substance. And each life is made by this substantial nature. Its form is concocted by its nature. This can be evidenced in the style of the written characters of Chinese words which are formed as collections of symbols that describe the essentials of the inner substantial nature of that word's components.

Survival is a natural instinct. Humanity's natural instinct for self-preservation is culturally defined through ritual. In fact, ritual forms the expression of humanity's deepest longings towards the world. Even if those longings or feelings be contaminated by human selfishness, ritual is where the deepest values of the human heart evidence the desire to be re-ordered, re-connected and even corrected. Something deep inside the human psyche aches to return to that lost state of harmony with the natural world. It is a state that may never have been known personally but is somehow recognized as existing somewhere out there, yet unattainable without the transformation of human artificiality and egocentrism. It is understood that the enchantments of nature can once again be experienced by the human creature. People can be united with nature only if they will give up their need to always be in control. The true nature of humans is like a flag waving in the wind. This unrestricted flow is the very nature of life itself. It is an effortless movement.

Yet because of the separation from this natural harmony, human moral codes must exist. But Chinese moral codes are subjective. Acceptance of a particular moral code is determined by its degree of adequateness within the given contextual circumstances. Behavior that is extreme, whether good or bad, is seen as uncontrollable. The highest standard of life does not come from transcending the world but is actually found in daily life, that is, a very natural form of human existence. The ideal and authentic life is not to be sought in humanity's artificial or mechanical design but in the midst of the natural world. Shangri-La is a place where humans can taste that longed-for harmony with the world yet it is only discovered by stumbling into it accidentally when lost along life's way. The design inherent in Chinese gardens, the world of the Book of Odes (the collection of Ancient Poems by Confucius), and the calm, strolling world of Lǎozǐ are some examples of this Chinese aspiration to return to harmony with the natural world.

Merit-Making in Chinese Naturalism

There have been various attempts to conceal the illusive world of Buddhism within the Chinese realistic natural order. One of these attempts is the teaching of Abbot JeeEu of Chinese Shang (Zen) Buddhism in the 6th century called the "One in Three World." This doctrine has been accepted as a classic of Chinese Buddhism. He said that the world is an unreal illusion yet humans make their lives within temporality. These two worlds (the illusive and the temporal world) meet in the present moment and it is this juncture together that creates a third reality (the world we live as real). The two worlds (illusive and temporal) are not contradictory but in present time the unreal world becomes real and the real can also become unreal if humans cannot endure it. The readiness and receptivity of the human mind is the sole determinant. In this view, merit is the key to making the unreal real. The virtue of gods attained through merit placates the mind of the human viewer into an unmoved state, so that even the constantly changing illusive world can be fixed at the present moment. To him or her color is no longer color, the unreal (or empty) is no longer unreal. And it could also be possible that the unreal may become real and vice versa.

Merit as the means to view the unreal as permanently real involves three steps: merit as moral code, merit as being seated, and merit as enlightened wisdom. Chinese Buddhist monks believed that merit could be achieved through various actions in life, however, all human efforts would fall short without the help of certain givens that shall be explained further. What follows are examples of two forms of merit-making widely accepted by the Chinese found in Pure-Land Buddhism and Zen Buddhism.

Merit in Pure-Land Buddhism

The merit in this school of Buddhism is only achieved on the condition that one's heart be pure from the contaminated world. And this heart is only possible by calling upon the name of Amitabha Buddha (in Chinese) or Amitayus Buddha (in Sanskrit), whose nature is being understood as "the unlimited life 無量壽" or "the unlimited light無量光." According to Damvan, the great monk during the Tang Dynasty, all of Buddhist scriptures can be categorized into two ways: "The Easy Path易行道" and "The Difficult Path 難行道." The world we live in has so many evil things that his school taught that there was no other option for most people than "The Easy Path." Damvan meant by this simply repeating the name of Buddha (Buddhamsmrti), Pusa 菩薩 as a way of attaining the light. This is not a burdensome merit-making practice for common people in their given settings. The land they are seeking to enter is the Pure Land. This blessed land has different names but the common denominator is that this land is without worries, a land without lust, anger, and stupidity.

Entrance into this world requires "leaving" or "going out" of this worldly setting that has been entangled in the lust-filled hearts of humanity. This is an action of an "instant moment" not something that must be attained through lengthy human effort of meritorious deeds. At once, the present world of evil can turn into the land of Buddha. The Sutra of Prajnaparamita or Hrdaya-Sutra teaches that true realization arises through the knowledge that this lust-filled world is unreal, a mere illusion. This world is nothing, void, and meaningless so that as a result the seeker of the truth must necessarily leave this world by calling with full trust upon the name of Helping Buddha, Pusa 菩薩. At once the world becomes nothing. But another world comes into reality in the newly transformed mind like a light shining through dark clouds.

Merit-Making and Zen Buddhism in China

The word "Zen" or "Shang" comes from "Diyana" of the Indian word translated into "Suna" in Chinese phonetics. "Diyana" refers to "calm thinking," "introspection," and "being still." This is the state of immersing oneself deeply into his or her inner being. In China, this word was translated into "Jung 靜" meaning "to be seated correctly." It is also called "Sayusoo 思惟修" meaning "training by thinking." So, the Chinese word for "Diyana" is understood by Chinese as "Zen-Jung 禪定."

Zen practice is one version of understanding the Noble Eightfold Path (*pa ariyo atthangiko maggo*). According to the Prajnaparampraj-hrdaya-Sutra, the Zen state is the fifth position of the six meritorious *paramita* (states of perfection or completion). The six states are: giving offerings (generosity), keeping the code (ethics), enduring hardships (forbearance), continuing forward (diligence), Diyana (concentration), and wisdom (insight). Here you see that the state of Zen is only one rung on the ladder below wisdom or self-realization. This merit is the state of almost, but not yet complete, perfection.

There are many branches in Zen Buddhism based on differences of how to attain self-realization. However, the common denominator is that they all follow the doctrine of "Seeing Buddha in Oneself." This understanding says that there is the seed of Buddha all over the universe. Realization may come to individuals who live in this world when Buddha is the key to their practices.

Zen Buddhism goes with Mahavaipulya Buddhavatamsaka Sutra or the Avatamska Sutra 華嚴經. The main teaching of this sutra is that the world we live in, the mind of humanity, and the Buddha are all one. In this view, the world is limitless. In even the smallest element there is the universe ("The world is not larger than the plum leaf"). One is everything and everything is in one. Therefore, the mind should not be bound by the size of things, places, or even rules. The mind should remain in a free state. According to this teaching, Zen followers believe that he or she embodies the sutra. The way of reaching the Buddha is within. The path is not made by effort but sudden recognition of the true-self ("Leap and the net will appear"). The Northern School of Zen Buddhism that emphasizes the sudden getting into self-realization is more satisfactory to Chinese followers.

To the Zen Buddhist any sutra is no more than a means of a direction for practice. However, the real way of knowing Buddha in oneself cannot be translated in words but only from mind to mind. To them, any path that carries certain merit is no more than a vehicle of transport towards an end, a boat available for crossing the river to the other side. The follower must seek to be free from even the charms of the meritorious means itself to find the heart of Zen ("To understand nothing takes time").

Chinese Buddhism in Chinese Naturalism

As shown in the previous sections, the nature of the doctrine of merit-making in both the Pure-Land School of Buddhism and Zen Buddhism is not about morality but rather the pursuit of wisdom. Merit-making was not understood as the key for steady progress in the process of reincarnation but as a means of reaching the other side of the world.

Since merit-making is merely the means of reaching the other side in the finding of the true self, it can be found within oneself. Here, the self-seeker does not need to get help from the transcendental world. It rather requires the attitude of mind to look at the world correctly. So, it can be said that the true nature of merit-making is not found in the divine but rather in the attitude of the hearts of human beings. Here, the human being is a part of nature.

Both schools of our study do not negate the virtue of merit-making. However, the real virtue of merit in these traditions can be found within the daily life of those who live in peace with their eyes focused towards the other side. In the School of Pure-Land Buddhism, the Land of Buddha is here and now to those whose eyes are open. Religious works are not a prerequisite for reaching the other side but a prison that captures the true soul of wisdom. In other words, in this tradition merit-making can be consider heresy to what Buddha has already provided.

So, it can be said that for the Chinese Buddhists in both schools, merit-making itself is understood as neutral, it can be good or bad in the end. The more important point lies within the heart of the truth seeker, the attitude of "dis-positioning" of the things they have, and separation from attachment ("If you love something hold it loosely"). Here, Chinese

Buddhist wisdom would promote developing an outlook of adequateness with whatever situation the follower finds him or herself situated.

Some Missiological Reflections for Christian Mission in Chinese Buddhists

Whether we, as outside communicators, accept or refuse all, part, or none of the worldview of the Chinese, it must be recognized that it is the soil in which the seed of the Christian gospel has been and is being planted. Some of us may become apologetic towards the gospel and desire to explain it in a certain way familiar to our own worldview. But look at the connecting points that exist between the Chinese and non-Chinese worldviews. For example, none of us can deny that there are some inherent indefinable types of kinship with nature in our own physical bodies. Thus, the nature of merit making whether found within Buddhism or labeled something else within Christianity is to a certain extent self-feeding, self-preserving. The self-feeding (or survival) can come up any time by human nature. Of course this chapter is not intended to defend or justify the universal instinct for self-preservation. However, let us be honest. All missionaries need to be mindful of their own (often unrecognized) self-feeding in their mission work and in the ways they are comfortable (and uncomfortable) in doing theology.

Jesus is the son of man but he does not end there. Jesus is also the son of God. He sent the Holy Spirit to us who are living on the earth. The Holy Spirit is here with us in our daily life. The Holy Spirit is not imprisoned within religious temples nor defined by our religious works but is free and sets us free by the truth. His name "Immanuel" means he is right here with us.

At times the gospel that foreign communicators preach comes from a static, logical, apologetic approach that seems too complicated and outside of the core philosophy (or worldview) of local people. This is definitely the case in China. Missionaries should remember that theology is the housing of the gospel. However, when that theology complicates the good news and changes it into incomprehensible concepts, it becomes a detention center. The sincerity of God's love is not a mechanical causal movement solving humanity's salvation problem but is actually many waves of constant movements towards the heart of God's creation. The good news desires to resonate with the deepest longings found in the heart of the hearer. This can be illustrated from the worldview values expressed in the Chinese character for the word "heart." The component parts of the character for this word are centered not on symbols for mechanical logic but on a very emotional symbol for a living being. This symbol is shown surrounded by the concept of wisdom represented by the movement towards the constantly changing world. Living within the movements of this world represents the Chinese heart. The gospel must speak to the worldview values of that heart.

The merit of Jesus is his living sacrifice. It should be understood more than a legal payment. Any religious doctrine or understanding should be appropriated in accordance to the needs of the followers. That is the difference between an apologetic sermon coming from the detention center of encoded theology and good news that touches the heart.

The new life God has given to us is real and blessed every moment. The merit of Jesus is for all aspects of human life itself, not merely to appease religious obligation. Joy in those who are the communicators should not be interpreted as being separated from this temporal life. It must be evidenced here and now. The kingdom of God is above but also within us.

Conclusion and Suggestions for Further Study

The nature of merit-making in Chinese Buddhism shown in the Pure-Land School and the Zen School is surely one acculturated by the worldview of the Chinese, particularly within Chinese naturalism. Some of the important characteristics of the nature of merit-making found in these two schools of Buddhism within Chinese naturalism include: wisdom seeking, the sudden awareness of inner recognition, the pursuit of the proper disposition of the mind, and the seeking of the means of attaining that reality that is intangible to the senses.

Religious life is a living thing such as a plant or a tree. Its seed should be sound and healthy but that seed also needs to be planted correctly in the given soil in order to grow. Merit-making has been present for many centuries in the heart of humankind as a guideline on how to live in the cultural soil of India. However, the Chinese cultural soil frees merit-making beyond these narrow boundaries.

There is something inside human beings that feels a kinship in one sense or another with the natural order. Christian missionaries should seek to promote this instinct in themselves and others when doing their work. Recognize that this instinct that is common to humanity is actually one example of the work of God found within every culture even before the missionary arrives as deep calling to deep. Those who present the gospel of Jesus Christ should be wary of subjugating seekers and followers to a cognitively bound form of the message or any other forms of spiritual or religious subjugation. Rather, they must allow themselves as model communicators to be the first of all to be set free by the truth of the good news that God is love here and now in the natural order. They must embody this message. Here Christian mission workers are in need of help from the Holy Spirit to be living testimonies of the sacrificial and sincere love of the Creator. The end of the gospel is the bringing of God's kingdom of heaven to earth today, not to obscure God as an illusion.

Jesus preached the gospel of the kingdom of God, which is near and within. Since Jesus the Son of God is with us, Jesus as the Son of Man was within us too. He is the Immanuel, his kingdom here on earth. The Holy Spirit abides in us as well; the glory of God is in his creation, the temporal but blessed reality. That is what we are. And we are privileged to be called now to share this wonderful reality within the world of Chinese naturalism, in celebration of the joy of life.

Bibliography

Bodde, Derk. *China's Cultural Tradition*. Hinsdale: Dryden, 1957.
Brown, Brian. "Towards a Buddhist Ecological Cosmology." In *Worldviews and Ecology: Religion, Philosophy and the Environment* edited by Evelyn Tucker and John A. Grim. 124–137. NJ: Associated University Presses, 1994.
Callicott, J. Baird & Roger T. Ames. *Nature in Asian Traditions of Thought*. N.Y: State University of New York Press, 1989.
Elwood, Douglas J. *What Asian Christians are Thinking: A Theological Sourcebook*. Quozon City: New Days, 1976.
Hall, David L. & Roger T. Ames. *Thinking from the Han: Self, Truth, and Transcendence in Chinese and Western Culture*. N.Y: State University of New York Press, 1998.
Jung, Jin Hong. *Yeollim kwa Datchim* (Open and Close). Seoul: Sanchurum, 2009.
Kang, Sa-Moon. *Kuyak eu Jayun Ihae* (*Understanding of Nature in the Old Testament*). Seoul: Dahankidock Suhae, 2005.
KeumKok, et al. *History of Chinese Thought*. Seoul: Eron Kwa Silchun, 1986.
Lee, Sung-Hee. *Mihakeuro DongAsia Eukda* (*Reading the East Asian by Aesthetic View*). Seoul: Silchun Munhaksa, 2012.
Lengar, Keshavaram N. and Rama P. Coomaraswamy. *Hinduism and Buddhism*. New Delhi: Indira Gandhi National Center for the Arts, 1999.
Li, ZeHou. *Is This the Time for Chinese Philosophy?* translated by YuJin Lee). Seoul: Geulhangari, 2013.

Part II: Cultural Perspectives

Nakamura, Hajime. *Ways of Thinking of Eastern Peoples, India-China-Tibet-Japan* edited by Philip P. Wiener. University of Hawaii Press. 1971.

7

An Indian Christian Dialogue with the Karmic Community

Bouvert Regulas

GENUINE OPEN AND HONEST dialogue between people of different faiths inspires confidence. Dialogue enables people to overcome misunderstandings. Through dialogue we see more clearly the distinctives of our own faith and the continuity and discontinuity with others. Evangelicals need to develop the use of dialogue and not react to it simply because it has been misused by some. All too often we are answering questions that people are not asking. A wide range of reading and getting involved in dialogue are necessarily needed for a committed Christian to respond to the thought-world of our Buddhist friends and neighbors. At the same time, Christian understanding should lead to the clear formation of a doctrine, which is biblical. Below is one example of dialogue addressing questions members of karmic communities may ask that evangelicals should be prepared to answer.

What is the Cause of Inequality in Life?

A young truth-seeker approached the Buddha and questioned him regarding the intricate problem of social inequality, "What is the cause, what is the reason, O Lord," he questioned, "that we find amongst mankind the short-lived and long-lived, the healthy and the diseased, the ugly and beautiful, those lacking influence and the powerful, the poor and the rich, the low-born and the high-born, and the ignorant and the wise?" The Buddha's reply was, "All living beings have actions (karma) as their own, their inheritance, their congenital cause, their kinsman and their refuge. It is karma that differentiates beings into low and high states." He then explained the cause of such differences in accordance with the law of cause and effect.

Karma, a word that came from the Sanskrit language, basically means "action." It doesn't describe the effect of our action – it's the action itself. We constantly generate it by our thoughts and their resulting actions. Our thoughts and actions become the cause that will eventually be followed by the effect. We have to live with the consequences of our actions. Karma, according to Buddhist tradition, is the way the universe teaches us the lessons we need to learn.

It is this doctrine of karma that gives consolation, hope, reliance and moral courage to a Buddhist. When the unexpected happens, and he or she meets with difficulties, failures, and misfortune, the Buddhist realizes that this is merely a reaping what has been sown, and is viewed as wiping off a past debt. Instead of resigning oneself, leaving everything to karma, he or she makes a strenuous effort to pull the weeds and sow useful seeds in their place, for the future is in one's own hands.

Those who believes in karma do not condemn even the most corrupt, for they too have their chance to reform themselves at any moment. Though bound to suffer in woeful states, they have hope of attaining eternal peace. By their own doings they have created their own hells, and by their own doings they can create their own heavens too.[1] Buddhists believe that we are the architects of our own fate.

Karma is action that produces results, which could be called 'merit.' It is like seeds planted in a field; no one knows for sure when they will ripen, but if they were planted, they will ripen. Demerit due to evil actions brings pain, punishment and suffering. Merit due to good actions or karmas bring pleasure, blessing and enjoyment. Buddhists are very concerned with merit-making through their deeds or thoughts, from their birth until their death. They strongly believe they ought to regularly make and gain merit, which in turn would bring them happiness, a peaceful life and other good things. They also believe that gaining merit will strengthen them to overcome any obstacles or misfortune they are suffering. They intend to gain more merit because they also believe their accumulated merit will help them to be in

---

1. Conre, *Buddhism*, 148.

heaven or a peaceful place after their death. More importantly, the merit they gain will help them to reach *nirvana* (divine peace beyond this world).

Merit has been translated from '*puṇya*' in Sanskrit and '*puñña*' in Pali. This concept is that which accumulates as a result of good deeds, acts, or thoughts and which carries over throughout the life or the subsequent incarnations. Such merit contributes to a person's growth towards spiritual liberation.[2] A common rule in making merit is to prepare one's mind and thoughts. The mind has to be purified and ready. Gaining merit must not bring any trouble or worry to oneself or others. There are three ways of making and gaining merit. They are (1) to give alms; (2) to maintain religious commandments in life, and (3) to pray. If all of these are perfectly met, it represents great merit making.[3]

How Do I Prepare My Mind for Proper Merit Making?

In the karmic traditions of Buddhism and Hinduism, merit or *punya* is that which purifies and cleanses the mind. Merit has the power of purifying the mind of greed, hatred and delusion. Merit can be looked upon as those actions that improve the quality of the mind. They tend to raise the level on which the mind usually runs, refining and purifying it of grosser mental defilements. It is the making of merit that ensures one to lead a balanced and a harmonious life. Another fruit of merit is that merit opens doors everywhere. The meritorious person generally finds their way unobstructed. Whatever work they take up, they are able to bring it to a successful conclusion.

In the *Paticca Samuppada* (Dependent Origination), the Buddha states that evil activities arise from ignorance. Associated with ignorance is its ally of craving (*tanha*), the other root of karma. Evil actions are conditioned by these two causes. Hinduism lays down three special pathsways (*margas*) of liberation from bad karma. People may follow any one of these *margas* according to one's inclination, temperament, character, attainments and reach the desired goal. These three *margas* are: *karma-marga, bhakti-marga, and jnana-marga.*

Karma marga (way of action) leads to liberation through self-purification of body, mind and self-realization (performance of disinterested actions *(nishkama karma)*. To perform "duties for duties' sake" without any

---

2. Harvey, *Buddhism*, 186.
3. Ibid., 186.

ulterior motive or gain, weakens one's feeling of pride and egoism *(ahankara)*. The terminating of *ahankara* is essential for liberation.

Bhakti marga or devotion to God is the second way which enables people to calm and pacify the senses and passions within oneself and turn them toward God. This will sublimate and ennoble them. The devotee dedicates everything he or she has, including ego, to God and in so doing removes obstacles for personal liberation.

The third way—*jnana marga* (way of wisdom) says *jnana* or knowledge of the self as the pure, free and immortal spirit in humans is of great help in effectively controlling the human senses and passions, and also destroying egoism *(ahankara)*. All these three ways help a person to attain *mukti* or *moksha*. Hence, each of these three is a distinct method of attaining liberation in its own specific way.

In the Hindu *Vedas* (1500–500 BC), the idea of sacrifice for the atonement of sin in order to attain moksha was very prevalent. Here is a statement from the Rig Veda, the oldest and most important of the Vedas, "Prajapati, Lord of creatures gave himself for them; he became their sacrifice." In the Satapada Brahmana, a commentary on the second most important of the Vedas, the Yajur Veda, says, "God would offer himself as a sacrifice and obtain atonement for sins." Stephen Neill says that even though "in later days, blood sacrifices ceased to be offered in the great temples of Hinduism; in early times they played almost a central role in worship". The nineteenth century Indian Christian theologian K.M. Bannerjesa, used the idea of Prajapati's self-sacrifice in his dialogue with educated Hindus.[4]

In Buddhism we do not find a clear definition of sin. Sin is some act that brings about reaction because of the law of karma. One may query what the purpose of the Buddhist prohibitions are. The prohibitions are tools to be used for aiding concentration so that ignorance may be dispelled. If there is a strict dichotomy between good and evil, it would serve as a hindrance to attaining liberation. For when one attains liberation one is delivered from the illusory belief in evil and good. In fact, since there is no God to obey or disobey there is no sin from which to be delivered.

According to Sankara *(advaita vedanta)* and his followers, the individual self is identical with *Brahman* or God. It is *maya* or ignorance that conceals this truth from the individual's view and makes him think that he is identical with the body and is different and separate from God. The study of the *vedanta* will lead to the realization of the truth that the individual self

---

4. Fernando, *The Supremacy of Christ*, 133

(*atman*) is one with the *Brahman*. When the false distinction between the self and *Brahman* disappears, the bondage will also vanish. This liberation is considered to be positive bliss. Liberation means identity of the self with the *Brahman; Brahman* is infinite, eternal bliss.[5]

In contrast to this, there is another view known as the *visistadvaita vedanta* view. According to Ramanuja, the bondage of the soul to the body is due to its *karma*. Humans learn that liberation is not attained by study and reasoning but only through God's grace. God bestows his grace on those who are sincerely devoted to God and constantly meditate on him. Anyone who thus realizes God is liberated from the body forever, without any possibility of rebirth. The liberated soul having pure consciousness becomes similar to God *(brahmaprakara)*, who is also pure and blissful consciousness. This goal is reached only after death.[6]

Dr. Thomas is a layman turned theologian from India, known as the spokesperson of liberal theology in the east. For many years, he has played a leading and creative role in the ecumenical movement, both in the World Council of Churches and also in the East Asia Christian Conference. Thomas himself is attracted to a faith, which issues in constructive social action, perhaps indeed a form of *karma marga*. He said, 'Our concern should be that spirituality and metaphysics serve moral regeneration of life, for 'humanisation' is inherent in the message of salvation in Christ.'[7] Thomas' interpretation of Christianity as *karma marga* in the light of suffering love can be seen most clearly. Thomas believes in social and political action, and to that extent we may call him a follower of *karma marga*. Certainly he has little sympathy for a thoroughgoing theology based on *bhakti* or *jnana*. He looks rather for a new type of *karma marga*, which will take full account of the power of sin, of the tragic aspect of life and of humanity's need for forgiveness if true humanity is to be restored in Christ. In the theology of M.M. Thomas *karma marga*, we must make it clear that the 'action' involved is chiefly action 'in the world', the action of loving *diakonia*.

Will the Karma of Parents Affect their Children?

In the Buddhist understanding, the karma of parents determines or affects the karma of their children. Physically, the karma of children is generally

---

5. Gnanakan, *Salvation*, 126.
6. Ibid., 127.
7. Ibid., 75.

determined by the karma of their parents.[8] Thus, healthy parents usually have healthy offspring, and unhealthy parents have unhealthy children. A child's karma is determined apart from itself—it forms the child's individuality, the sum-total of its merits and demerits accumulated in innumerable past existences. For example, the karma of the Buddha-to-be, Prince Siddhartha was certainly not influenced by the joint karma of his parents, King Suddhodana and Queen Maya. The glorious and powerful karma of our Buddha-to-be transcended the karma of his parents which jointly were more potent than his own.

It is stated in the Dhammapada that not in the sky, nor in mid-ocean, or entering a mountain cave is found that place on earth where one may escape from (the consequences of) an evil deed.[9] One is not bound to pay all the past arrears of one's karma. If such were the case emancipation would be impossible. Eternal recurrence would be the unfortunate result.

When the disciples asked Jesus with regard to a man born blind (John 9:1–3), Jesus answered them, he became blind not because he sinned, nor his parents. He explained that this special calamity was not the result of special criminality or transgression. Not that both were guilty of original sin, and had committed actual transgressions; but Christ's answer is to be considered agreeable to the design of the question. The sense is that it was not any sin that either of them had committed, whilst he was in the womb, or previous to his birth; the cause of this blindness was otherwise, all such irregularities and afflictions arise from sin, and the fall of humankind.

Can a Person Transfer their Merit to Another?

The origin and the significance of the transference of merit is open to scholarly debate. Although this ancient custom still exists today in India and many Buddhists countries, very few Buddhists who follow this ancient custom have understood the meaning of transference of merits and the proper way to do it. Scholar Heinz Bechert dates the Buddhist doctrine of transfer of merit (Sanskrit: *puṇyapariṇamana*) in its fully developed form to the period between the 5th and 7th centuries AD. However, Sree Padma and Anthony Barber note that merit transfer was well established and a very integral part of Buddhist practice in the Andhra region of southern India. In addition, inscriptions at numerous sites across South Asia provide

---

8. Harvey, *Buddhism*, 89.

9. Devasthan, *Theology of Buddhism*, 208

definitive evidence that the transfer of merit was widely practiced in the first few centuries AD.[10]

The basic Buddhist scripture, the Dhammapada, says, "Purity and impurity depend on oneself. No one can purify another" (verse 165). There is no place for seeking the assistance of a higher being. Yet in practice Buddhists seek to transfer merit to those who have died through almsgiving *(dana)*. This practice of merit transference *(pattidana)* is present in a more formal way in the less orthodox Mahayana branch of Buddhism.[11]

According to the Theravadan tradition, it is very difficult to fathom the principle of accumulating merit or *punya karma*, as well as the popular practice of transferring merit to one's departed loved ones. Like many other things in Buddhist practices and rituals, *punya karma* also has the hallmark of a vestigial remnant of Hinduism. Accumulation of merit has minimal input on purification of one's mind, which is the cornerstone of the Buddha-dharma. There is mystery and a degree of *lobha* (lust or desire) when one collects merit hoping for a better life, as practiced and often preached today. Why make a case for one's relatives when there is supposedly no "self?"[12]

That sort of merit transfer eventually turns into a semi-magical substance you can earn and donate to the needy like money. This sort of a practice allows one to not take credit for what good things you have done. If you have a Mahayana bent, you may wish to refocus on why you were doing meritorious things. Do we perform meritorious acts to gain enlightenment or do we refuse to become fully enlightened until everyone is enlightened?

Dependence on human merit of effort, therefore, will make assurance of salvation impossible because humans are never good or acceptable enough for God to accept us. The bankruptcy of human morality as a basis for acceptance before God is readily acknowledged by Paul:

> I know that nothing good lives in me, that is, in my sinful nature. For I have the desire to do what is good, but I cannot carry it out. For what I do is not the good I want to do; no, the evil I do not want to do—this I keep on doing. What a wretched man I am! (Rom 7:18–19, 24)

To transfer merit does not mean that a person is deprived of the merit originally acquired by the good deed. On the contrary, the very act of 'transference' is a good deed in itself and hence enhances the merit already

---

10. Ibid., 47.
11. Fernando, *The Supremacy of Christ*, 130.
12. Devasthan, *Theology of Buddhism*, 82.

earned. The Buddha declares that one of the duties of children towards their dead parents is to transfer merit to them. There is no decrease of merit to him who transfers it thus; on the contrary, there is only an increase. Under this category would fall the transference of merit to the dead.[13]

The Buddha says that the greatest gift one can confer on one's dead ancestors is to perform 'acts of merit' and to transfer these merits so acquired. He also says that those who give also receive the fruits of their deeds. The Buddha encouraged those who did good deeds such as offering alms to holy men, to transfer the merits which they received from their departed ones. Alms should be given in the name of the departed by recalling to mind such things as, "When he was alive, he gave me this wealth; he did this for me; he was my relative, my companion, etc." (*tirokuddha Sutta—khuddakapatha*).[14]

Buddhism prioritizes our merit, but Christianity gives much emphasis on the grace of the Almighty God. According to Christianity our effort to attain salvation is futile. We cannot achieve it by our human merit. Even in Hinayana Buddhism which claims to be the system of liberation by self-effort, when the Buddhist repeats the worlds "I take refuge in the Buddha, I take refuge in the Sangha, I take refuge in the Dhamma" there is an elevation of the Buddha to a level of a deity and as a factor in salvation.[15]

Are there Karmic Worldview Values Found in Christian Scripture?

The foundation of Buddhism, the Four Noble Truths, begins with an affirmation about suffering: all existence entails suffering or *dukka*. The Buddha's understanding of suffering here is akin to the biblical understanding of frustration or futility in Ecclesiastes and Romans 8:18–25. Buddha said suffering is caused by craving or *tanha* (the Second Noble Truth). The misfortunes one faces are the result of negative karma accrued in previous and present births. The Buddha saw suffering as ceasing when craving ceases at nirvana (the Third Noble Truth), and he presented his eight-fold path or *marga* as the way to extinguish craving (the Fourth Noble Truths). As Buddhism is a non-theistic religion, Buddhists do not have to grapple with

---

13. Conre, *Buddhism*, 148.
14. Gnanakan, *Salvation*, 76.
15. Devasthan, *Theology of Buddhism*, 208.

the theological problem of having to reconcile the problem of evil with the existence of a supreme God.[16]

We may conclude then that religion is both the path to God and a stumbling block to finding him. Religion reflects both the truths of God's general revelation and mankind's rebellion against God's lordship in creation. We gladly acknowledge that the religions of the world contain truth about God and his proclamation of the gospel. Paul clearly did this at Lystra; he used the people's understanding of God as Creator as his starting point. In his address to the Areopagus, he quoted with approval the pagan poets who had a true understanding of humanity created in the image of God. Many evangelists in India have been able to use their knowledge of Sanskrit, the Hindu scriptures, and the poetry of the Indian saints to good advantage. Narayan Vaman Tilak, the Brahmin convert who became the Charles Wesley of Marathi hymnology claimed that he came to Christ "across the bridge of Tukaram."[17]

The resurrection has always been associated with the great triumph of Christ. The christological hymn of Philippians 2 presents this victory immediately after presenting the humiliation of Christ,

> Therefore God exalted him to the highest place and gave him the name that is above every name, that at the name of Jesus every knee should bow, in heaven and on earth and under the earth, and every tongue acknowledge that Jesus Christ is Lord, to the glory of God the Father (Phil 2:9–11).

This victory of Christ gives us the boldness to follow him as Lord of our lives and pay whatever price to do it. This is how the disciples, especially Peter, were transformed into bold people, after they saw the risen Lord. With the victorious Christ as their Lord they were willing to pay the price of obedience.

Christ died and made salvation possible once and for all. Anyone who believes in the Lord Jesus Christ will be saved by grace, not by works (karma). Nobody will be saved unless God reveals Himself to him (John 1:12; 3:16; Rom 10:9–10). We humans will be saved from sin and curses only through confession, not by our own merit making.

On the other hand, we have to deal with moral guilt. Sinful acts are always a violation of divine law. Due to sin, humanity falls short of the

---

16. Fernando, *The Supremacy of Christ*, 187.
17. Ibid., 40.

divine expectation. "For all have sinned and fall short of the glory of God" (Rom 3:23). Having fallen short of the divine standard, we therefore stand convicted and guilty before God. Paul, speaking within the Graeco-Roman and Jewish contexts, views salvation in a variety of ways: forgiveness, redemption, reconciliation, adoption, victory over the kingdom of darkness, and justification. However, when he speaks of the central message of the Gospel, he emphasizes justification, devoting ample space to its presentation, primarily in the letters to the Romans and Galatians and partly in 2 Corinthians 5:18–21, and Philippians 3:10f. The truth that God pardons and accepts repentant sinners is at the heart of the biblical message, and sets Christianity apart from other religions as the religion of pardoning grace and saving faith.

A recently influential theological system, pioneered in Roman Catholic circles, is associated with Karl Rahner, Hans Kung and Raimundo Panikkar. Like Barth, these people, stress the efficacy of the work of Christ, see salvation extending to people independent of explicit faith in Christ. They took a further step, however, which Barth would have firmly denounced. They saw the 'sacraments' of other religions as a means of salvation. Practices like Buddhist almsgiving and Hindu rites were viewed as sacraments which bring salvation. Rahner described the saved people of other religions as 'anonymous Christians'. Kung refers to the non-Christian religions as the 'ordinary' way to salvation whereas Christianity is a 'very special and extraordinary' way to salvation.[18]

A brilliant Hindu scholar, Pandita Ramabai (1858–1922), who was committed to improving the lot of women in India, began a movement to help in this and often gave lectures on the topic of karma and moksha (work and salvation). She became friendly with a Christian English woman, principal of a teacher training school, who agreed to teach her English, and through whom she was introduced to the New Testament. She was deeply impressed by Christ's loving and courteous attitude toward women. Soon, though she was a Hindu, she began to quote almost exclusively from the gospels in her lectures. She later went to England and, as a result of meeting a community of Anglican sisters, was baptized as a Christian. But she had not yet grasped the meaning of salvation by grace through faith. She changed her religion because she had become a follower of Jesus. Many

---

18. Ibid., 173.

years later she experienced the joy of a personal relationship with the Saviour Jesus, which made her one of God's great agents of revival in India.[19]

The apostle Paul first lived a life which was against God. He was a persecutor of the Christian church in the New Testament. But God loved him and changed him. He became a chosen vessel in the hand of God. He was one of the important apostles of the New Testament church. The Lord used him to plant many churches in the then known world. Moreover, he was able to write many epistles to the churches that had been established by him.

In Kerala, India, there was a notorious thief named Rajan. He had stolen idols from Hindu temples and was never caught. Later somebody shared the gospel with him and he was saved. All his sins were washed away. No punishment remained according to his past works (karma). This is the peculiarity of the message of the gospel of Christ. Our past sins, done in ignorance, will never be remembered. They will never affect the person in the life after death, as he or she became a new person in Christ. The Bible says that if anyone is in Christ, he is a new creation (2 Cor 5:17).

Is there a Creator God who will Judge Us According to our Karma?

As long as we live, breathe, and reincarnate, the Buddhists teach that we will continue to create karma. It is nearly impossible to completely eliminate karma. Elimination can only be accomplished after achieving moksha or nirvana, the states of our souls evolving to perfection. With moksha you will have fulfilled all the missions of your soul and will not reincarnate again. And very few people throughout history have achieved nirvana while still in their physical bodies.

According to Buddhism, the fundamental cause of suffering is ignorance regarding the true nature of existence. The Christian faith would claim that it is rebellion against God that is the root cause of the human predicament. It is therefore, a creation-fall-centered message that will speak to the Buddhist way of thinking.[20] The Buddhist definition has no vertical dimension to it. Even though the law of karma is behind the retribution, sin is committed against one's own self and not against any supreme being. Here we need to proclaim human depravity and moral accountability to

---

19. Ibid., 64.
20. Ibid., 158.

a holy God. The Buddhist anthropology of the person as a sum of states, weakens moral accountability. Since the law of karma is the final point of orientation of all things, true repentance must involve the rejection of the supremacy of the law of karma and submission to the authority of Christ the omnipotent Lord.

What Does Free-will Mean to a Buddhist?

Refuting the erroneous view that "whatsoever fortune or misfortune experienced is all due to some previous action," the Buddha said:

> So, then, according to this view, owing to previous action humans will become murderers, thieves, unchaste, liars, slanderers, covetous, malicious and perverts. Thus, for those who fall back on the former deeds as the essential reason, there is neither the desire to do, nor effort to do, nor necessity to do this deed, or abstain from this deed.[21]

We understand that God of the Bible gave free-will to human beings in order that they might choose right or wrong. This is nothing to do with a person's past, but each one is responsible for him or herself. In eternity, everyone will be rewarded according to his deeds (Matt 16:26).

In Buddhism, sin does not move the heart of God or knock hard on God's door. In contrast, the grace of Jesus Christ is costly grace. Jesus Christ had to suffer and die upon the cross on Calvary for the sins of humankind and for the redemption of all people. It is through the karma of repentance that people may receive forgiveness. After receiving forgiveness, it is only through the sublimated karma of love that Christians can advance.

The belief that all physical circumstances and mental attitudes spring solely from past karma was what Buddha contradicted. If the present life is totally conditioned or wholly controlled by our past actions, then certainly karma is tantamount to fatalism determinism, or predestination. If this were true, free will would be an absurdity. Life would be purely mechanistic, not much different from a machine. Being created by an almighty God who controls our destinies and predetermines our future, or being produced by an irresistible karma that completely determines our fate and controls our life's course, independent of any free action on our part, is essentially the same. The only difference lies in the two words God and karma

---

21. Devasthan, *Theology of Buddhism*, 152.

is that one could easily be substituted for the other, because the ultimate operation of both forces would be identical. Such a fatalistic doctrine is the Buddhist law of karma.

Is There an Intermediate Stage Right after Death?

In Buddhist understanding, when a sentient being leaves one existence, it is reborn either as a human being, a celestial being, (Deva or Brahma), an inferior animal, or a denizen of one of the regions of hell. The sceptics and the ignorant people held that there are intermediate stages—*antrabhava*—between these; and that there are beings who are neither of the human, the celestial, the Deva or the Brahma worlds, nor of any one of the stages of existence recognized in the scriptures but are in an intermediate stage.[22] Some assert that these transitional stages are possessed of the Five Khandhas (Five Aggregates) which are: matter *(rupa)*; feeling *(vedana)*; perception *(sanna)*; mental-activities *(sankhara)*; and consciousness *(vinnana)*.

The Bible does not speak of an intermediate stage in which the human soul rests. Eccl 12:7 says that "then the dust shall return to the earth as it was, and the spirit shall return to God who gave it." Matthew 25:46 says that "And these will go away into eternal punishment; but the righteous into eternal life."

Is Nirvana Possible within Christianity?

The so-called Buddhist progression into nirvana, the absolute, is in reality a regression into the void.[23] The biblical proclamation of salvation as the bliss of fellowship with God and the ecstasy of union with one's maker, though it seems to be contrary to the Buddhist notion of salvation, may be the most appropriate doctrine to speak to the Buddhist void.

The ultimate goal, even of the Mahayanist, is total extinction, although there is minimization of the opposition between nirvana and *samsara*. As in Hinayana, in Mahayana too, the concept of nirvana is divided into two spheres: (a) active nirvana (*apratisthita*) wherein the individual has attained sainthood but chooses not to become extinct but rather to live on as a transcendent bodhisattva and (b) static nirvana (*pratisthita*) wherein

---

22. Harvey, *Buddhism*, 189.
23. Ibid., 98.

the liberated one loses individuality at the moment of death and is now in the absolute.[24]

The realization or awareness that one is already liberated does not arise to consciousness because of ignorance and craving. Therefore, in order to attain liberation these two preventative causes must be rooted out. The realization is that *sunyata* (emptiness) is the reality in all appearances. Even buddhahood and nirvana are seen as illusory ideas useful for the purpose of attaining liberation. This realization alters the attitude of the person radically.

The doctrine of the Buddha is a path or vehicle used to cross from the shore of worldly experience, ignorance, suffering and craving to the other side of transcendental wisdom. This is liberation from suffering or extinction. The Four Noble Truths explain the origin and cessation of suffering and the Eight-Fold Path enumerated the way that leads to the cessation of suffering. The way to deliverance is called the Middle Way because it teaches that in order to attain liberation one must avoid two extremes—self mortification on the one hand and sensual indulgence on the other. The Middle Way is the humanistic ethic; it is rooted in discipline and self-reliance and hence its appeal to intellectuals.

Nirvana is not a place but a state of non-being. It speaks of non-reality while the Christian doctrine of salvation speaks of reality, reality in the ultimate. While in heaven, according to Christianity, corruption puts on incorruption, and mortality puts on immortality. In the concept of nirvana, one moves into the formless and the void. One speaks of fullness of life while the other speaks of the extinction of life and non-becoming. The Buddha asked people to work out their own salvation without any objective teleology as is found in the biblical revelation. So, the obvious gaps between the Buddhist and Christian concepts of salvation are evident and there is no way to minimize the difference, only to present the all-sufficient Christ.

The total dissimilarity between the nature of salvation in Buddhism and Christianity is evident when we see the Buddhist concept of the person. The individual is merely an aggregate of the five *khandhas* mentioned earlier. There is no real, objective individuality. Salvation itself is the realization of this no-selfness (*anatta*) and the awareness of voidness (*sunnyata*). We could say that Buddhist salvation is obliteration of the individual personality. The belief in the individual personality is considered an erroneous belief within Buddhism. The nature of salvation experience

---

24. Gnanakan, *Salvation*, 150.

in Buddhism has nothing to do with experiencing deliverance from sin or receiving forgiveness. The relentless, impersonal law of karma operates and one stores up or diminishes one's capacity of merit by good works. The moment of salvation is the eradication of ignorance and desire, even the desire to be liberated, rather than freedom from sin.[25]

Buddhism negates the concept of eternal life and discourages speculation as to the beginning and end of the world. The reason is that it is assumed that such speculation does not contribute positively towards the goal of achieving liberation. The contrast in regard to the ultimate state in Buddhism and Christianity is quite stark. Nirvana is extinction or non-becoming while the ultimate state in Christianity is fullness of becoming in heaven.

The ultimate reality of nirvana is formless and empty while in Christianity the ultimate is a personal God with whom is salvation and the restoration of true fellowship for all people. The Absolute is a personal creator God.[26]

How Can One Be Forgiven Through the Sacrificial Death of Christ?

Buddhism is proud of the fact that it has a means of salvation that is based on self-deliverance through knowledge and wisdom. Even the Buddha did not ask for faith in himself nor in his teachings. What is necessary to attain liberation is to understand the Four Noble Truths and follow the Noble Eight-Fold path by right action. The self-deliverance of Buddhism is based on the law of karma, cause and effect. It is ethical retribution through *prajna* (wisdom), *samadhi* (concentration) and *sila* (morality). There is no principle of grace or forgiveness, strictly speaking. Even though ultimate liberation is the fruit of one's own doing in recourse to other powers such as bodhisattvas there is an accommodation of this position. The bodhisattvas look after the ones who seek their help graciously. The transference of karmic merit alters the self-deliverance concept substantially, even though the liberating insight has to be gained ultimately by the follower.[27]

The message of sacrifice for sin can make Christianity appear as an abhorrent bloody religion to Buddhists who are taught to revere all kinds

---

25. Ibid., 156.
26. Ibid., 156.
27. Ibid., 157.

of life. But they find the life of Jesus very attractive. This opens them to the Christian message which may ultimately lead them to accept the gospel and believe the message of the cross. This concept of sacrificing for others is found even in religions hostile to the idea of Christ dying for sins. Stephen Neill refers to "the immense part that the idea and the practice of sacrifice have played in the thoughts and the worship of the human race as far back as we can trace clearly human consciousness."[28]

Irenaeus' view of God's redemption is presented in his most comprehensive idea of the *recapitulation,* that is the restoring and the perfecting of creation by the work of Christ as head of a new humanity. It is God's new way of restoration, not by overturning, but by continuing and fulfilling creation. The history of the old Adam needs to be repeated in a totally different direction by the new Adam.[29]

Sin is infinitely evil before God, and we humans are totally impotent to achieve our own salvation. In addition, only by faith in Christ can anyone be given all the gracious benefits of salvation. Due to sin, we face a two-sided existential problem. On the one hand, we are morally corrupt, so corrupt and distorted, we are unable to purify ourselves. St. Augustine best represented the Pauline concept of humanity's moral corruption and bondage to sin in the following statements: (1) Being created in God's image, it was possible for Adam not to sin, (2) After the fall, it was impossible for humans not to sin; (3) After conversion, it is possible for the believer to sin, and (4) After resurrection, it is impossible for the saint to sin.[30]

It is burdensome when religious activities are repeated constantly to the point where they create guilty feelings and become tiresome. It is even worse when they lack any prospect of the assurance of salvation. The biblical concept of salvation can fully serve as good news to free people from the burden of Buddhist (or any other religion's) laws, as well as from inadequate righteousness, faith and obedience to that law. Believers should make their presence felt in a positive, constructive way in the community, with a high sensitivity to those around them. Through prayer, assembly, education, health and social projects, a Christian creates an openness to the mind and the lives of her Buddhist friends and family members. With extreme sensitivity, they live and speak out their faith.

---

28. Fernando, *The Supremacy of Christ*, 132.
29. Ibid., 51.
30. Gnanakan, *Salvation*, 63.

The constant uplifting of this aspect of the biblical concept of salvation, namely, the sovereign act to declare humanity's righteousness by God will present an opening into Buddhist minds. It has to be proven that God's action, including the provision of a Savior, the preparation for the arrival of the Savior, the sacrifice of the righteous Savior, the proclamation of the good news of righteousness by faith, and the ethical removal of the condemnation in the day of judgement, are all the sovereign act of the divine. The object and the content of saving faith in Christianity is the person and the finished work of Jesus Christ on Calvary as the substitution for sin. This view counteracts the one held by Buddhism. The question, therefore, is how the great grace of God in Christ can be understood and accepted in the Buddhist mind.[31]

Salvation must be seen as the dethronement of the existing center of one's life and the enthronement of Christ. Since the overriding emphasis of Buddhism is self-deliverance, the doctrine of justification by faith has particular relevance and importance in the content of the message. The experience of being "born again" can be more easily understood by Buddhists if it is presented as "enlightenment" (*buddhi*), about the Lord Jesus Christ and his power.

We are privileged to obtain forgiveness through Jesus Christ. The death of Christ also motivates us to forgive others who have harmed us. Louis XII had many enemies before he became king of France. After becoming king, he had a list made of those who had tried to harm him, and marked a large black cross against each of their names. When they knew this, his enemies fled, taking it as a sign that the king was going to punish them. But the king allayed their fears and promised them pardon. He said he put the crosses beside each name to remind them of the cross of Christ.[32]

Buddhism teaches that sinful people may be justified on the basis of each one's inherent or earned righteousness. This is impossible, however, because humans can never be good or righteous enough to be acceptable to God. As the prophet declared, "All of us have become like one who is unclean, and all our righteous acts are like filthy rages; we all shrivel up like a leaf, and like the wind our sins sweep us away" (Isa 64:6). "We have already made the charge that the Jew and Gentile alike are all under sin" (Rom 3:9) "so that every mouth may be silenced and the whole world held accountable to God" (3:19). The bankruptcy of self-righteousness as the

---

31. Fernando, *The Supremacy of Christ*, 105.
32. Fernando, *The Supremacy of Christ*, 105.

basis of acquittal before God is clearly shown. The blood of Jesus Christ God's son cleanses us from all sin (1 John 1:7).

Is Christ the Supreme Bodhisattva?

In the proclamation of the salvation message would it not be appropriate to proclaim Christ as the immortal, infinite, uncreated, un-originated, supreme bodhisattva? Christ's *kenosis,* incarnation, substitutionary death and glorious resurrection generated an infinite quantum of *kusala* (merit) which is able to cancel the evil (*akusala*) of all humanity. When Christ is seen as the supreme merit Transferor, he is seen also as Savior. We must go on and affirm that he is the only savior also. This karmic Christology may be the answer the Buddhist void is waiting for.

At the very heart of the Christian gospel is the belief that Jesus is God incarnate. Christianity is founded upon the person and work of Jesus; Buddhism is based not on the person but on the teachings of the Buddha. Buddhism and Hinduism teach that salvation is attained through what one does; Christianity says salvation is based on what Christ has done. Hindu and New Age pantheism say we are all part of the divine. Christianity says that we are created by God, who is transcendent and separate from us.

Humankind not only seeks after God but rebels against God at the same time. This predicament is seen in the goal of vedantic religion. "*Aham Brahma asmi*," (I am God). This goes to the heart of the nature of the fall, as Kraemer noted.[33] If idolatry is the collective religious expression of human depravity, then it is inherent in all religious expressions including those which deny idolatry such as Islam, Judaism and Christianity in particular. All religious traditions can fall prey to idolatry.

The philosophic systems of the so-called higher religions are generally stumbling blocks to the gospel of God's grace to all. The law of karma in Buddhism, "people reap what they sow" is a wonderful starting point for preaching the true nature of salvation. The awareness of ethical principles, order, discipline and desire as a cause of suffering in Buddhism are all entrance points for the gospel.

The heart of the good news of the gospel is encapsulated in John 3:16. God does not want anyone to perish but everyone to come to repentance (2 Pet 3:9). God in his eternal love created humans male and female, in his own image so that they might enter into a relationship of holy love with

---

33. Gnanakan, *Salvation*, 40.

their creator God and walk in fellowship with him. The biblical record from Genesis to Revelation is the story of this universal and steadfast love.

With the coming of Jesus Christ, the Incarnate Son of God, the central focus is the exclusiveness of faith in him. His own claim is unequivocal, "I am the way, the truth, and the life. No one comes to the Father except through me" (John 14:6). He is the only way to God. As Peter expressed it, "there is one God and one mediator between God and mankind, the man Christ Jesus" (1 Tim 2:5). The so-called gods worshipped by others are either non-existent beings, or they are the agents of demonic powers. Thus unbelievers are without God and without hope in the world. To the Asian mind this exclusiveness is intolerable, Christian boasting is not in the fact that God has chosen us for we are insignificant people, but we find glory in the cross of Christ—a stumbling block to the Hindus and foolishness to the Buddhists.

Christ's wonderful characteristics of holiness and marvelous power, as fully acknowledged by the Buddhists, can serve as meeting points of thought that cross-bearers can make use of, to explain his right to impart righteousness to those who receive him as personal Savior. These are parts of the content of faith in the concept of salvation that can attract the attention of Buddhists.

Jesus fulfils the aspirations of Buddhism and many parallels between the Buddhist scriptures and the Old Testament. Today this is how he approaches Buddhists. Our point then is that even though sacrifice sounds strange to some, our deepest instincts agree with it. We could trace these instincts to remnants of the image of God in each human and to the original revelation of God to the human race. We can preach Christ crucified. We should convince all that we will be saved not through our merit, rather we will attain our salvation (*moksha*) through the grace of the Lord Jesus Christ.

Conclusion

Obviously, there is so much more to be said than can be covered in this chapter. This brief example should be a start for other questions and conversations. Genuine and open dialogue with people of other faiths is essential to our evangelistic task. Evangelical theologians and mission practitioners in Asia must take their initiative in the formulation of the doctrine of salvation and all other doctrines from the Scripture according to their particular

Asian contexts. Let us be faithful to the teachings of the Scripture and at the same time be sensitive to our own cultural contexts in such a way that we may be able to communicate the gospel more effectively to all people. Through dialogue let us listen and learn to what God is saying to us and to the world.

Bibliography

Conre, Edward. *Buddhism: Its Essence and Development.* New York: Harper and Row, 1959.
De Silva, Lynn A. *Buddhism: Beliefs and Practices in Sri Lanka*, Colombo: De Silva, 1974.
Devasthan, Jyot. *Theology of Buddhism.* Delhi: Dominant, 2000.
Fernando, Ajith. *The Supremacy of Christ.* Bangalore: Theological Book Trust, 1996.
George. Author's interview with this Missionary among the Andaman Buddhists, 2016.
Gnanakan, Ken. *Salvation: Some Asian Perspectives.* Bangalore: Asia Theological, 1992.
Harvey, Peter, editor. *Buddhism.* New York: Continuum, 2001.
Radhakrishnan, S. *Indian Philosophy.* New York: Oxford University Press, 1999.
Pongi. Interview with this Buddhist monk, Port Blair, Andaman and Nicobar Islands, India, 2016.
Schmidt-Leukel, Perry. *Buddhism and Christianity*, Delhi: ISPCK, 2005.

8

How Cultural Reciprocity Practices Reinforce Merit-Making Affecting the Experience of God's Grace

Sheryl Takagi Silzer

As a third-generation Japanese American, I didn't realize the extent to which my Asian reciprocity practices contributed to merit-making values that were embedded in my soul. I felt driven to work and do things that I thought were required of a missionary and did not know how to say "no" when asked to take on extra assignments. After twenty-five years of cross-cultural service I was diagnosed with cancer. My illness caused me to examine the reasons for my drive to work, and in the process I discovered that my Asian cultural practices hindered me from experiencing God's grace.

This chapter describes how the Asian cultural practice of reciprocity fosters merit-making that hinders a person's experience of God's grace. It first looks at Asian cultural reciprocity practices and compares these practices with karmic merit-making beliefs. Then it compares the cultural practices and the karmic beliefs with Scripture to reveal how cultural reciprocity practices keep people from experiencing God's grace. A greater understanding of how Asian cultural practices influence Buddhist practices can assist Christ followers to present the good news of God's grace to people in karmic communities who are acculturated to live up to societal expectations and to earn favor from others.

Part II: Cultural Perspectives

Asian Cultural Reciprocity Practices[1]

Although sociologists, anthropologists, and other scholars have examined reciprocity in many different cultures, the theories they developed come from a non-Asian perspective based on a single person with individual choice and freedom.[2] These individualistic perspectives define reciprocal practices as a transaction in which some kind of exchange takes place that does not imply reciprocation[3] and does not imply a long-term relationship.[4] The non-Asian focus of these studies has also been on the material aspects of giving. In Mauss's seminal book, *The Gift*, he says "exchange and contracts take place in the form of presents."[5] Reciprocity is also defined in terms of an equal return, a transaction or an exchange. However, the way that reciprocity works in Asian relationships is quite different, and therefore may not be adequately understood.[6]

In Asian cultures, reciprocal practices form the basis for relationships that combine benefits, favors, and/or benevolence. It is a sign of friendship to have an on-going debt or obligation of return that can never be fully repaid.[7] If the debt is fully paid, that signals the end of the relationship.[8] Although there is a sense of back and forth of reciprocity, the return may also be given to someone else who the person knows.[9] Asian reciprocal practices also have a moral sense of right and wrong.[10] See below for examples of reciprocity.

The Asian view of reciprocity grows out of the definition of the person in relationships rather than as an individual person. Markus and Kitayama describe the Asian self as an interdependent self and the American self as

---

1. The term "Asian cultures" in this paper focuses on the East Asian cultures of China, Japan, and Korea while the term "non-Asian" primarily refers to a North American or western perspective.

2. Yu, "Confucius Relational Self," 282.

3. MacCormack, "Reciprocity," 91.

4. Yeung and Tung, "Achieving Business Success," 55.

5. Maus, *The Gift*, 3.

6. Adloff and Mau, "Giving Social Ties," 95; Yen et al., "Exploring the Mediating Role of Trust," 172.

7. Being indebted for a kind act is not considered a mark of friendship or an on-going relationship in non-Asian (or American) culture.

8. Lebra, *Japanese Patterns of Behavior*, 91.

9. Moody, "Serial Reciprocity," 131.

10. Yang, *Gifts, Favors, & Banquets*, 68.

an independent self.[11] Asian relationships are fixed at birth, while American relationships are chosen by the individual. The Asian person derives identity from their relatedness to others rather than to themselves. With the interdependent self "the emphasis is attending to others, fitting in, and harmonious interdependence... rather than attending to the self by discovering and expressing their unique inner attributes." Hwang uses the phrase "Chinese relationalism" to define the Chinese based persons-in-relation.[12]

Hofstede found that his four dimensions of culture did not adequately describe Asian cultures and, as a result of studying Chinese culture, added a fifth dimension—long term orientation necessary for relationships. This dimension includes an "ordering of relationships by status and having a sense of shame."[13] These characteristics are also found in cultures that have been described as "hierarchical." A Hierarching culture has Strong Structure (relationships ordered by various categories such as status, gender, age, social class, etc.) and Strong Community (where people have a sense of honor or shame from expectations to uphold the reputation of the group).[14]

In the Asian social hierarchy everyone has a place and everyone knows their place. With a set and stratified social structure, there are also clearly defined social roles and expectations for a person's behavior in their role.[15] A person's identity is derived from belonging to a particular family/group or community and is validated by fulfilling the expectations of their stratified social role. Hierarching cultures also have a strong sense of loyalty and trust with others in their group and a strong sense of distrust of people who are not in their group.[16] Loyalty and trust develop over time as group members fulfill their social obligations to share and reciprocate resources, both material and spiritual.

The Asian stratified society is shaped by the five hierarchical Confucian relationships (rulers and subjects, parents and children, husbands and wives, older and younger people, and friends with friends). This hierarchy determines people's social roles and the expected behaviors of each role.[17] These roles also follow the natural course of the universe based on the fam-

---

11. Markus and Kitayama, "Culture and the Self," 224–226.
12. Hwang, "Face and Favor," 170.
13. Robertson, "The Global Dispersion of Chinese Values," 236.
14. Shin and Silzer, *Tapestry of Grace*, 142–143.
15. Douglas, "The Normative Debate," 142–145.
16. Ibid., 138–140.
17. Schwartz, 1985, 67–68.

ily unit. When people behave according to their social role, it is believed that society will be more harmonious and that disagreements and conflicts will be minimized.[18] When people behave according to their social role, they also develop a particular virtue creating a sense of morality in fulfilling their social obligations.[19]

The cardinal virtue for all relationships is filial piety, which is repayment or reciprocity by the child to the parent for the care, provisions, emotional support, etc. that they received during their upbringing. The repayment of one's social obligation is not only for material resources but is also for spiritual resources such as protection, loyalty, and respect.[20] This filial behavior is a model for the expected behavior of any person towards anyone who is older or has a higher status. As such, one's parents provide a model for the child to behave appropriately towards others in society.[21] If a child does not behave appropriately, the parents are blamed for not teaching the appropriate behavior.

As people fulfill the expectations within each of the five relationships, they develop specific virtues in each relationship.[22] The ruler develops benevolence in his relationship with his subject, while the subject develops loyalty. The father develops kindness, while the child develops filial duty. The husband develops righteousness, while the wife develops submission. The elder brother develops gentleness, while the younger brother develops deference.[23] Fulfilling social roles develops the virtues that characterize a moral man as well as characterize the relationships people have. As such, the expectation for fulfilling Asian social roles establishes a moral system.

Behavior that favors people with whom one has a close relationship can be termed benevolence (*ren*); respecting those for whom respect is required by the relationship is called righteousness (*yi*); and acting according to previously established rites or social norms is called propriety (*li*).[24]

The essential characteristic of Asian social roles (relationships) is reciprocity, that is, giving back what you have been given or providing help for others as you have received help. Reciprocity is based on a sense

---

18. Tu, "Confucius and Confucianism," 12.
19. Ibid., 256.
20. Hwang, "Face and Favor," 170.
21. Lai, "*Confucian Moral Thinking.*" 258.
22. Cheng, *New Dimensions of Confucian and Neo-Confucian Philosophy*, 222.
23. Hwang, "Face and Favor," 170.
24. Ibid., 168.

of indebtedness that generates obligations that are guided by one's social role. Filial piety is the basis for Asian social roles and is expressed through fulfilling the expectations of a person's social role. Some specific ways that children can reciprocate care to their parents is to honor and obey them in their daily lives, produce male heirs, honor their ancestors, and mourn and offer sacrifices after that person has died.[25] As a person first learns to reciprocate within the family, they then know how to act towards others.

In society, these relationships take on a more complex structure, which in Chinese is called *guanxi* 關係 or 系 (*kwankye* in Korean and *kankei* in Japanese). The two characters in *guanxi* represent "gate" and "connection."[26] Su says that *guanxi* is based on two codes: one is the code of brotherhood and the other is the code of reciprocity. Originally people pooled and exchanged resources in order to survive and the practice continues to this day within *guanxi*.[27]

These reciprocal practices not only enable the person to fulfill the obligations of their social role but also strengthen the relationship. Qi describes *guanxi* relationships as reflecting social norms for interpersonal behavior that includes reciprocity and obligation.

> *Guanxi* involves personal connections between individuals in their formation and maintenance of long term relationships which follow implicit social norms . . . These norms include: *xinyong* (trustworthiness), *mianzi* (face), *renqing* (norms of interpersonal behavior), reciprocity and obligation.[28]

Hwang describes the complexity of reciprocity practices as follows:

> [N]orms of reciprocity *(bao)* are intense, but these norms are heavily shaped by the hierarchically structured network of social relations (*guanxi*) in which people are embedded, by the public nature of obligations, and by long time periods over which obligations are incurred through a self-conscious manipulation of face and related symbols.[29]

Throughout a person's life, family members care for one another by sharing resources, both physical and spiritual, and that sharing comes with

---

25. Li, "Shifting Perspectives," 21.
26. Yeung and Tung, 1996, 54–65.
27. Su et al., "Enabling *Guanxi* Management in China," 303.
28. Qi, "Guanxi, Social Capital and Beyond," 309.
29. Hwang, "Face and Favor," 944.

the obligation to reciprocate that strengthens and maintains the relationship over time. This pattern expands to include others outside the family as a person develops a relationship with people they meet in their place of birth, school, or workplace. As each person develops relationships, they have access to more resources. As a person develops a relationship with another person, they also have access to the people in the other person's network. Anyone in your network can be an intermediary by introducing you to people in their network. The value of this practice is that an intermediary person can connect people who are unfamiliar but who have gained trust from fulfilling their obligations.[30] Intermediaries can also share knowledge or provide access to knowledge.[31] These *guanxi* relationships are so foundational that they often take priority over organizational or legal law to protect obligations.[32]

As these reciprocal exchanges foster connections between individuals, they also develop a sense of warmth, emotion, and trust. That is, as a person gives and reciprocates, he can be judged to be trustworthy if he gives and reciprocates appropriately. This develops a feeling of warmth or emotional connection between the individuals.

There are different ties of *guanxi* relationships depending on the nature of the relationship. In each tie the reciprocity practices have a different base. The first group is the family relationship or what are called "expressive ties" in which relationships not only have an emotional *renqing* component but are also considered permanent and stable. What is given is that which is perceived to be necessary for living. There is no limit to what can be given and there is not a set time frame for reciprocity.[33]

Due to globalization and the availability of goods outside the family network, another tie of *guanxi* relationships is called "instrumental ties" that include people outside the family network that are not intended to be part of a long-term relationship or have an emotional component that develops trust. The purpose of instrumental ties is to obtain material goals that do not have the same emotional component as the expressive tie as

---

30. Bian and Ang, "Guanxi Networks and Job Mobility in China and Singapore," 985.

31. Zhou et al., "Internationalization and the Performance of Born-Global SME's," 677.

32. Chang, "The Dilemma of *Renqing* Processes," 483.

33. Hwang, "Face and Favor," 949–950.

they are unstable and temporary. The exchange should be equal and paid as agreed.[34]

The third tie is called "mixed ties" which are a combination of the above two and includes people from one's home area, school, neighbors, relatives, colleagues, and teachers. This group is not as strong as family ties that last forever but they last as long as there is frequent interaction between the two parties. This tie operates by what is called the rule of *renqing* (obligation, favor) and *mianzi* (face).

It is also important to know how to reciprocate in such a way that you are viewed as a trustworthy and moral person. This includes when, what, and how to reciprocate or how your actions reflect face work. As you reciprocate you develop a reputation. If you do it well or according to social expectations, your reputation remains strong. When you share resources with those who are not as fortunate, your reputation also gets enhanced. Yeung and Tung say that "the primary deterrent against immoral behavior or illegal behavior is shame."[35] Relationships take time to develop, enabling a series of reciprocal interactions that builds up a person's trustworthy reputation. This enables other people to observe your behavior and they can vouch for your reputation. Barbalet speaks of reciprocity as requiring "public visibility" and "third party sanction."[36] If others do not consider your actions appropriate to your position, they sanction you by shaming you.[37] They do this by gossip or even by public disclosure in the media. This results in the loss of face.[38]

Face work is necessary not only "to maintain face but to also do face work in front of others within the same social network."[39] As a result "an individual's *mianzi* is a function of their perceived social position and prestige within their social network."[40] A person can have ascribed status due to their family reputation, place of birth, age, etc. or they can achieve status from use of knowledge, experience, wealth, authority, etc. that benefits oth-

---

34. Ibid., 950–952.

35. Yeung and Tung, "Achieving Business Success in Chinese Confucian Societies," 55, 57.

36. Barbalet, "The Structure of Guanxi," 52.

37. Yeung and Tung, "Achieving Business Success in Chinese Confucian Societies," 55–57.

38. Barbalet, "The Structure of Guanxi," 52.

39. Hwang, "Face and Favor," 960.

40. Ibid., 961.

ers. In the Chinese relational society, it is necessary not just to look at the individual alone but also to their relationships, networks, as well as material status markers such as possessions. When a member of one's group is suffering the loss of face, it is important to know how to save face as well as to give face. It is easier to address face loss when a person has built up a store of social capital or *renqing* by doing things for others.[41]

Asian reciprocal relations are quite complicated and are very different from non-Asian reciprocity where it is often sufficient to say, "thank you" for a gift received or a favor done on a person's behalf with no similar expectation of reciprocity. The different definition of the person—individual or part of a group—creates the context for giving. With the collective definition of the person in Asia, favors are done or gifts are given with the expectation that they will be reciprocated at some time in the future. If this reciprocity is not done appropriately, others will disapprove and the person needs to correct their actions in order to save not only their own face but to also save the face or reputation of the group to which they belong. The potential long-term nature of a relationship can be cut short abruptly if the proper anticipated response is lacking. Favors and gifts are not necessarily returned to the person but can be given to someone else in the person's network.

The Asian person fulfills their social role through reciprocity practices. Buddhist beliefs in good works and merit-making karma also align with Confucian social roles through the cultural practice of reciprocity. That is, as a person shares or reciprocates, they fulfill the social expectations of their role as well as earn merit or karma.[42]

Merit-Making Karmic Beliefs

The Confucian social hierarchy establishes the framework for how reciprocity works by fulfilling the obligations of one's social roles. Buddhist beliefs provide the motivation for reciprocal obligations and merit-making karma. By doing good works, people receive the benefit of increased karma that they believe will lead to nirvana or a better situation in the next life. Karma can be described in terms of one's past and present deeds and is similar to a reward.[43] As work or activities, karmic activities also have a

---

41. Ibid., 961.
42. Shin and Silzer, *Tapestry of Grace*, 152.
43. Walsh, "The Economics of Salvation," 360.

"residual effect, trace, or result"[44] that is both physical and psychic.[45] That is, karmic activity is not just the action but also the effect of the action. The effect is not just energy expended but also contains some psychic elements of the person. Shin and Silzer also describe Asians in terms of the integration of spiritual and material.[46] If there is a concentration of good karma, the results will be more beneficial than if the concentration is negative. That is, actions that bring a sense of well-being and happiness lead to good karma, while actions that lead to negative emotional states such as worry, dissatisfaction, or various kinds of suffering lead to negative karma.[47]

Buddhism seeks to free people from suffering by explaining its causes due to the impermanence of life.[48] The Four Noble Truths help people recognize the source of the suffering and how to get rid of it. The first Noble Truth is that suffering *dukkha* (worries and anxieties) exists from life itself (birth, illness, death, being separated from a loved one, etc.). The second Noble Truth is that the cause of this suffering (worries and anxieties) comes from desiring the wrong things. The third Noble Truth is that these wrong desires can be replaced by doing the right things. The fourth Noble Truth explains the way to do the right things through the Eightfold Path of Truth that can lead to nirvana (quietude, a calm and tranquil state).[49]

The things that people do are their actions. Both past and present actions form people's karma. Each action is either good or bad. When people view their actions in terms of cause and effect, they do things to increase or enhance their karma. Ariyabuddihiphongs cites the three main activities of Buddhists as doing good deeds, observing the five precepts, and meditating.[50] All of these activities result in merit-making karma.

Although these merit-making activities appear to focus on the individual, the Asian Buddhist is always aware of the social context for his or her activities. In fact, they view meditation as a means to break away from individualism or narcissism.[51] There is also an aspect of social recognition

---

44. Ghose, "'Karma' and the Possibility of Purification," 266.
45. Kalghatgi, "The Doctrine of Karma in Jaina Philosophy," 229.
46. Shin and Silzer, *Tapestry of Grace*, 124.
47. Gyatso, *Buddhism in the Tibetan Tradition*, 32–33.
48. Bhagat, *Ancient Indian Asceticism*, 160.
49. Kishimoto, "Some Japanese Cultural Traits and Religions," 115.
50. Ariyabuddihiphongs, "Buddhist Belief in Merit," 192.
51. Epstein, *Thoughts Without a Thinker*, 48.

that validates one's karma.[52] People validate their karma by telling stories about their karma and receive affirmation from those who hear their stories.[53] They also believe that doing good things or earning merit will also negate past bad deeds.[54]

Similar to Confucian thinking, Buddhists also view the world through an integrated and interdependent lens.[55] Everything in the world is connected, including humans to nature as well as the people who have already passed on. The difficulty for some non-Asians to understand the Buddhist concept of no-self arises from the heritage of dualistic thinking that separates the spiritual from the physical.[56] The collective focus of Asian culture comes not only from Confucian beliefs and practices but also from Buddhist merit-making karmic beliefs and practices. These religious influences shape Asian reciprocity practices that are very different from non-Asian cultures.

In contrast to a dualistic philosophy, Buddhism defines the person as a "no-self" rather than an autonomous individual that Buddhism considers an illusion.[57] Voerhoeven says that Asians and non-Asians are actually talking about two different things in terms of the self, "Ātman referred primarily to a presumed philosophical and metaphysical entity, not to a psychological and empirical concept of the "self" used in contemporary Western discourse."[58]

This different definition of the self is compatible with the Confucian self that is also not self-focused but other-focused or interdependent.[59] This collective perspective needs to be taken into consideration when looking at Buddhist practices in Asia. Although the focus appears to be on the individual who does good works in order to achieve nirvana, what the individual does also affects the collective.

---

52. Keyes and Daniel, *Karma: An Anthropological Inquiry*, 268.
53. Carlisle, "Synchronizing Karma," 201.
54. Adamek, "The Impossibility of the Given," 135.
55. Voerhoeven, "Buddhist Ideas about No-Self and the Person," 95.
56. Campbell, "Self or No-Self: Is There a Middle Way?" 10.
57. Lancaster, "Self or No-Self? Converging Perspectives from Neuropsychology and Mysticism," 516.
58. Voerhoeven, "Buddhist Ideas about No-Self and the Person," 94.
59. Markus and Kitayama, "Culture and the Self," 224–246.

Voerhoeven says in Buddhism the problem of the self is that it becomes attached to the things of this world and that leads to suffering.[60] This is one reason why Buddhism is attractive in the consumer world as a reaction to the individualistic focus to obtain more. In order to minimize suffering, the no-self person turns their thoughts to others and acts compassionately on their behalf. In other words, Buddhist virtue includes both "overcoming the attachment to self and acting compassionately on behalf of others."[61]

Engaging in these three activities enables a person to mature their karma. A person needs "both meritorious deeds and meditative acts" to get to nirvana.[62] Karma is what shapes a person's destiny in terms of nirvana and rebirth as well as determines the happiness or suffering that a person experiences.[63] Karma refers to both the initial act and the reward or punishment that results from that act.[64] Karma encompasses, "The type of birth, human and non-human, length of life, happiness and suffering etc. experienced as being the consequences of specific acts done by a being in his previous existences."[65]

There are a number of ways a person can give to mature their karma (making merit), although some of the giving is more effective than others. The most common and effective way to give is to provide food for the monks every morning, as well as to provide the necessities for the temple and the monks.[66] Merit was originally instituted to "maintain monastic buildings and to meet the daily needs of the monk and nuns."[67] The belief is that giving will accumulate merit for their future lives.[68]

Other ways that people can enhance their merit (*gongde*) is by giving money to fund construction of Buddhist temples believing that they will continue to receive merit from the ones who come to pray and learn there. Some also believe they receive as much merit from helping to construct

---

60. Voerhoeven, "Buddhist Ideas about No-Self and the Person," 96.
61. Swearer, "Buddhist Virtue, Voluntary Poverty, and Extensive Benevolence," 71.
62. Reynolds, "Ethics and Wealth in Theravada Buddhism," 15.
63. Krishan, "Doctrines of *Karma*," 163.
64. Gombrich, "'Merit transfer' in Sinhalese Buddhism," 204.
65. Krishan, "Doctrines of *Karma*," 200.
66. Reynolds, "Ethics and Wealth in Theravada Buddhism," 71–72.
67. Walsh, "The Economics of Salvation," 359.
68. Ariyabuddihiphongs, "Buddhist Belief in Merit, 194.

schools and hospitals as they do by giving to Buddhist temples.[69] Providing furnishings such as murals and images for the Buddhist temples are other ways to earn merit. In these instances, not only do the creators of these items who have built the temple receive merit, but the commissioners and the people in general do as well.[70]

A person can also make merit by giving food not only to Buddhist monks but also to the poor. In this giving, the receiver as well as the giver receives merit. That is, the one who receives enables the giver to be released from their attachment to their material possessions.[71] It is also believed that the more you share the more merit you gain.[72] A person can give away or transfer merit to others, including the deceased, in an attempt to enhance their next life. Both the giver and the receiver benefit[73] and "the act of transferring merit increases the original merit accumulated by the donor."[74]

Fischer also noted that people believe there is a connection between the amount of money given and amount of merit received. That is, the more one gave to the temple or the clergy, the more merit the giver will receive. His research also showed that the clergy gave more attention to wealthy visitors than others who were less wealthy. Explanations were that finances also provided protection as well as merit.[75]

There is also the belief that those in a higher position of authority and power have more karma at their disposal. The king's actions in Thailand are believed to benefit (grant karma to) not only himself, but also his people, and the guardian spirits. This kind of karma is referred to as "overflow karma."[76] In the past, governments who acted favorably towards Buddhism were considered to receive merit that also benefited the general populace.[77]

Other ways of giving or gaining merit are:

---

69. Fischer, "The Spiritual Land Rush," 148.

70. Schmidt, "Initial findings on the *Wat Suthat*," 589.

71. Bowie, "The Alchemy of Charity," 472.

72. Gómez, "Buddhism as a Religion of Hope," 10.

73. Gombrich, "'Merit transfer' in Sinhalese Buddhism," 212; Keyes and Daniel, *Karma: An Anthropological Inquiry*, 270.

74. Malalasekera, 1967, 360

75. Fischer, "The Spiritual Land Rush," 150–151.

76. McDermott, "Is There Group Karma in Theravāda Buddhism?" 69.

77. Smith, *Religion and Politics in Burma*, 168.

> [B]y giving a seat (to a person) one gets a very high position, by bestowing food one secures health and wealth, by the gifts of clothes, one acquires good complexion (varṇa) and property, the gift of conveyance procures for the giver special happiness and that of lights begets power of vision, by giving a house one gets all sorts of property.[78]

Walsh cites the Chinese Buddhist cannon as listing "seven ways that the layperson can experience merit: help build a temple or pagoda, plant trees, give medicine to the ill, build strong boats, repair bridges, build irrigation canals, and build public toilets."[79]

Similar to Confucian reciprocity practices, Buddhism also views karma in terms of obligation and debt such as to their parents in terms of "karmic obligation" or "karmic debt." If their parents are no longer living, people can gain karma by giving food or money to the temple instead of to their parents.[80]

Ariyabuddihiphongs' research on merit among Thai Buddhists in Bangkok found that their beliefs about merit influenced their religious activities as well as their life satisfaction.[81] The belief of the effectiveness of merit on their karma motivates people to continue in their merit-making efforts.

People can also get bad karma from bad actions, but good actions are considered to be stronger than bad actions due to the remorse a person may have about his bad deeds later.[82] Bad actions can come from "voice, mind, and body" and include greed and anger.[83] They can also come from violating the 5 *sila* (moral precepts) of "harming, stealing, lying, sexual misconduct, and the use of intoxicants."[84]

The way that Buddhists address the attachment to self is to develop compassion for others through merit-making karma. Merit-making is not only an individual activity; but a person's good deeds affect others. Social obligation to the group/community/nation motivates good deeds.

---

78. Cited from the *Vimānavatthu* commentary of Dhammāphala (5th–6th Century AD).

79. Walsh cites Jinjirô, Takakusu and Kaigyoku Watanabe, eds. "Taishō Sinshû daizôkyô." Tokyo, Taishô Issaikyô Kankai. T 683, v.16, 777a–778c.

80. Carlise, "Synchronizing Karma, 212–213.

81. Ariyabuddihiphongs, "Buddhist Belief in Merit, 209.

82. Krishan, *Karma Vipaka*," 205.

83. Reynolds, "Ethics and Wealth in Theravada Buddhism," 15.

84. Ibid., 16.

Part II: Cultural Perspectives

Comparison of Confucian and Buddhist Reciprocity Practices

The above sections have briefly described Asian reciprocity practices as influenced by Confucian and Buddhist beliefs. Confucian social roles provide the framework for how a person is born with a social obligation to reciprocate. The expectation is for reciprocity practices to be learned in the childhood home. A person is born indebted to his parents for the care and provisions they have provided. The care and protection from the parents are to be reciprocated by loyalty and respect for the parents as well as by providing for their physical needs, especially when they get old. If the child or person fulfills the expectations of the Confucian hierarchical ideals, the reputation of the group is maintained. If the reciprocity practices do not follow Confucian hierarchical ideals, the group's face is lost and the person needs to engage in face saving activities.

This practice of care for others in one's family is extended to the rest of society. In a Strong Community society people observe how well each person fulfills the reciprocal practices of their social role. If they do not reciprocate appropriately, they will be disciplined in some way because they have caused the group to lose face as well. The complexity of reciprocity is illustrated in the concept of *guanxi,* which again means one person has potential influence or access to a great number of people and resources.

Likewise, the collective focus of Buddhism provides the motivation for reciprocity that benefits the group as well as the individual. That is, a person can engage in activities (*karma*) and these activities enable them to lead to a better life in the future. Doing things for the religious community enhances one's *karma* the most. Hearing a person's stories about their karmic activities also validates their good karma. By doing good deeds people are able to receive a spiritual reward that impacts not only them but also others. Buddhists' belief in reciprocity motivates them to karmic-making merit.

Reciprocating with group members strengthens and maintains a person's identity and sense of belonging to their group. As a person is cared for, he or she learns to care for others as well. People from Strong Community cultures are more aware of the others in the group—who they are, what their needs are, how they are feeling, etc. However, at the same time, there is not a similar sense of responsibility for those who are not in one's own group.

Comparison with Scripture

The concept of reciprocity is found throughout Scripture. There are a number of verses that command reciprocity as found in the Golden Rule, "So in everything, do to others what you would have them do to you, for this sums up the Law and the Prophets (Matt 7:12).

Other references specifically give instruction for the kinds of reciprocal actions: love one another (John 13:34), honor one another (Rom 12:10), do not judge one another (Rom 14:13), have equal concern for one another (1 Cor 12:25), serve one another (Gal 5:13), do not provoke or envy one another (Gal 5:26), carry one another's burdens (Gal 6:2), and be kind and compassionate (Eph 4:32).

There are also a number of passages that speak of reciprocity in terms of what we sow we will reap: 2 Cor 9:6–8; Gal 6:7–10. If we honor God with what He has given to us, He will increase our blessing: Matt 25:21, 23; Luke 6:38.

Scriptures also indicate the importance of the family and family relationships. A number of references give instructions similar to the Confucian hierarchy:

> Subject to ruler: Rom 13:1–7; 1 Tim 2:1–3; Titus 3:1; 1 Peter 2:13–14; Heb 13:17

> Child to parent: Exod 20:12, Deut 5:16; Prov 6:20; Eph 6:1–3; Col 3:20

> Wife to husband: Eph 5:23–24; Col 3:18; 1 Pet 3:1–22;

> Younger to older: 1 Pet 5:5; Titus 2

> Friend to friend: Prov 17:17; John 15:12–15

Missiological Implications

When I began to learn more about Asian culture and Confucian social role expectations and Buddhist merit-making, I began to see how my drive to work was a result of underlying Asian reciprocity practices. I was driven to do good works and unconsciously making merit, but my motivation was not because of God's grace. As a result, I drove myself to do more than I was physically, emotionally, and spiritually able. As I read Scripture, I interpreted the verses on submitting to others from a cultural perspective rather than from a biblical perspective. That is, I submitted out of duty to an authority figure rather than from a desire to please God. In fact, the drive to work came from my belief that I needed to work to be acceptable to God. Because I did not understand that God loved me for who I was as created in his image, I felt the need to do things to gain his approval.

My drive to work also created unintended consequences. When I was not able to complete everything that I agreed to do, I became very frustrated and felt bad about myself. It did not occur to me I was over-committing myself and that I could never do all those things. As a person in a lower role, I was socialized to say "yes" to whatever an authority figured asked of me. I did not know how to say "no." Growing up I had not learned to disagree with older people or even to disagree with my peers. This created the need to please other people by doing more things (good works).

I was also very disappointed when God did not reciprocate my good works (twenty-five years of missionary service) with good health but rather with bad health (cancer diagnosis). I thought I had enough good works that it would not result in something bad like cancer. I began to realize that my view of myself and God were influenced by my Asian Confucian and Buddhist heritage and, therefore, I was not able to experience God's grace or His peace, joy, love, longsuffering, etc.

When dealing with Asians and helping them think through their Confucian and Buddhist influences, it will be important to help them understand how their own culture (influenced by Confucian and Buddhist beliefs) shapes how they do things—for good works or for God.

There are a number of missiological implications for a better understanding of East Asian reciprocity practices coming from Confucian and Buddhist influences.

The first implication that needs to be addressed is how Confucian social roles address only the outward behavior of submission but do not address the inward bitterness that develops from having to submit, thus preventing the experience of God's grace. Changing one's motivation to submit to being motivated by God's love will be a challenge to people who have submitted their whole life without dealing with this bitterness.[85]

A second implication is how the Gospel is presented and perceived through the different definition of the person. When the definition of the person is based on the individual, salvation is viewed from the perspective of individual choice apart from one's group. Jackson Wu discusses how

---

85. Andrew Sung Park has written on this bitterness or *han* in Korean.

salvation from a Chinese perspective can be better understood through the concept of honor and shame and saving God's face instead of doing good works.[86] Honor and shame arise from the concept of belonging to the group and speak to the heart of East Asian cultures. God also perfectly fulfills the Confucian roles of the ideal father, leader, parent, brother, and friend. Fulfilling one's social role as unto God enables us to experience God's grace.

Buddhist Strong Community cultures will also have difficulty moving from their original family group to another if the other group does not have similar reciprocity practices that help them take care of their needs as well as enhance their group identity. Zimmerman-Liu states that new believers need a new identity going from "children of the devil to sons of God."[87] Strong Community or Collective Asians view the world as an integration of the physical and spiritual aspects, while Weak Community non-Asians view the world from the separation of the body and the spirit. This difference determines what is important. For Asians, relationships are important, and the Gospel needs to be demonstrated through the lives of the people who are presenting the Gospel message. However, non-Asian cultures tend to focus on information or the truth of the Gospel presented clearly but do not necessarily demonstrate the truth through relationships.

A third implication is how grace is defined culturally. Shin compares the Western concept of unilateral grace with the Asian concept of bilateral or global grace coming from the Asian cultural view of reciprocity.[88] He suggests that both perspectives have aspects of the truth. From the western perspective we learn that there is nothing we can do to earn God's grace and from the Asian perspective we know that we need to reciprocate what God did for us. It is not good works but what God did for us. A greater understanding of these two perspectives will result in a deeper understanding of God's grace. The suggestion is to develop humility to learn from the other in order for both to better understand God's grace. One perspective does not have the full understanding of God's truth.

This chapter only touches on a few of the missiological implications, but these implications arise from major cultural differences that need more time and reflection than can be included in this short article. Each of the three implications need further research.

---

86. Cf. Wu, *Saving God's Face*.
87. Zimmerman-Liu, "From 'Children of the Devil' to 'Sons of God. 4.
88. Shin, *Tapestry of Grace*, 52–53.

Part II: Cultural Perspectives

Bibliography

Adamek, Wendi L. "The Impossibility of the Given: Representation of Merit and Emptiness in Medieval Chinese Buddhism." *History of Religions* 45:2 (2005) 135–180.

Adloff, Frank and Stephen Mau. "Giving Social Ties, Reciprocity in Modern Societies." *European Journal of Sociology* 4:1 (2006) 93–123.

The Analects XV: 23.

Ariyabuddihiphongs, Vanchai. "Buddhist Belief in Merit (Puṅṅ), Buddhist Religiousness and Life Satisfaction among Thai Buddhist in Bangkok, Thailand." *Archiv für Religionspychologie/Archive for the Psychology of Religion* 31:2 (2009) 191–213.

Barbalet, Jack. "The Structure of Guanxi: Resolving Problems of Network Assurance." *Sociological Theory* 43 (2014) 51–69, 52. Published online 13 November 2013.

Bhagat, Mahadeo Gopal. *Ancient Indian Asceticism*. New Delhi: Munshiram Manoharlal, 1976.

Bian, Yanjie and Soon Ang. "Guanxi Networks and Job Mobility in China and Singapore." *Social Forces* 75:3 (1997) 981–1005.

Bowie, Katherine A. "The Alchemy of Charity: Of Class and Buddhism in Northern Thailand." *American Anthropologist* 100:2 (June 1998) 468–481.

Campbell, John T. "Self or No-Self: Is There a Middle Way?" *The Journal of Pastoral Care* 53:1 (Spring 1999) 7–18.

Carlise, Steven G. "Synchronizing Karma: The Internalization and Externalization of a Shared Personal Belief." *Ethos* 36:2 (June 2008) 194–219.

Chang, Ling-Hsing. "The Dilemma of *Renqing* Processes: Interpretations from the Perspective of *Guanxi* of Chinese Cultural Society." *Behaviour and Information Technology* 31:5 (2012) 481–493.

Cheng, Chung-Ying. *New Dimensions of Confucian and Neo-Confucian Philosophy*. Albany, NY: SUNY, 1991.

Douglas, Mary T. "The Normative Debate and the Origins of Culture." In *Risk and Blame: Essays in Cultural Theory*. 124-148. London: Routledge, 1992.

Epstein, Mark. *Thoughts Without a Thinker: Psychotherapy from a Buddhist Perspective*. New York: Basic Books, 1995.

Fischer, Gareth. "The Spiritual Land Rush: Merit and Morality in New Chinese Buddhist Temple Construction." The Journal of Asian Studies 67:1 (Feb 2008) 143–170.

Ghose, Lynken. "'Karma' and the Possibility of Purification: An Ethical Psychological Analysis of the Doctrine of 'Karma' in Buddhism." *The Journal of Religious Ethics* 35:2 (June 2007) 259–289.

Gombrich, Richard. "'Merit Transfer' in Sinhalese Buddhism: A Case Study of the Interaction between Doctrine and Practice." *History of Religions* 11:2 (November 1971) 203–219.

Gómez, Luis O. "Buddhism as a Religion of Hope: Observations on the 'Logic' of a Doctrine and its Foundational Myth." *The Eastern Buddhist* 32:1 (2000) 1–21.

Guan, Xing. "The Teaching and Practice of Filial Piety in Buddhism." *Journal of Law and Religion* 31:3 (2016) 212–26.

Gyatso, Geshe Kelsang. *Buddhism in the Tibetan Tradition*. London: Penguin/Arkana, 1984.

Hwang, Kwang-Kuo. "Chinese Relationalism: Theoretical Constructions and Methodological Considerations." *Journal for the Theory of Social Behavior* 30:2 (2000) 155–178.

Hwang, Kwang-Kuo. "Face and Favor: the Chinese Power Game." *American Journal of Sociology* 92:4 (January 1987) 944–974.

Kalghatgi, T. G. "The Doctrine of Karma in Jaina Philosophy." *Philosophy East West* 15:3/4 (June-October 1965) 229-242.

Keyes, Charles F. and E. Valentine Daniel. *Karma: An Anthropological Inquiry.* Berkeley, CA: University of California Press, 1983.

Kishimoto, Hideo. "Some Japanese Cultural Traits and Religions." In *The Japanese Mind: Essentials of Japanese Philosophy and Culture* edited by Charles A. Moore, 110-121. Honolulu, HI: University of Hawaii Press, 1967.

Krishan, Y. "Doctrines of *Karma, Mokṣa, Nisskāma, Karma* and the Ideal of "Bodhisattva." *Annals of the Bandarkar Oriental Research Institute* 70:1/4 (1989) 163–180.

———. "*Karma Vipaka.*" *Numen* XXX: 2 (1983) 199–214.

Lai, Karyn L. *"Confucian Moral Thinking."* Philosophy East & West 45 (April 1995) 249–272.

Lancaster, Brian. "Self or No-Self? Converging Perspectives from Neuropsychology and Mysticism." *Zygon* 28:4 (2005) 507–526.

Law, Bimala Charan. *Heaven and Hell in Buddhist Perspective.* Delhi: Bhartiya, 1973.

Lebra, Takie Sugiyama. *Japanese Patterns of Behavior.* Honolulu, HI: University of Hawaii Press, 1976.

Li, Chenyang. "Shifting Perspectives: Filial Morality Revisited." *Philosophy East and West* 47:2 (Aug 1997) 211–232.

MacCormack, Geoffrey. "Reciprocity." *MAN* 11:1 (March 1976) 89–103.

Malalasekera, Gunapala Piyasena. "Transference of Merit in Ceylonese Buddhism." *Philosophy East West* 17:1-4 (1967) 85–90.

Markus, Hazel Rose, and Shinobu Kitayama. "Culture and the Self: Implications for Cognition, Emotion, and Motivation." *Psychological Review* 98:2 (1991) 224–253.

Mauss, Marcel. *The Gift: The Form and Reason for Exchange in Archaic Societies.* London: Routledge, 1990.

McDermott, James P. "Is there Group Karma in Theravāda Buddhism?" *Numen* XIII:1 (1976) 67–70.

Moody, Michael. "Serial Reciprocity: A Preliminary Statement." *Sociological Theory* 26:6 (June 2008) 130–151.

Park, Andrew Sung. *The Wounded Heart of God: The Asian Concept of Han and the Christian Doctrine of Sin.* Nashville, TN: Abingdon, 1993.

Qi, Xiaoying. "Guanxi, Social Capital and Beyond: Toward a Globalized Social Science." *The British Journal of Sociology* 64:2 (2013) 308–324.

Reynolds, Frank E. "Ethics and Wealth in Theravada Buddhism: A Study in Comparative Religious Ethics." In *Ethics, Wealth, and Salvation: A Study in Buddhist Social Ethics.* 59–76. Columbia, SC: University of South Carolina Press, 1990.

Robertson, Christopher J. "The Global Dispersion of Chinese Values: A Three Country Study of Confucian Dynamism." *Management International Review* 40:3 (2000 3rd quarter) 253–268.

Schmidt, Luke. "Initial Findings on the *Wat Suthat*: Presence, Power, and Merit-Making in the Vihara Murals and Inscriptions." *Religion Compass* 4:10 (2010) 588–605.

Schwartz, Benjamin I. *The World of Thought in Ancient China.* Cambridge: Harvard University Press, 1985.

Shin, Benjamin C. and Sheryl Takagi Silzer. *Tapestry of Grace: Untangling Cultural Complexities of Asian American Life and Ministry.* Eugene, OR: Wipf and Stock, 2016.

Part II: Cultural Perspectives

Silzer, Sheryl Takagi. *Biblical Multicultural Teams: Applying Biblical Truth to Cultural Differences*. Pasadena, CA: William Carey, 2011.

——— "How Buddhist Spirituality Influences/Shapes Asian Cultural Practices: Missiological Implications." *Seeking the Unseen: Spiritual Realities in the Buddhist World* edited by Paul H. de Neui. 101–122. Pasadena, CA: William Carey, 2015.

Smith, Donald Eugene. *Religion and Politics in Burma*. Princeton, NJ: Princeton University Press, 1965.

Su, Chenting, Ronald K. Mitchell and M Joseph Sirgy. "Enabling *Guanxi* Management in China: A Hierarchical Stakeholder Model of Effective *Guanxi*." *Journal of Business Ethics* 71 (2007) 301–319.

Swearer, Donald K. "Buddhist Virtue, Voluntary Poverty, and Extensive Benevolence." *The Journal of Religious Ethics* 21:1 (Spring 1998) 71–103.

Tu, Weiming. "Confucius and Confucianism." In *Confucianism and the Family* edited by Walter H. Slote and George A. DeVos, 3–36. Albany, NY: SUNY, 1998.

——— "The Ecological Turn in New Confucian Humanism." *Daedalus* (2001) 243–264.

Verhoeven, Martin. "Buddhist Ideas about No-Self and the Person." Religion East & West, 10 (October 2010) 93-112.

Walsh, Michael J. "The Economics of Salvation: Toward a Theory of Exchange in Chinese Buddhism." *Journal of American Academy of Religion* 75:2 (June 2007) 353–382.

Wu, Jackson. *Saving God's Face: A Chinese Contextualization of Salvation through Honor and Shame*. Pasadena, CA: William Carey, 2013.

Yang, Mayfair Mehui. *Gifts, Favors, & Banquets: The Art of Social Relationships in China*. Ithaca, NY: Cornell University Press, 1994.

Yen, Yu-Fang; Jung-Feng Tseng, and Hsing Kuo Wang. "Exploring the Mediating Role of Trust on the Relationship of *Guanxi* and Knowledge Sharing: A Social Network Perspective." *Asian Pacific Journal of Human Resources* 522 (2014) 173–192.

Yeung, Irene E.M. and Rosalee L. Tung. "Achieving Business Success in Chinese Confucian Societies: The Importance of *Guanxi*." *Organizational Dynamics* 25:2 (1996) 54–65.

Yu, Jiyuan. "Confucius Relational Self and Aristotle's Political Animal." *History of Philosophy Quarterly* 22:4 (October 2005) 281–300.

Zhou, Lianxi, Weiping Wu, and Xueming Luo. "Internationalization and the Performance of Born-Global SME's: The Mediating Role of Social Networks." *Journal of International Business Studies* 38 (2007) 673–690.

Zimmerman-Liu, Teresa. "From 'Children of the Devil' to 'Sons of God.' The Reconfiguration of *Guanxi* in a 20th Century Indigenous Chinese Protestant Group." Working Paper 215-4, UC San Diego Department of Sociology, 2015.

9

Christianity Viewed Through Karmic Eyes in Sri Lanka

G.P.V. Somaratna

A HISTORY OF OVER two millennia has deeply rooted Buddhism in the culture of the Sinhalese. It acts as a rallying point for the Sinhala-speaking population. The contemporary Buddhist population is well instructed in Buddhist doctrine through the government-sponsored system of education and the mass media.[1] In this study, we attempt to explain how Christian charity (*agape*) is viewed politically by the Sri Lankan interpretation of Buddhist merit-making (*punya karma*), and how this had led to violence against Christians.

Attention in this chapter is given mainly to Buddhism as it is the established dominant religion in Sri Lanka. Although the Hindus, who comprise about fifteen percent of the population also believe the concept of karma in their religious life, they have not been given the main attention in this study. Buddhism in Sri Lanka is the Theravada form. It is different from Christianity which is divided into several denominations. This unity of Buddhism makes it easy to grasp the religious doctrines and practices of the Buddhist population in the country. The distinguishing factor is that it is an ethnic religion.

The public display of religion is encouraged by the state. National media encourages the practice of Buddhist teachings through regular

---

1. Obeyesekere, *Karma and Rebirth*, 1.

preaching programs. The state-sponsored system of schools imparts Buddhism to the children of Buddhist parentage. Over ninety-five percent literacy in the country enables the Buddhists to be deeply aware of Buddhist teachings. Therefore, the concept of karma is well known among Sri Lankan Buddhists as it is one of the foundational teachings of Buddhism. Even an illiterate person would know what the Buddhist teaching of karma means for his life and society.

How Tolerant is Buddhism?

The Buddhists are proud of Buddha's comments regarding other religions. The tolerant attitude displayed in the *Kalama-Sutta* is often quoted in academic gatherings as well as public and political arenas to show that Buddhism is tolerant of other religions. It is true that Buddhism is generally regarded as a tolerant religion. It is a religion that places emphasis on practical methods for cultivating spiritual awareness and on the importance of finding the truth for oneself. Its hallmarks are loving-kindness (*metta*), compassion (*karuna*), sympathetic joy (*mudita*), equanimity (*upekkha*).[2] Walpola Rahula states:

> This spirit of tolerance and understanding has been from the beginning one of the most cherished ideals of Buddhist culture and civilization. That is why there is not a single example of persecution or the shedding of a drop of blood in converting people to Buddhism, or in its propagation during its long history of 2500 years. It spread peacefully all over the continent of Asia, having more than 500 million adherents today. Violence in any form, under any pretext whatsoever, is absolutely against the teaching of the Buddha.[3]

However, history does not support this statement. Preaching and practice very often do not agree. In practice, the situation has not always been as harmonious as the theory would have us believe. There have been several clashes over doctrine in the history of Buddhism in Sri Lanka. Writing about Buddhist behavior Faure states: "Tolerance of the other is practical only when the otherness is reduced to sameness."[4] The history of

---

2. Buswell, *Encyclopaedia of Buddhism*, 458; Powers, *Introduction to Tibetan Buddhism*, 5.

3. Rahula, *What the Buddha Taught*, 5.

4. See Faure, *Unmasking Buddhism*, part III.

Buddhism in Sri Lanka has not been peaceful despite the rhetoric of Rahula who apparently wishes to convince the Western readership, giving an appearance of harmonious relations with other religions. There have been acts of violence against other religions directed, fomented or inspired by Buddhists.[5] The attitude toward animist religions is often cited as a classic example of Buddhist tolerance. Even in this process the local gods have been made a part of the Buddhist pantheon while others are demoted to the rank of demons to be subjugated through suitable rituals.[6]

"Militant Buddhism" may be an oxymoron, but it is a fact of life in Sri Lanka. It has been a source of violent repressive action in recent decades. Buddhist revivalism since the nineteenth century in Sri Lanka took place among the Sinhalese to counter Christian missionary influence. Fear of the country's Buddhist hegemony being challenged by Christian evangelism had driven Buddhist monks in the eighteenth century to demonize Christianity.[7] The trend has continued. One popular monk recently compared Christian missionary activity to terrorism.[8] Many Buddhist leaders have clandestinely supported the conduct of anti-Christian violence.[9] In the last three decades, the number of attacks against Christian churches has increased, with extremist Buddhist clergy leading the violence in many areas. Anti-Christian violence has included "beatings, arson, and acts of sacrilege, death threats, and violent disruption of worship, stoning, abuse, unlawful restraint, and even interference with funerals."[10] There have been continued sporadic attacks on Christian churches by Buddhist extremists who accuse Christians of conducting "unethical" or "forced" conversion by enticing the poor. The Pew Research Center listed Sri Lanka among the countries with very high religious hostilities in the year 2012. Buddhist monks intensified violence against Muslim and Christian places of worship during the last two years of the Rajapaksa regime.[11]

---

5. Jerryson & Juergensmeyer, *Buddhist Warfare*, 24.

6. Cf. Faure, *Unmasking Buddhism*, part III.

7. Young and Senanayake, *The Carpenter-Heretic*, 7.

8. http://christianaggression.org/2016/04/27/lanka-red-alert-on-terrorists-and-evangelists/.

9. Tambiah, *Buddhism Betrayed*, 46.

10. http://dbsjeyaraj.com/dbsj/archives/46253.

11. Recently the destruction and arson of a church in a suburb of Colombo was headed by a well-known scholar monk.

In spite of these episodes of violence, monks continue to preach non-violence and toleration as the characteristic of Buddhism, thereby creating an effective verbal cover-up for the militant activity that is going on. This also shows that there is a clear gap between the preaching of toleration and practice of discrimination. In particular, there is a clear connection, described below, between the Sri Lankan Buddhist teaching on the concept of merit-making (*punya karma*) and the promotion of violence against practitioners of the Christian faith.

Concept of Karma

The doctrine of Theravada Buddhism is considered to be an intellectual philosophy. The dogma of karma is one of the fundamental truths which is deeply embedded in the minds of devotees. It is at the center of Buddhist eschatological thinking.[12] It is a crucial element in traditional Buddhist thought; without it Buddhism is inconceivable. The root meaning of 'karma' is action. In both Hindu and Buddhist thought, the concept refers to the moral consequence of human action. These two religions make the doctrine of karma an explanation for how certain aspects of one's present experience are the outcome of acts in previous lives in the cycle of birth and death.

They believe that karmic heritage will manifest itself in different types of actions.[13] For the Buddhist, "it is the Buddha's solution to the problem of evil."[14] In the Buddhist theory of karma, this word is used in connection with volitional acts which find expression in thought, word, and deed which would be good, evil or neutral. In the *Cula-kammavibhanga Sutta*, *cetana* (will) is a necessary condition for such acts to be morally good, evil or neutral.[15] Conscious volition (*cetana*) is necessary for such acts to be morally good (*kusala*), evil (*akusala*) or neutral (*avyakara*). Thus, karma is volitional action. *Cetana* would determine the goodness or badness of these acts.[16] In simple language, karma means that if one does morally good (*kusala*) deeds, good will come to you, now and hereafter. If one does morally bad (*akusala*) deeds, bad will come now and hereafter. It is like sowing

---

12. Obeyesekere, *Karma and Rebirth*, 1.
13. Keyes, *Buddhist Politics*, 13.
14. Gombrich, *Sinhalese Buddhism*, 204.
15. Cf. *Cula-kammavibhanga Sutta*, 135.
16. Jayatilleke, *The Message of the Buddha*, 140.

good seeds to reap a good harvest. If the seeds are bad, one will reap a bad harvest. The philosophers call it the law of cause and effect. Every cause has an effect. It is a law of moral causation. Karma is a process, action, energy and force.[17] These actions may find expression in bodily behaviour (*kaya kamma*), verbal behaviour (*vaci kamma*) and psychological behaviour (*mano kamma*).

According to Buddhism, the world is the result of the karma, or actions, of the beings who inhabit it.[18] It continues to play an essential role in the thinking and action of modern Buddhists today. It is said that Theravada Buddhists have two soteriological goals. The distant goal is the attainment of nirvana. It consists in the escape from the cycle of birth and death, which they call samsara. The immediate goal is a good life in the heavens or on earth while existing continuously in the samsara.

Impersonal Law

The law of karma is a cosmic law that all crimes are suitably punished and all good deeds are suitably rewarded in the long run.[19] Karma is a doctrine to the effect that the worldly order has a moral order by which all affairs are conducted ethically, automatically creating a fair distribution of punishments and rewards. Thus, the pain and happiness humans experience are results of their own deeds, words and thoughts reacting on themselves. There are no supernatural forces to influence karmic results. Buddha stated that karma is neither predestination nor determinism. People will reap what they have sown. There is nothing other than the karma themselves and their fruits which again produce new acts without any actor or agent to determine a person's destiny.[20] Buddhism adopts rebirth on the grounds that one must assume a continuum of lives in order to account for the rewards of the virtuous and the punishments of the wicked.

Karma is based on the Buddhist concept of time. Time is eternal and Buddhism calls it samsara. It is endlessly cyclical or cakra. Therefore, karma does not always result in an immediate response. This is important in dealing with Christians, as there is no continuation of life in samsara because the Christian concept of time is linear, not cyclical.

---

17. Dhammananda, *The Buddhist Path of Wisdom*, 88.
18. Gyatso, *Modern Buddhism*, ix.
19. Gombrich, *Merit Transference*, 214.
20. Panikkar, *The Law of Karma*, 27.

PART II: CULTURAL PERSPECTIVES

Explaining Inequality

The concept of karma has apparently perpetuated social inequalities in Buddhist societies. According to Buddha, "It is karma that differentiates beings into low and high states." As karma may be good or bad, so may the fruit be good or bad. Though it may not be clear to us now, all such inequalities among all sorts of beings, including human beings, come about because of the karma they have made individually. Each person reaps his own fruits. In the *Cula-kammavibhanga Sutta*, a Brahmin student, Subha, asks Buddha for an explanation, stating:

> Master Gotama, what is the reason, what is the condition, why inferiority and superiority are met with among human beings, among mankind? For one meets with short-lived and long-lived people, sick and healthy people, ugly and beautiful people, insignificant and influential people, poor and rich people, low-born and high-born people, stupid and wise people. What is the reason, what is the condition, why superiority and inferiority are met with among human beings, among mankind?[21]

The answer of Buddha was "Student, beings are owners of karmas, heirs of karmas, they have karmas as their progenitor, karmas as their kin, karmas as their homing-place. It is karmas that differentiate beings according to inferiority and superiority."[22] According to some modern Buddhists, these views of Buddha on karma justify the social inequalities based on caste. Therefore, some political leaders in the Buddhist world have proposed alternative ways of thinking about karma in order to avoid some of the problems of traditional Buddhist teaching on the subject.

One example can be seen in the writings of B. R. Ambedkar. His primary enemy was the Hindu caste system. Ambedkar reinterpreted the theory of karma in order to explain the cause of suffering of the untouchables community in India. Contrary to the accepted idea in the Buddhist teaching, Ambedkar says that it was not the misdeeds of their past lives that they suffer but the exploitation by the so-called high castes through an unjust social system. According to him, a person's unfortunate conditions are not the result of karma or ignorance and craving, but result from "social exploitation and material poverty together with the cruelty of others."[23]

---

21. Cf. *Cula-kammavibhanga Sutta*, MN. 135.2.
22. Ibid., 135.
23. King and Queen, *Engaged Buddhism*, 47.

Ambedkar's vision for liberation of the untouchables seemed impossible if traditional teachings on karma were maintained. As a consequence, Ambedkar dropped discussion of these aspects of karma from his interpretation of Buddhism.

Aung San Suu Kyi (b. 1945), the leader of the democracy struggle in Myanmar, had stated that one of the greatest difficulties her movement faces is that the Burmese people typically think karma means fate. According to this view, the suffering of Burmese masses at the hands of the military dictatorship was the result of their past karmic actions. Some people believe that there is nothing they can do to prevent it but bear it until that karma has been exhausted, at which point their suffering will end automatically. Unlike Ambedkar, who veers away from the teachings of Buddha as recorded in the scriptures, Aung San Suu Kyi and many other Buddhist modernists remain on solid scriptural ground. They argue that the understanding of karma as passivity is contrary to the teachings of Buddha.

Buddha emphasized many times that any teaching that makes people believe that there is no point in making an effort to engage in spiritual practice is contrary to his teachings and indeed a wicked teaching that no one should accept. Buddha's teaching was to encourage people to strive for liberation. He discouraged people from wondering about their karmic inheritance. Just as the attainment of Ambedkar's goals requires a change in thinking about karma, so too is Suu Kyi's thinking about karma. Her view was that the change of thinking in respect of karma is a necessity for sufficiently large numbers of Burmese to actively engage in the struggle for democracy for their liberation.[24]

Similar views on the impact of karma regarding social inequalities have been expressed by the Thai feminist trainer Ouyporn Khuankaew.[25] In spite of intellectual and political reinterpretation of the concept of karma, the traditional deterministic views of karma have continued to be important in Buddhist thought and practice.

Karma, Caste and Conversion

The caste system still prevails in the Sri Lankan Buddhist society. In the recent past, there was opposition to the conversion of the Rodi caste to Christianity. This movement to Christian conversion derived its religious

---

24. Veliath, *Buddha and Jesus*, 280–281.
25. Norsworthy, *Understanding Violence*, 146.

motivation from the statement of the Buddha that karma classifies beings in terms of low and high (*kamman satte vibhajati yadidan hina panitattaya*) found in the *Cula-kammavibhanga Sutta*.[26] Rodi is one of the outcaste social groups amongst the Sinhalese people of Sri Lanka. There have not been any Buddhist temples to serve them spiritually. When the Kitusewana (Christian) Fellowship began working among them in the 1980s there was great opposition.[27] The church building of kadjan leaves was burnt down and the two Christian workers were beaten severely. Buddhist leaders have justified their actions against Christian evangelists on the grounds that the low castes are in that position because of the result of their karma. The common belief is that any action against it would be an attempt to disrupt the social order based on the law of karma.

Social Welfare

The real origin of social welfare took place with Christian missionary activities in Sri Lanka. Later it became a part of the political process and parliamentary politics that widened the scope of welfare programs found in the country today. The practice of changing governments through electoral process has degenerated into an acrimonious competition for social welfare. Successive governments have sought the NGOs to assist them in welfare activities within the country.

In contemporary Sri Lanka, many NGOs are religious in orientation while many others, which are ostensibly secular, have strong religious sympathies.[28] NGOs have had a long history in Sri Lanka, beginning as "local counterparts of organizations affiliated with Christian missionary efforts in the British overseas empire."[29] They were involved in social service and welfare activities as well as poverty alleviation activities.[30] Many NGOs operating in Sri Lanka are interested in evangelization.[31] Such NGOs receive funds from abroad. These organizations, being Christian, receive negative treatment by the Buddhists, who interpret any social service through kar-

---

26. Cf. *Cula-kammavibhanga Sutta*, MN. 135.20.
27. Interview with Pastor Adrian DeVisser of Kitusewana Church, Welisara, Sri Lanka, on 10 December 2016.
28. Perera, *The Dynamics*, 106.
29. Samaraweera, *Politics*, 4.
30. Ibid., 5.
31. Perera, *The Dynamics*, 115.

mic eyes. There is a clash of worldviews in this respect. For Buddhists, these social services are meritorious acts, while for Christians it is a command of Christ to help those in need. Therefore, misinterpretations are bound to occur.

Grace and Karma

Grace is a one of the fundamental teachings of Christianity. The common definition of grace is the unmerited favor of God toward humanity. Grace is a relational concept. One cannot understand it without belief in the creator God and his personal involvement in the affairs of the world. All references in the Bible emphasize the free character of grace.

Salvation in the Christian faith is a gift given by God without consideration of the merit of people. Therefore, grace and karma are incomparable. Under the rule of karma there is no hope apart from what we can do for ourselves by our own effort. The Bible teaches that we are sinful by nature, and left to ourselves we will do evil, and thus deserve punishment. Grace, however, does what we cannot do. It gives us eternal life that we have not earned and gives us God's Spirit to help us do good.

In the New Testament grace means God's love in action towards those who merited the opposite of love. The story of the prodigal son in the Bible shows the loving father as a symbol of God (Luke 15:11–32). In contrast to the concept of karma where one has to earn his salvation, grace means God taking steps to save sinners who could not do anything to save themselves. While karma operates as a self-sustaining mechanism as natural universal law, without any need of an external agency, grace shows the opposite of it. Grace is an essential part of God's character of benevolence, love and mercy. Thus, God forgives and blesses in spite of the fact that humans do not deserve to be treated well or dealt with generously. The Bible repeatedly calls grace a gift (Eph 4:7).

Since salvation is a gift from God we cannot offer anything in return for the gift. We can only offer our gratitude. One way of expressing that gratitude is in our love for God. Grace is associated with agape love. Christianity teaches that agape is the love originating from God for humankind as well as the human reciprocal love for God.

This concept applies to the acts of benevolent giving by Christians. There is no cost to the person who receives the gift. Since it is a gift, the receiver does not owe anything in return in the Christian environment which is based on grace. There is no cost to the recipient as the giver transfers full ownership to the one who receives. Therefore, in the giving of a gift, the Christian giver voluntarily forfeits his ownership willingly, so the recipient would profit from it.[32] The act of giving has nothing to do with the receiver's merit or any inherent quality (2 Tim 1:9–10).

As the Christian religion is based on human's relationship with God, the word grace also is connected to that relationship. In the New Testament, the word translated as grace is the Greek word *charis*. Because God loves us, and because his innocent son satisfied his justice, God can give us his eternal life, his righteousness, and his forgiveness for all of our sins. By God's grace through faith in his son we are given what we do not deserve. While karma locks a person into a cycle of retributive justice, God breaks that cycle with his grace. While karma guarantees that a person gets what he deserves, grace guarantees that a person can get what he does not deserve. Buddhism teaches self-deliverance. "You are the lord of your fate, the doer of your deeds; it is you who brings yourself into heaven or hell, or Nirvana."[33] On the other hand, grace cannot be earned. Salvation is a gift from God, not our achievement through good karma. Salvation is the most extraordinary expression of God's grace.

There are differing theories within Christianity of how grace is attained. Catholics and Reformed Protestants understand the accomplishment of grace in significantly different ways. It has been described as the main concept that divides Catholicism from Protestantism, and Calvinism from Arminianism. Catholic doctrine teaches that God uses the vehicle of the sacraments, carried out in faith, as a primary and effective means to enable a Christian to receive God's grace.[34] Sacraments carried out in faith are the tangible method through which God's grace becomes personally received by the participant. Reformed Protestants, generally, do not share this view with regard to the transmittal of grace. They favor a less institutionalized method.

Christian Charity and Merit Making

In the King James Version of the New Testament, the word *agape* is translated in some places as "charity" which has a modern meaning of giving to

---

32. Peiris, *Fire and Water*, 14.
33. Almond and Otto, *Buddhism and Christianity*, 90.
34. Ryrie, *The Grace of God*, 10–11.

meet the needs of the less fortunate. However, giving to the needy is based on the statement of Jesus expressed in Matthew 25:40: "The King will reply, 'Truly I tell you, whatever you did for one of the least of these brothers and sisters of mine, you did for me.'"

Christians from the beginning have had a habit of practicing charity. The missionaries viewed charity as an expression of agape love. Food, clothing and medicine were supplied to those unable to work through want and disease. A host of people were thus saved from falling victims to hunger and disease.[35] During the malaria epidemic of 1934–35 in Sri Lanka, some Christian churches were turned into hospitals when the epidemic intensified and peaked in April 1935.[36]

The Buddhist concept of merit-making is an area in which most misunderstanding takes place with regard to Christian charity. Merit is one major concept attached to karma in Buddhism. It is a power which accumulates as a result of good deeds, acts, and thoughts.[37] Merit is generally considered to be fundamental to Buddhist ethics; merit-making is important to Buddhist practice. Merit brings good and pleasant results, determines the quality of the next life and contributes to a person's growth towards nirvana. In addition, merit is also shared with a deceased loved one, in order to diminish the deceased's suffering in their new existence. Despite modernization, merit and merit-making remain essential in traditional Buddhist countries.

Christian Grace Misinterpreted Under Karmic Law

There are several occasions where Christian charity was interpreted through a karmic point of view. If the meritorious aspect is lacking in an act of giving, Buddhists speculate other motives to be in operation. Therefore, in many cases Christian help is seen as inducement for conversion, since Buddhists engage even in social work in order to gain merit. This misunderstanding is enhanced when help is given to poor laity who are at the bottom of the category of the merit-making field (*punya kheta*) in Buddhism.

According to a study undertaken by Barend Terwiel in 2001, Thai Buddhists were asked to place the main items of what they thought would

---

35. Mateer, *The Land of Charity*, 309.
36. Kohn, *Encyclopedia of Plague and Pestilence*, 377.
37. Bodhi, *Dana, the Practice of Giving*, 4.

give them the most merit in the correct order. Their answer was: 1. Becoming a monk, 2. Contributing enough money for the construction of a monastery, 3. Having a son ordained as a monk, 4. Making excursions to Buddhist shrines throughout the country, 5. Contributing towards the repair of a monastery, 6. Giving food daily to the monks and giving food on holy days, 7. Becoming a novice, 8. Attending a temple on all holy days and obeying the eight precepts on these days, and 9. Obeying the five precepts at all times. These findings are relevant to Sri Lanka as well to a great extent. In this list one may notice that giving to the poor, needy, outcaste, fatherless and marginalized is not important. Such people do not belong to the field of merit where the devotees' action would bring them the highest meritorious results.[38] Christian help, on the other hand, is usually targeted at this group.

In 1957, the services in government hospitals of the Roman Catholic nuns of the Holy Family Sisters of Bordeaux were terminated, since the Buddhists believed that their compassionate work led to the conversion of Buddhists.[39] In 2005, in the aftermath of the Tsunami disaster, the Baptist Church in England wished to build one thousand houses in a village in the South Western coastal area of Sri Lanka. A Buddhist monk who led a movement against the Christians, demanded that a Buddhist temple be built in the proposed village; if not, they would not allow any construction activities. The Baptists withdrew from the village in the Sinhala Buddhist area and moved to the Tamil Hindu area in the northeast of the island. The Buddhist opposition again was that the aid would be an inducement for conversion of poor people.

Evangelism

The practice of evangelism presupposes that people are freely entitled to choose the religion which they prefer. At the same time, however, it also raises tense questions about belonging to a particular community in Asian societies. This disturbs the social coherence within a given society. The current era of globalization has added new issues to this question of changing religions. There are ways in which contemporary contexts of religious pluralism in Asia both enable and threaten any project of evangelism.

---

38. Cf. Terwiel, *Monks and Magic*.
39. Stirrart, *Power and Religiosity*, 41.

The growth in popularity of evangelical and Pentecostal charismatic Christianity over the last three decades has heightened worries among Sinhala Buddhist nationalists over the extent of the economic, political and social effects of Christian activities in Sri Lanka. The Buddhists perceive Christian charity as unethically purposed work. They assume that the help given by a Christian individual or an organization to socially and economically disadvantaged people is a surreptitious method of making them adopt Christianity. In this protectionist view, when charity is given to someone who is materially impoverished or socially disadvantaged, the Buddhist perception is one-sided, as they interpret Christian charity from the Buddhist karmic worldview. Thus, the decision of a person to convert to Christianity would be interpreted as being a decision taken under conditions of duress. It is treated as a conversion elicited under circumstances where unethical methods were used.[40]

Buddhists who oppose Christian conversions argue that "force, allurement, and other fraudulent means" have been used to convert people to Christianity (Anti-Conversion Bill of May 28, 2004). Christian evangelists see their religious activity in the island as the work of salvation mission. The Buddhist and Christian views on 'salvation' are dramatically different. Buddhists are critical of the means, methods and the types of targets chosen as subjects of evangelism.[41] This is caused by differences in their metaphysical, cosmological and practical ideas about proper ways to pursue their missions. The two groups are at opposite extremes.

Alarmed by the view that Christianity, with the force of its global network, could potentially supplant Buddhism, a set of vociferous Buddhist monks, vowing to create legislative measures to ban 'unethical conversions,' formed a political party in 2004. Many Buddhist extremists are critical of Christian charity as allurement to attract the poor. Thus, Christian charity and humanitarian aid from individuals, churches and NGOs are looked upon as forces actively threatening Buddhism. As we noted earlier, some segments of Sri Lankan Buddhists have vigorously resisted any form of material support given by Christians as inducement. Yet, these features of Christianity are attractive to many contemporary Sri Lankans who are in need of social and material assistance.

The concern that Christians wield material influence through access to charitable capital form the foundation of the conflict between Buddhist

---

40. Feener, R. Michael and Juliana Finucane, editors. *Proselytizing*, 223.
41. Ibid., 224.

nationalists and evangelical Christians. Charity is also deplored by the Buddhists as a tool of the mission strategy of the new Pentecostal and charismatic groups. Charitable work is widely viewed by Buddhist nationalists as a practice intended to encourage church attendance by poor Buddhists. Although there may be incidents of attaching charity to the missionary agenda by some individual Christians, for many Christians charity is an act to uplift the poor and not laden with evangelistic motives.

These Christians assert that their generous engagement in charitable work and social justice activism is motivated by their love for God. They claim that they put their faith into practice. Therefore, it should be understood as selfless acts intended to strengthen their own faith. They also insist that charity is an act through which they seek to contribute to the pluralistic society in Sri Lanka.

Worldview Misunderstandings

The following example illustrates how the redemption and lift experienced by a rural Christian community was viewed by outsiders as manipulation of the poor through foreign material help. A pastor from Minuwangoda went to Seeppukulama, a remote village in the North-central province of Sri Lanka in 2014. He and his wife decided to remain in the village in order to express Christian love. They found that there were no toilets in the entire village. The pastor and his wife were used to using toilets, while the villagers were not.[42] Therefore the pastor decided to build a toilet. When he started digging a pit in his compound the villagers also came to help him. While digging the pit they suddenly found water. The villagers requested that he make it a well as they had to go very far to collect water for daily usage. Then they began to dig another pit at a considerable distant from the well. As a result the villagers now have a toilet and a well. This achievement was the result of free community labor guided by the pastor.

Those who did not have any dealings with the pastor's work began to speculate about the contribution made to these sympathizers of Christianity after the appearance of the pastor. They noticed that the pastor and his wife came from Colombo and that now there were improvements in the village. Other villagers also gradually thought of building their own toilets.

---

42. Their habit was to go barefooted to the forest for toilet activities. Therefore, worm and other infections were common. The introduction of the use of a toilet gradually reduced worm-borne diseases.

The pastor helped them within his capacity. Once he brought a squatting pan from Colombo for a villager's toilet when he returned from a trip. The householders helped each other in the work. Now, in a village that for years did not have toilets, when another pastor came from Colombo, toilets began to appear in several houses. Outsiders who observed the development began spreading rumors, saying that there was aid coming from outside through this Christian worker.[43]

Another example: The devotees of a Buddhist temple had donated a part of their land some distance from the temple premises. The land lay barren for nearly ten years without being made use of by the monk of the Buddhist temple. Later the same donors, who had embraced Christianity, donated another portion of the same land to the church. The pastor mobilized the believers and made it an economically useful place for the people. The monk of the temple instigated some Buddhist villagers and organized an attack on the pastor and the Christian community, accusing them as recipients of foreign funds who were trying to betray the nation. In both these cases, misunderstanding occurred due to two different worldviews.

As a result of the Christian presence, the villagers who were impacted by it began to show considerable improvement in their lifestyle. Their houses became clean; the children performed better in school, and household goods also began to increase. In these villages, the contribution to family coffers was usually made by women. Often men were the consumers of the income created by their wives with very little contribution of their own to the family coffers. They used to waste money on items of quick gratification. They had a lot of spare time to waste with their friends in drinking illicit liquor and smoking. As Christian influence infiltrated the family through female believers, their lifestyle began to change. Gradually, with the attendance of women in worship services, the men also became less troublesome. The despicable habits of men gradually disappeared. The time previously wasted in unproductive activities was spent on work.

The other villagers who did not take part in the Christian community noticed an improvement in the church goers. Vendors of illicit liquor and drug suppliers lost a part of their income. Their interpretation was that these men were getting some assistance from a foreign donor. They assumed that the pastor was doling out a part of what he got to the members of the village in order to convert them.

---

43. Interview with Pastor Asitha de Silva of Free Church Minuwangoda on 16th December 2016.

Part II: Cultural Perspectives

Charity as Threat

People who are brought up in the Buddhist culture usually are unable to see someone helping others without getting anything in return. The view of the Buddhist is that the gods are dependent on humans for merit, while humans seek help from them by transferring a part of their merit earned. The purpose of offering any assistance to someone or some worthy cause is to receive reward for themselves. This is determined by the karmic view of making merit. If the merit-making purpose is lacking, there would be other motives. The Buddhists see the help given by Christians in villages as having a hidden agenda. They do not believe that a person who saw a poor man would give some help without getting something in return. Therefore, cases where a person among the poor embraces Christianity and experiences 'redemption and lift' have been interpreted as the "unethical conversion of poor Buddhists."[44] The members of a newly formed political party of Buddhist monks, known as Jatika Hela Urumaya, have demanded the Sri Lankan government several times to pass a bill in Parliament banning 'unethical conversions' carried out among poor Buddhists.

Again, this is how many Buddhist monks view Christian charity. The Buddhists cannot believe that others give help to people without an ulterior motive. The donor has to have the intention of getting something in return. If anyone experiences improved socio-economic standards, the usual Buddhist interpretation would be that there is some outside help. In fact, the personal upliftment of the new Christian has no connection with any material help from the church but with the change in their outlook on life.

Unlike a Christian pastor, a visit by a Buddhist monk to a house of a devotee is rare. It would be only for an alms-giving ceremony that he may visit a house with a retinue of monks. On a rare visit, if the monk comes to a house he has to be given special attention, with the house being made ritually suitable for the occasion. When monks pay a visit to a lay home, the householders have to offer gifts to him. Meritorious acts performed with monks are very expensive and they are beyond the possibilities of a poor villager. Nevertheless, the visit of a monk is considered a meritorious one to the family. Pastoral visits will be misinterpreted through the karmic lens this way as well: if not coming for merit making, then what?

Even the language expresses these values. 'Thank you' is not a part of traditional Buddhist vocabulary. They usually say, "May you gain merit."

---

44. Deegalle, *Politics*, 93.

The amount of merit gained varies according to the spiritual purity of the recipient. As we noticed earlier, the ordinary villager does not fall into this category of field of merit (*punya kheta*). In the mind of Buddhists, when there is no merit to be gained, there is no meaning in giving. Giving without any return is alien to the karmic mind. In such cases they may even interpret the recipient's condition as good karma from a previous existence. In such cases, Christian influence becomes suspect.

Missiological Implications

Christian evangelists must be aware of the different worldviews when they engage in social service activities among Buddhists in Sri Lanka. The karmic worldview of Buddhism, as a system, requires its adherent to be devoted to exploring a set of principles that will earn him or her a meritorious state that they hope will lead to the end of suffering. There is no divine presence involved in their religious philosophy. In Christianity, it is required to love God and obey his commandments through a relationship with Jesus Christ, and to spread the good news to others so they too may be saved.

For Buddhists who work on the principle of karma, charity to the poor is at the bottom of their merit-making process. Karma has no relational concept. Christians, on the other hand, work on the principle of agape love, which is not a reward-seeking sentiment. Buddhists find it hard to understand the principle of grace (*charis*) which is an unmerited, unearned, undeserved gift. Therefore, Buddhists will continue to have a suspicious attitude with regard to ecumenical and evangelical Christians who engage in social services.

One has to remember that grace in Christianity and karma in Buddhism are core concepts of each religion. Therefore, they are non-negotiables. Since they are two opposite doctrines one has to expect continued misunderstandings and misinterpretations which would lead to clashes.

Bibliography

Almond, Philip C. and Rudolf Otto. "Buddhism and Christianity: Compared and Contrasted." *Buddhist-Christian Studies*. 4 Hawaii: University of Hawaii Press, (1984), 87–101.

Bodhi, Bhikkhu, editor. *Dana, the Practice of Giving: Selected Essays*, Kandy: Buddhist Publication Society, 1990.

Buswell, Robert E. *Encyclopaedia of Buddhism*, Vol. I, New York: Macmillan, 2004.

Part II: Cultural Perspectives

Cula-kammavibhanga Sutta (Majjhima Nikaya) MN 135; PTS: M iii 202. http://www.accesstoinsight.org/tipitaka/mn/mn.135.nymo.html.

Deegalle, Mahinda. "Politics of the Jatika Hela Urumaya Monks: Buddhism and Ethnicity in Contemporary Buddhism." *Contemporary Buddhism*, 5-2 (2004) 83–104.

Dhammapada: The Buddhist Path of Wisdom, translated by Acharya Buddharakkhita, Kandy: Buddhist Publication Society, 1985.

Egge, James R. *Religious Giving and the Invention of Karma in Theravada Buddhism*, Richmond, Surrey: Curzon, 2002.

Faure, Bernard. *Unmasking Buddhism*, London: Wiley Blackwell, 2009.

Feener, R. Michael and Juliana Finucane, editors. *Proselytizing and the Limits of Religious Pluralism in Contemporary Asia*, New York: Springer, 2014.

Gombrich, Richard. "Sinhalese Buddhism: A Case Study of the Interaction between Doctrine and Practice." *History of Religions* 11-2 (January 1971) 203–219.

———. "Buddhist Karma and Social Control." In *Comparative Studies in Society and History*. Cambridge: Cambridge University Press, 1975.

Gyatso, Geshe K., *Modern Buddhism: The Path of Compassion and Wisdom*. New York: Tharpa, 2011.

Hresko, Tracy. "Rights Rhetoric as an Instrument of Religious Oppression in Sri Lanka." *Boston College International and Comparative Law Review*. 29-1 (2006) 123–133.

Jathika Hela Urumaya. *Prohibition of Forcible Conversion of Religion Bill* (draft), May 22, 2004.

Jayatilleke, K. N., *The Message of the Buddha*. Kandy: Buddhist Publication Society, 2000.

Jerryson, Michael and Mark Juergensmeyer. *Buddhist Warfare*. New York: Oxford University Press, 2015.

Jootla, Susan Elbaum. "Right Livelihood: The Noble Eightfold Path in the Working Life." In *Buddhist laymen: Four essays*, edited by R. Bogoda. Kandy: Wheel, 1990.

Keyes, Charles F. "Buddhist Politics and Their Revolutionary Origins in Thailand." *International Political Review*. 10-2 (April 1989) 121–142.

———. "Introduction: Popular Ideas of Karma." In *Karma: An Anthropological Inquiry*, edited by Charles F. Keyes and E. Valentine Daniel. Berkeley: University of California Press, 1983.

King, Sallie B., and Christopher S. Queen, eds. *Engaged Buddhism: Buddhist Liberation Movements in Asia*. Albany: State University of New York Press, 1996.

Kohn, George C. *Encyclopedia of Plague and Pestilence: From Ancient Times to the Present*, New York City: Facts on File, 1995.

Mateer, Samuel. *The Land of Charity: A Descriptive Account of Travancore and Its People, with Especial Reference to Missionary Labour 1835–1893*. Sydney: Wentworth, 2016.

Matthews, B. "Christian Evangelical Conversions and the Politics of Sri Lanka." *Pacific Affairs*. 80-3 (Fall 2007) 455–472.

Muller, Edward. *The Atthasalini: Buddhighosha's Commentary on the Dhammasangani*. London: PTS, 1887.

Norsworthy, Kathryn L., Understanding Violence against women in Southeast Asia: a group approach in social justice work. *International Journal for the Advancement of Counselling*, 25: 145–56.

Obeyesekere, Gananath. *Karma and Rebirth: A Cross Cultural Study*. Delhi: Motilal Banarsidass, 2006.

Oddie, Geoffrey. *Hindu and Christian in South-East India*. London: Rutledge, 1991.

Panikkar, Raymond. "The Law of Karma and the Historical Dimension of Man." *Philosophy East and West*. 22–1 (Jan. 1972) 25–43.
Peiris, Aloysius. *Fire and Water: Basic Issues in Asian Buddhism and Christianity*. New York: Orbis, 1996.
Perera, Sasanka. "The Dynamics, the Impact, Rhetoric and the Politics." *Dialogue*. XXV–XXVI (1998–1999) 104–124.
Perera, Sasanka. *Living with Torturers*. Colombo: International Centre for Ethnic Studies, 1995.
Powers, John. *Introduction to Tibetan Buddhism*. Snow Lion, 2007.
Rahula, Walpola. *What the Buddha Taught*. New York: Grove Weidenfeld, 1959.
Ryrie, Charles C. *The Grace of God*. Chicago: Moody, 1963.
Samaraweera, Vijaya. *Politics, National Security and Vibrancy of NGOs*. Colombo: Law and Trust Society, 1997.
Stirrart, R. L. *Power and Religiosity in a Post-Colonial Setting*. Cambridge, UK: Cambridge University Press, 1992.
Tambiah, S. J. *Buddhism Betrayed: Religion, Politics, and Violence in Sri Lanka*. Chicago: University of Chicago Press, 1992.
Terwiel, Barend J. *Monks and Magic: An Analysis of Religious Ceremonies in Central Thailand*. London: Curzon, 2001.
Veliath, Cyril, editor. *Buddha and Jesus: An Anthology of Articles by Jesuits Engaged in Buddhist Studies and Inter-Religious Dialogue*. Kelaniya, Sri Lanka: Tulana Research Centre for Encounter and Dialogue, 2015.
Wright, Dale S. "Critical questions towards a naturalized concept of karma in Buddhism." *Journal of Buddhist Ethics*. 11 (2004) 77–93.
Young, R. F. and Senanayaka, G. S. B. *The Carpenter-Heretic: A Collection of Buddhist Stories about Christianity from 18th Century Sri Lanka*. Colombo: Karunaratne and Sons, 1998.

10

Prapheni Heet Sibsong
The Tradition of Merit-Making with Ethical Commitment to the 'Other'

Dipti Visuddhangkoon

In Isan, the Northeast of Thailand, Prapheni Heet Sibsong or the twelve-month Thai-Isan tradition has formed the main doxastic structural bedrock and conceptual framework based upon which all socio-cultural, religious and ethical values are enacted and brought to full realization. The ceremonies incorporated in Prapheni Heet Sibsong create conditions of veritable relationship with oneself and others in the community. The calendrical ceremonies that have given social meaning to the passage of time by creating monthly cycles oriented mostly towards seasonal variations with its impact on agro-based economy, have imposed a cultural order on nature as well as ethical behavior-orientation on both the laity and monastics as a whole. Each of the ceremonies recalls and commemorates the basic beliefs of Isan people and its annual celebration establishes a link between past and present, as if the original events, for instance, the Bodhisattva's life events (as re-enacted through verbal narration in the Boonphravet ceremony) are happening over again. The series of these traditional ceremonies start with Boonkhaokam in the first month and ends with Boonkathin in the twelfth month. Here we shall briefly describe each of the twelve traditions before highlighting two, namely Boonkumkhaoyai and Boonpravet, for a detailed analysis.

The Twelve Ceremonies

The first of the traditions, Boonkhaokam, is an after-harvest ceremony and starts approximately in mid to late November every year. Since this ceremony is directly related to the spiritual purification of monks, the activities that mark the ceremony involve intensive practice of dhamma such as listening to sermons, practicing of vipassana meditation, reading dhamma books, and more.

The second in the list is Boonkhunlarn or Boonkumkhaoyai. This will be discussed in some detail following this overview in order to understand the concept of ethical commitment to the 'Other' which is deeply embedded in the way of life of the Isan people. Like Boonkhaokam, Boonkhunlarn or Boonkumkhaoyai is also a post-harvest ceremony marking the beginning of the winter season in early January. The main activity of the ceremony involves merit-making by offering the giant paddy heap by the villagers. Monks are invited to individual households for chanting and blessing the harvest and the granary.

The third ceremony, Boonkhaojee, starts at the end of February or early March. While villagers take great delight in offering roasted egg-coated newly harvested sticky rice cakes (*khaojee*) to the monks, the aroma of which pervades every home, merit-making is performed in observance of the great event of the Buddha's time through the celebration of the Magha Puja Day.

The fourth ceremony in the series is Boonphravet, falling in the month of March. This particular ceremony, discussed in detail below, is the heart of Prapheni Heet Sibsong. During this ceremony, monks are invited to chant the Vessantara Jataka, the story of The Great Birth.

Following this great ceremony is the traditional Thai New Year celebration, Boonsongkran, that is marked by great festivity and many commemorative activities like merit-making, sand pagoda construction, bathing of Buddha statues, pouring water in the palms of Buddhist monks, honoring ancestors' bones (*bangsakul*), releasing fish, birds and turtles for accumulation of merit through these wholesome actions, and more.

The next ceremony, immediately after the cool splashing of water at Songkran, is one of opposite temperamental feeling that corresponds to the gradual seasonal changes with increase in temperature and aridity as summer approaches. This ceremony is called Boonbangfai or the Rocket festival and falls in the month of May. This festival originated from the influence of multi-cultural beliefs, an eclectic mixture of Buddhism, Brahmanism and animism with its emphasis on belief in spirits and fertility cults. Merit-making, as a part of this festive occasion, is a direct Buddhist influence. Invoking the celestial deity Indra and appealing for rain is a purely Brahmanical doxastic practice. Worshiping the guardian spirit is an animistic influence. The competitive shooting skyward of homemade rockets on temple premises bears significant resemblance to symbolic values ingrained in indigenous fertility cults.

The ceremony that immediately follows the jubilation of the Rocket Festival is one of ablution and cleansing, both at the spiritual/mental level as well as bodily/physical level, and is known as Boonchamha or Boonberkbaan. During this ceremony, villagers take sand, small stones and water in a big jar and white consecrated thread to the central hall of the temple to be blessed by the monks and which are then carried back home as symbols of ablution and purification. Moreover, Buddhist monks are invited to chant for two consecutive nights, and on the third day, a meal is offered to them.

The next ceremony, starting in late July or early August, marks the commencement of the Buddhist Lent and is known as Boonkhaophansa. On the full moon during this ceremony, Asalha Puja is celebrated to commemorate the Buddha's deliverance of the First Sermon.

The ceremony that follows the Buddhist Lent is Boonkhaopadabdin, conducted with the purpose of dedicating merit to one's dead relatives and distant ancestors so as to alleviate the suffering of those who must have descended to the woeful abodes or lower realms of pain and misery. As part of this ceremony, villagers offer different food items such as: rice, sweets, fruits, areca palm and betel leaf, all well wrapped up in banana leaves, to the spirits of dead ancestors at early dawn in the village monasteries and wish them well-being and a good future life. Since Boonkhaopadabdin falls in the ninth month, most devotees usually make offerings of nine banana-leaf-wrapped packs to the spirits of the deceased. This ceremony in a way re-enacts the Buddha's advice to King Bimbisara to make merit and offer food to dead ancestors.

The ceremony that follows Boonkhaopadabdin is similar in spirit and is known as Boonkhaosak. Villagers make merit as usual and bring items to offer the monks with their names tagged on the offerings. Once any monk or novice accepts the offering, then a section of it is taken back home to be offered to the guardian spirit (*Phi-tahaek*) on the homestead and also to the dead ancestors for their well-being as well as the villagers' own happiness and prosperity.

The ceremonial sharing of food for ancestors is followed by the ceremony to mark the end of the Buddhist Lent, known as Boonorkphansa and falls in the month of October. Great ritualistic offering of alms food to monks (*Takbatra-devo*) is organized to mark the end of the Buddhist Lent.

And immediately following the end of the Buddhist Lent, the last Prapheni Heet Sibsong ceremony is the robe-offering ceremony, known as Boonkathin. Ceremonial presentation of yellow robes and other necessary items to monks is the hallmark of this final ceremony in the entire corpus of Prapheni Heet Sibsong.

Two Common Ceremonial Ends

While each of the traditional ceremonies is important in its essence and codified meaning and can be considered complete in itself, what impresses the present writer most is the subtle connection between each of the ceremonies. Taken in its sequential entirety, we recognize that the corpus of Prapheni Heet Sibsong begins with the ceremony of Boonkhaokam, the monastics' self-purification period and ends with Boonkathin, the annual robe-offering ceremony. Monks are the spiritual leaders of society and to play this specific role it is indispensable for them to lead a pure and chaste life. In order to lead a pure life, both in letters and spirit, monastics are expected to be mindful of all their actions—verbal, bodily and mental. Any minor and major offences of monastic disciplinary codes (except for the most severe that lead to immediate disrobing and dismissal) have to be amended through undergoing an extended period of perseverance and penance as laid out in the Vinaya Pitaka.

The entire corpus of Prapheni Heet Sibsong thus logically starts with the mindful awareness of living up to the ideals of a truly spiritual and renunciant life with diligence and full-hearted dedication through participation in Boonkhaokam and thereby setting the ideal example before the lay Buddhist community, who constantly supports the monastics' material needs of food, shelter and clothing. The trajectory of this mindful awareness connects itself to the other end of the corpus; monks as spiritual leaders are befitted to receive the annual robe-offering from the laity.

Part II: Cultural Perspectives

On the two ends of the conceptual framework of Prapheni Heet Sibsong, thus stand the monastics as spiritual watch guards over the field of merit. Moreover, within these two ends various ceremonies are inserted that help train lay devotees to follow the spiritual path through emphasis on cultivation of such qualities as generosity, mindfulness, loving-kindness, and more. While Boonkhaojee and Boonkumkhaoyai highlight the good deed of sharing the best part of one's hard-earned fruits of labor with monastics and community members, Boonkhaopadapdin and Boonkhaosak bring to the fore the sharing of relished items for the departed. It is thus clear that ethical responsibility does not get limited to living subjects alone but is repatriated to distant and absent entities in some unknowable realm, thereby reinforcing the idea of merit-making with ethical commitment to the other, either living or absent. While rooted in the present, devout Buddhists dedicate merit to those past (dead ancestors) with the wish that the departed ones' future (a future that is already distanced and can never be intelligibly explored by the devout), be better and worthy. Within the conceptual framework of all the ceremonies in Prapheni Heet Sibsong the connection of past, present and future time and the effect of one's actions on self and others are endorsed. We shall now discuss in some detail two of the ceremonies that epitomize the cultivation of generosity, loving-kindness and responsibility towards the 'Other'.

Boonphravet

The Boonphravet ceremony, that marks the fourth lunar month and falls approximately in the month of March, is the most important ceremony in the entire corpus of Prapheni Heet Sibsong or twelve-month Thai-Isan tradition. The unique feature of this traditional ceremony is that specialized and trained monks are invited to different temples for chanting the Vessantara Jataka[1] (known in Thai as Vessantdorn Chadok). This is the story of

---

1. Of the 547 Buddhist stories (Jātakas) illustrating the previous lives of the Buddha, the Vessantara Jātaka is the most popular in Thailand and has long been delineated in both poetry and visual arts. The Great Birth story relates the penultimate incarnation of Buddha as Prince Vessantara, the Bodhisattava. The core action of the story revolves around Prince Vessantara's perfection of the meritorious act of charity or *dāna*, which began with his generous act of donating the magical rain-giving white elephant to the drought-stricken denizens of the city of Kalinga. This act outraged his own subjects and resulted in his banishment from the kingdom by his father, King Sonjay. His exile expedited the next phase of generous acts that unrolled initially with the whole-hearted

Mahachat or The Great Birth. This particular Jataka tale which delineates the penultimate birth-story of the Buddha as the Bodhisattva, before being finally born as Gotama Buddha, is extremely popular all throughout Thailand. The Mahachat sermon text is rich both in religious and linguistic information. Its religious significance is clear from the fact that it provides the foundational base of moral perfection, epitomized in the character of the Bodhisattva. The text provides innumerable examples of proverbs and didactic messages that listeners can reflect upon and bring into practice in day to day life in order to accumulate merit and enrich their lives in spiritual terms. The arrangement of Boonphravet involves a lot of time-consuming and expensive preparation on the part of the host temple and for the lay devotees. To offer help and support with every stage of arrangement is an act of merit-making symbolizing self-sacrifice, dedicated effort and devotional zeal. The delivering of the sermon is an auspicious event and begins at early dawn so that the entire sermon can be delivered on a single day. Monks who have voices in a high range train themselves to delineate the entire story (in thirteen sections) in a unique recital style infused with distinct rhythms.[2] As recital-narrators, sung-sermon practitioner monks

---

donation of all his earthly and palatial belongings to suppliants from every stratum of society. Eventually it culminated with the giving away of his two beloved children, Kanha and Chali to the glutton Brahmin, Chuchok and his wife, Matsi to the deity Indra, who approached Vessantara disguising himself in human form.

2. In order to delineate the story effectively, sung-sermon practitioner monks have devised many different literary, stylistic and narratological techniques that have positively affected the proliferation, preservation and continuation of the tradition of this oral narrative form. These techniques have also helped to infuse great enjoyment, merry-making, spiritualism, subliminal bliss and solace to the process of listening to the sermon. Stylization represents the creativity of the practitioner monks in actual narrativization of the Mahachat sermon. The many different rhythms that have evolved over time represent stylistic features that are unique of the Isan Mahachat sermon. The most common style of rhythm used by monks while chanting from manuscripts is *Thamnong-nai-phuk-nai-mud*, literally translated into English as "tying-wrapping rhythm". It has the compositional characteristic of *Rai*, a traditional form of Isan verse. It is probable that this original rhythm has branched off with subtle variations at different localities throughout the northeastern region. A practitioner monk may master any one of the following three styles or all three depending on the locale, individual choice, ability and training. i) *Thamnong Lom-phad-phrao* is a rhythm that resembles the drifting of coconut palm fronds in the breeze. It is a slow kind of rhythm requiring alternate strong and weak or mild voice modulation similar to the effect of wind on coconut palm fronds. This rhythm is typical of Ubon Ratchathani province. ii) *Thamnong Chang-thiem-mae* is a rhythm that resembles the movement of the elephant calf along the side of its mother. In this rhythm, the voice is alternately pressed and released but without complete release; sung at alternately high and low pitch but without producing the sound "eei-eei".

follow the story along each of the thirteen sections known as *kan* that totals to one thousand verses or *Gāthā* expanding over time and space and uphold the values of compassion and generosity, qualities that are reflected in the character of the bodhisattva in the story.

Compassion is one of the four divine qualities[3] that Buddhism emphasizes. It is believed that the Buddha himself practiced compassion and its corollary, charity to the highest possible level during his penultimate birth as the bodhisattva before being finally born as the Buddha. Human life would not only be spiritually dull and drab, but also all too brutal, if there was an absolute lack of compassion. Compassion is a great virtue, the cultivation of which helps to keep vices like greed and selfishness at bay while bringing to full realization the ethical responsibility towards others. Such unwholesome mental states as egocentricity, egotism and megalomania can find suitable cures through the practice of compassion. When mindfully practiced to the highest level, it can purify one's body and mind leading to complete annihilation of all sorts of clinging and attachment. Only then the path of true renunciation can be tread upon. It is compassion that gave rise to other supremely admirable qualities in the Bodhisattva (Prince Vessantara) such as loving-kindness, generosity, charity, selflessness, self-sacrifice, honesty, endurance, patience, moral courage and determination.

Corresponding to the content of the Vessantara Jātaka, sung-sermon practitioner monks have improvised a unique style of rendition that renders the narration of the entire story very effective. Through their rendition the Bodhisattva, who is the epitome of moral perfections, becomes a living example and a perennial source of inspiration to lay devotees. Thus, it can be ascertained that sung-sermon practitioner monks play a significant role in propagating Buddhism amongst the laity. Usually the entire village community collaborates to help arrange the ceremony. It is a common belief among lay Buddhists in Northeast Thailand that one who listens through the entire thirteen sections of the Vessantara story on a single sitting

---

This rhythm is typical of Khonkaen and Chaiyaphum. *iii) Thamnong Kaah-ten-kon* is a rhythm that resembles the movement of a crow along lumps of clay. In this rhythm, the voice is rendered as slow and fast alternately similar to a crow's to and fro jumping, flying off, and landing movement around lumps of mud in the paddy field. This rhythm is typical of Roi-et province. Since it originated in the Suwanaphum district, it is also known as Suwanaphum rhythm.

3. The four divine or heavenly qualities or sublime states of mind known as *Brahmavihāra* that Buddhism emphasizes are *mettā* (loving-kindness), *karunā* (compassion), *muditā* (empathy or sympathetic joy) and *upekkhā* (equanimity). For a clear exposition of this, cf. Payutto, 1995, 236–238.

accumulates enormous merit that ensures future birth during the time of Ariya Mettaiya.[4] The practitioner monks who are invited by host temples to deliver the sermon not only help unite the villagers in merit-making but also open up this opportunity to lay devotees to accumulate merits for the future. The ceremony is infused with great enjoyment, merry-making, spiritualism, subliminal bliss and mental solace. Didactic interpolations interspersed throughout the Mahachat sermon text direct the listeners to universal truths with an emphasis on realization of these truths through practice along the moral path. Mahachat practitioner monks would devote enough time in the course of delivering the sermon to clarify and repetitiously stress them so as to inspire and encourage the laity to put into real practice in life.[5] Suppose the Mahachat sermon delivering ceremony ceases

---

4. This belief has arisen from a non-canonical sutta called the *Phra Malai Sutta*. The content is as follows:
Thou all must inform educable beings
Whosoever desires to meet the Future Buddha (Ariya Mettaiya)
Ought to revere the teachings
The Mahachat sermon
Be frequently organized
The 1000 verses therein be worshipped
With ritual item in 1000 sets
Listen to it entirely on a single day.

5. Repeated words and phrases in the original Isan version are maintained in our translation below from Sutasarapimol, 8–10.

All listeners, brethren dear	Father and mother, reflect upon this
Consider deeply about charity	all generous deeds you have done.
Did you gain mental benefits from them?	I welcome you to introspect it.
Have your meritorious acts made you happy?	Smile and be happy always.
Observe it, see it.	When you donate and distribute
Your mind delights	begets felicity through and through.
Whenever you donate	it is a great benefit
Meritorious action is reckoned thus.	All are welcome to continue the effort.
Accumulate merit gradually	little by little it will increase.
When you die this shall be your asset.	Gain great merits.
Everyone has to die	nobody can live forever
All beings in the vast world	none can escape from death
But when you transmigrate	to another realm
Everything would depend on your action.	Good and bad all depends on your action solely.
Whoever has done good deeds	has goodness accumulated.
When dead these actions will lead to heaven.	Ascend to heaven and reside there.
Whoever has done evil deeds	these actions will let you
Descend to hell	full of suffering and lamentation.
All virtuous people	men and women engage in generous action.
Accumulate morality and generosity.	The reward you gain is certain.

to exist in the future due to a lack of nurturing ambience and changing lifestyle, it would inevitably lead to a hiatus in the entire corpus of Prapheni Heet Sibsong that forms the warp and woof of the Isan way of life.

Boonkumkhaoyai

Boonkumkhaoyai (previously known as "Boonkhunlarn"), literally translated into English as 'merit-making by offering the giant paddy heap', marks the second lunar month and falls approximately in the month of January. It is an ancient traditional ceremony that is held at the end of the harvest season in order to create harmony and mutual co-existence among all people in the village. The historical origin of the ceremony can be traced back to the inspiration drawn by Isan people from the story of the previous lives of both Kondañña, the first disciple of the Buddha to attain arahantship and Subhadda Paribbāchaka, a lay devotee who was the last person to be enlightened immediately before the passing away of the Buddha.[6] In Boonkumkhaoyai, villagers co-operate to form the giant paddy heap by donating unhusked rice for the purpose of supporting and promoting various projects related to community welfare and propagation of Buddhism. Viewed from the socio-ethical perspective, this particular agro-based ritualistic

---

Accrue good deeds there would be no suffering.	The world will extol in your praise
All are welcome to do good.	People will admire you.
Deviate from all evil actions	it will reduce your value
Making you devoid of value in yourself.	Only good and evil exist in this world.
All other animals	like herds of cattle
And herds	of elephants
All decay and decompose	but their skin, tusks, and bones
Still have some value.	They can be sold and bought.
When people die all's over	just cremate the body.
Nothing remains	that could be sold or bought
Just like the poetry that has taught	Every poem a Thai poet has ever composed
I leave this to all you laity	for you to consider and reflect upon.
Bull, oxen, buffalo, elephant	that are old and unworthy of any work
Their tusks, horns	still bear importance and value in body
But when humans die	the whole body is valueless
Only good and evil actions persist	to adorn the world.
The entire human populace	when dead and decomposed
Goodness and evil still exist	permanent in essence.
Offer this message to each of you	read and investigate this dhammic truth.

6. Chob Desuankhok, "From Boonkhunkao or Boonkhunlarn to Boonkumkhaoyai," 204–205.

ceremony seems to epitomize the culture of merit-making ingrained in the traditional Thai-Isan way of life.

The originators of Boonkumkhaoyai were humble folks who tilled the soil. Their descendants and bearers of the lineage and rich heritage of the land who have successfully carried on the tradition until the present era are farmers too. Since the ceremony originated in rural Isan, where the majority of the population engages in farming as the chief means of livelihood, it can be assumed that right livelihood is endorsed in the very concept of Boonkumkhaoyai. Topographically, Northeast Thailand is a dry and arid region with scant resources, but the farmers are an industrious lot and generally reap harvest twice a year. They mostly grow glutinous rice, the staple food of the region. And in Boonkumkhaoyai they generously give away a section of the produce that they have reaped with much toil and labor. Every grain of rice that they accumulate and donate for public welfare projects comes from effort, endeavor and perseverance. The tradition-bound rural Isan society that is relatively restrained upholds the philosophy of sufficiency in economy and cherishes the culture of giving. Their approach to life, which is so clearly reflected in the traditional ceremony of Boonkumkhaoyai, manifests what Bhikkhu defined as 'Dhammic Socialism'. According to this philosopher-monk, Dhammic Socialism (*dhammika sangha-niyama*) has three basic principles: the principle of the good of the whole, the principle of restraint and generosity, and the principle of respect and loving-kindness.[7] Dhammic Socialism, which is said to characterize the original moral condition (*sila-dhamma*) of individuals and society, is a hallmark of Boonkumkhaoyai. The participants in Boonkumkhaoyai have loving-kindness deeply rooted in their hearts; otherwise they would have been reluctant to share the fruits of their extreme toil and labor. The desire to share implies sacrifice, which in turn originates from an innate feeling of loving-kindness and compassion towards others. Mettā or loving-kindness is one of the four divine qualities that Buddhism upholds. The vices of greed and selfishness that are rampant in today's consumerist culture can find suitable cures through the practice of loving-kindness. When mindfully practiced to the highest level, this virtue, which is rightly called heavenly abiding, can purify one's body and mind leading to complete annihilation of all sorts of clinging and attachment. A major chunk of the Isan populace, still very much inspired by the richness of the traditional Buddhist way of life and thinking is guided by these qualities to a great degree. Therefore,

---

7. Bhikkhu, *Dhammic Socialism*, 33–34.

despite material paucity in life, the village folks engage in different types of generous acts of which Boonkumkhaoyai is a distinct example. No matter how poverty-stricken Isan people might be, they do not pay lip service to religious ideals, but are real practitioners of loving-kindness, at least at the level of *dānamaya* or meritorious action of giving.

Merit-making is part and parcel of the Thai Buddhist way of life in general and traditional Isan lifestyle epitomizes it fully. One can make merit, especially of the *dānamaya*[8] type or meritorious action consisting in giving, in diverse ways such as by offering alms, food, yellow robes and other requisites to monks, by making cash-donations for the construction of monks' dwelling places (*kuti*) and temples, by financially supporting the ecclesiastical education of monks and novices, by bearing the cost of publication of dhamma books, by contributing to a funeral ceremony and last but not least by giving one's time and labor for various activities in a monastery. It is very interesting to observe how Isan people have traditionally entwined their lives with the culture of merit-making although in some urban settings[9] this has been adversely affected by rapid modernization, consumerist culture and capitalistic modes of growth. On the other hand, Isan people, have successfully preserved the culture of merit-making by still adhering to its pristine values and practicing it within the folds of the twelve-month tradition of Prapheni Heet Sibsong. Therefore, merit-making still exists as a spontaneously thriving customary practice and has not yet turned out to be a fetish or a means to 'barter' for merit. On every occasion of Boonkumkhaoyai ceremony, village folks are seen to circumambulate the giant paddy heap three consecutive times holding *tonphapa*,[10] yellow-robes and other offerings in their hands, before offering them to individual monks. On each such occasion, lay devotees rejoice in merit-making as they are aware that by doing so they are supporting the monastic order and are joining hands in the propagation of Buddhism. Their joint collabora-

---

8. *Dānamaya* is only one of ten bases of meritorious action. For a list of all ten see Payutto, *Dictionary of Buddhism*, 109–111.

9. One instance that immediately comes to mind is Wat Phra Dhammakāya that has fetishized the cult of accumulation of merit to an unprecedented degree while willfully misconstruing the teachings of the Buddha, especially the concept of non-substantiality (*anattā*). This temple has become a 'haven' for a section of ultramodern and affluent Thais who would prefer to go for an illusionary crystal ball meditation technique rather than make a sincere effort to understand and practice along the Three-fold training (*tisikkha*) in the true sense.

10. A makeshift toy tree made of straw with many branches into which devotees pin bamboo with currency notes.

tive action is effective in keeping the age-old tradition of their forefathers alive. In the long run, the continuity of such collective effort will make the flame of dhamma glow with ever more incandescence rendering Buddhism a living tradition. The various socio-ethico principles that form the foundational base of Boonkumkhaoyai manifest to a great extent the philosophy of living for the 'other'.

Boonkumkhaoyai is thus a Buddhist paradigm of balanced living based on holistic principles through which the great ideal of the Buddha's teaching, 'for the good of the many, for the happiness of the many, out of compassion for the many' (*bahujanahitāya bahujanasukhāya lokānukampāya*) is manifested in microcosm. This is a tradition that is exemplary enough to be emulated in its exact form or in a modified version by any concerned people.

Moral benefits Participants in Boonpravet and Bunkumkhaoyai Reap

As in any act of generosity, participation in Boonpravet and Boonkumkhaoyai is conducive to mental well-being and brings great happiness, satisfaction and solace to the humble devotees. Arrangement of the ceremonies and participation in them is regarded as a spiritual undertaking that is conducive to ethical practice and observance of the precepts. The observance of the precepts and realization of the significance of dhamma in life pave the way for deletion of defilements and temptations. When the path is clear and devoid of defilements, the mind gets ripe for higher spiritual attainment such as right understanding and right thought which form the foundational base of wisdom and that which eventually leads to ethical commitment towards the 'other'. Participation at both the ceremonies is enlivening since appreciative understanding of the Bodhisattva's ideal of absolute generosity through the Boonphravet story and generous sharing of a part of the harvest as in Boonkumkhaoyai give rise to an attitude of endurance, sharing and priority of others' needs even in the face of personal hardships in life. The attitude of endurance and tolerance beget patience and forbearance. Participation in both the ceremonies is a merit-making act that involves direct contribution towards social welfare giving rise to radicalization of sincerity—sincerity to the act of merit-making, to the age-old traditions and to the propagation of Buddhism not only for the good of oneself but also for others. Both the ceremonies involve collective undertaking that unites all participants giving rise to social harmony and solidarity. Mutual interdependence and harmonious co-existence are acknowledged and put into practice through the organization of the ceremonies. Thus, the concept of 'my/mine' gets reduced when people take part in such community and collective welfare-based ceremonies. The desire to donate unmilled rice to form the giant paddy heap emerges from the cultivation of loving-kindness and compassion and when the effort is seen to directly contribute to social and religious welfare it gives rise to empathetic joy. Participation in the ceremonies enhances the potentiality of accumulation of merits. Even if one cannot see the result of such good actions directly, the preceding benefits in themselves can be regarded as the direct result of the meritorious act.

Conclusion

The various socio-ethical values that form the foundational base of Prapheni Heet Sibsong strongly impacts daily life, due to the philosophy of 'the-Self-for-the-Other' cherished by the Isan people.[11] Through each of the ceremonies integrated with the twelve different months of year, representation (for example, the heap of donated paddy) and conceptuality (the idea of generosity as a merit-making act) capture every aspect of meaning lived out in life. Responsibility for the 'Other' is being perpetually focused as the significant reason for action. Through the traditional enactment of each of the ceremonies, innate capacities to be affected by the 'Other' are built up and the distance between myself and the Other diminished, whether the 'Other' is an immediate living reality or a distant absent-presence as in the case of a deceased relative. The traditional acts and activities of Prapheni Heet Sibsong run parallel to many teachings in the Pali Canon that are full of recognition of the self's relational dutiful recognition and ethical-behavior orientation towards the 'Other,' as for instance, the emphasis on development of all-encompassing loving-kindness (metta) in the Metta Sutta.

In our technologically well-connected global village of today, for the entire global community to exist in harmony and mutual respect, the revitalization of this philosophical stance so well manifested through Prapheni

---

11. The philosophy of ethical commitment to the 'Other' is deeply embedded in the Buddhist way of life although in the context of Western philosophy it has only recently gained prominence through the theological justification and ethicization of the concept in the writings of Levinas.

Heet Sibsong, is not only beneficial in the short term, but also indispensable in the long run for true understanding, harmonious co-existence, and solidarity. With rapidly changing global patterns of travel and migration and new emerging scenarios of cross-cultural encounters, every country is becoming a place where diverse socio-cultural and religious elements are perpetually merging and taking a dynamic form. Keeping in view the fact that the realization of such ideal slogans like 'unity in diversity,' 'tolerance for the different,' 'one vision, one identity and one community' are not easy endeavors. In this chapter, we have taken note of the full-blown manifestation of the philosophy of ethical commitment to the 'Other' as manifested through Prapheni Heet Sibsong and hope that by highlighting the richness embedded in a marginalized cultural context we can bring to possibility, however hypothetical, its universal applicability in the context of the global community as a whole. The Buddhist paradigm of balanced living based on holistic principles through which the great ideal of the Buddha's teaching, 'for the good of the many, for the happiness of the many, out of compassion for the many' (*bahujanahitāya bahujanasukhāya lokānukampāya*), is manifested through each of the traditional ceremonies. Therefore, I believe that Prapheni Heet Sibsong is exemplary enough to be emulated in its exact form or a modified version by any individual or community. If it is difficult to implement in exact form due to various cultural barriers, one can at least imbibe the core essence of the ceremonies in spirit and practice in a way that is appropriate in one's own socio-cultural and religious context manifesting the underlying principles of commitment to selfless giving, communal welfare and ethical commitment to the 'Other.'

Bibliography

Bhikkhu, Buddhadāsa, *Dhammic Socialism*, 2nd ed. Translated by Donald K. Swearer. Bangkok: Thai Inter-Religious Commission for Development, 1993.
Buddhist Legends Part I, Translated by Eugene Watson Burlingame. Cambridge: Harvard University Press, 1921.
Chob Desuankhok, "From Boonkhunkao or Boonkhunlarn to Boonkumkhaoyai." In *Kawpaikabboon*, Khonkaen: Mahachulalongkornrājavidyālaya University: (Jan–Mar 2009), 18–19.
De Silva, Lily. *The Self-Made Private Prison*, Kandy: Buddhist Publication Society, 1990.
Dipti Mahanta, *A Critical study of the Mahachat Sung-Sermon from Isan*. Research Monograph, Bangkok: Buddhist Research Institute, 2009.
———. "Boonkumkhaoyai: An exemplary model of Buddhist Economy." In *UNDV Conference Proceedings*. Bangkok: Dion Peoples, 2009.

Part II: Cultural Perspectives

Jaruwan Thammawat, *Characteristics of Isan Literature*, Mahasarakham: Srinakharinvirot University, 2521.

Kawpaikabboon, Special Issue Jan–Mar, Khonkaen: Mahachulalongkornrājavidyālaya University, 2009.

Kornfield, Jack and Paul Breiter, editors. *A Still Forest Pool: The Insight Meditation of Achaan Chah*. Illinois: Theosophical, 1985.

Levinas, Emmanuel, *Totality and Infinity: An Essay on Exteriority*, translated by Alphonso Lingis. Pittsburgh, PA: Duquesne University Press, 1969.

Payutto, P.A. *Buddhadhamma*, Albany: State University of New York Press, 1995.

———. *Buddhist Economics*, Bangkok: The National Identity Board, 1994.

———. *Dictionary of Buddhism*, Bangkok: Mahachulalongkornrajavidyalaya University Press, 2000.

Samyutta Nikāya: The Grouped Discourses, PTS Edition.

Sutasarapimol, *Phimpha Laeh Mahāchat 13 Kantha Isaan version* พิมพา แหล่มหาชาติ ๑๓ กัณฑ์ สำนวนอีสาน, Khonkaen: Klangnanatham, BE 2549.

Walpole, Rahula, *What the Buddha Taught*, Bangkok: Haw Trai Foundation, 1990.

www.ingramcontent.com/pod-product-compliance
Lightning Source LLC
Chambersburg PA
CBHW060605230426
43670CB00011B/1977